Deployment with Docker

Apply continuous integration models, deploy applications
quicker, and scale at large by putting Docker to work

Srdjan Grubor

BIRMINGHAM - MUMBAI

Deployment with Docker

First published: November 2017

Production reference: 1201117

Published by Packt Publishing Ltd.

Livery Place
35 Livery Street
Birmingham
B3 2PB, UK.

ISBN 978-1-78646-900-7

www.packtpub.com

Credits

Author
Srdjan Grubor

Reviewer
Francisco Souza

Commissioning Editor
Vijin Boricha

Acquisition Editor
Rahul Nair

Content Development Editor
Sharon Raj

Technical Editor
Prashant Chaudhari

Copy Editor
Stuti Srivastava

Project Coordinator
Virginia Dias

Proofreader
Safis Editing

Indexer
Aishwarya Gangawane

Graphics
Kirk D'Penha

Production Coordinator
Aparna Bhagat

About the Author

Srdjan Grubor is a software engineer who has worked on projects large and small for many years now, with deployment sizes ranging from small to global. Currently, he is working on solving the world's connectivity problems for Endless OS as a cloud engineer and was one of the first people to become a Docker Certified Associate. He enjoys breaking things just to see how they work, tinkering, and solving challenging problems. Srdjan believes that there is always room for philanthropy in technology.

Acknowledgments

I'd like to thank every person and company that has spent time working on open source software that has enabled me and countless others to improve their lives and learn things through its use—don't ever stop contributing!

As for personal appreciation for help on this book, I'd also like to thank:

- My family for being the most awesome family one can ask for
- My girlfriend for being the best partner ever and also keeping me sane through the stress of writing this book in my limited spare time
- Dora (the kitty) for making me take breaks by sitting on the laptop keyboard
- Galileo (the sugar glider) for being the cutest rebel pet in the world
- Endless for introducing me to open source software and encouraging me to contribute back
- So many others that would fill pages and pages of this book

Thank you all from the bottom of my heart!

About the Reviewer

Francisco Souza is a Docker Captain and a senior software engineer working with video and container technologies at the New York Times. Prior to that, he worked with the open source PaaS Tsuru, created back in 2012 and later adapted to leverage Docker for container deployment and management. Other than video and containers, Francisco also likes to explore topics related to concurrency, parallelism, and distributed systems.

He has also contributed as a reviewer to *Extending Docker, Russ McKendrick, Packt* and *Docker Networking Cookbook, Jon Langemak, Packt*.

www.PacktPub.com

For support files and downloads related to your book, please visit www.PacktPub.com. Did you know that Packt offers eBook versions of every book published, with PDF and ePub files available? You can upgrade to the eBook version at www.PacktPub.comand as a print book customer, you are entitled to a discount on the eBook copy. Get in touch with us at service@packtpub.com for more details. At www.PacktPub.com, you can also read a collection of free technical articles, sign up for a range of free newsletters and receive exclusive discounts and offers on Packt books and eBooks.

https://www.packtpub.com/mapt

Get the most in-demand software skills with Mapt. Mapt gives you full access to all Packt books and video courses, as well as industry-leading tools to help you plan your personal development and advance your career.

Why subscribe?

- Fully searchable across every book published by Packt
- Copy and paste, print, and bookmark content
- On demand and accessible via a web browser

Customer Feedback

Thanks for purchasing this Packt book. At Packt, quality is at the heart of our editorial process. To help us improve, please leave us an honest review on this book's Amazon page at https://www.amazon.com/dp/1786469006.

If you'd like to join our team of regular reviewers, you can email us at customerreviews@packtpub.com. We award our regular reviewers with free eBooks and videos in exchange for their valuable feedback. Help us be relentless in improving our products!

I would like to mainly dedicate this book to you, the reader, as you were my primary motivation for writing this book and always kept me typing. Without the thought that someone would use this material to learn new things, the book itself would not have been written at all.

Table of Contents

Preface

Microservices and containers are here to stay, and in today's world Docker is emerging as the de facto standard for scalability. Deploying Docker into production is considered to be one of the major pain points of developing large-scale infrastructure and the documentation that you can find online leaves a lot to be desired. With this book, you will get exposure to the various tools, techniques, and workarounds available for the development and deployment of a Docker infrastructure in your own cloud, based on the author's real-world experiences of doing the same. You will learn everything you wanted to know to effectively scale your deployments globally and build a resilient and scalable containerized cloud platform for yourself.

What this book covers

Chapter 1, *Containers – Not Just Another Buzzword*, examines what the current approaches are to deploying services and why containers, and Docker specifically, are eclipsing other forms of infrastructure deployment.

Chapter 2, *Rolling Up the Sleeves*, covers all the necessary steps to set up and run a small local service based on Docker. We will cover how to install Docker, run it, and get a quick overview of the Docker CLI. With that knowledge, we will write a basic Docker container and see how to run it locally.

Chapter 3, *Service Decomposition*, covers how to take the knowledge from the previous chapter and use it to create and build additional of a database and an app server container, mirroring simple decomposed microservice deployments.

Chapter 4, *Scaling the Containers*, talks about scaling horizontally with multiple instances of the same container. We will cover service discovery, how to deploy one to make the scaling of a module transparent to the rest of the infrastructure, and its various pros and cons depending on the implementation, with a quick look into horizontal node scaling.

Chapter 5, *Keeping the Data Persistent*, covers data persistence for your containers. We will cover node-local storage, transient storage, and persistent volumes and their intricacies. We will also spend a bit more time on Docker image layering and some pitfalls.

Chapter 6, *Advanced Deployment Topics*, adds isolation and messaging to the cluster to increase the security and stability of the services. Other security consideration in Docker deployments and their trade-offs will be covered here.

Chapter 7, *The Limits of Scaling and the Workarounds*, covers all the issues that you might come across as you scale beyond your basic RESTful service needs. We will dig deep into the issues that you will find with default deployments and how to work around them with minimal hassle, along with handling code version changes and higher-level management systems.

Chapter 8, *Building Our Own Platform*, helps us build our own mini **Platform-as-a-Service (PaaS)** in this chapter. We will cover everything from configuration management to deployment in a cloud-based environment that you can use to bootstrap your own cloud.

Chapter 9, *Exploring the Largest-Scale Deployments*, covers what we built up, and extends into the theoretical and real-world examples of the largest-scale deployments of Docker it also covers any development on the horizon that the reader should keep an eye out for.

What you need for this book

Before you start with the book, make sure you have the following:

- Intel or AMD-based x86_64 machine
- At least 2 GB of RAM
- At least 10 GB of hard drive space
- Linux (Ubuntu, Debian, CentOS, RHEL, SUSE, or Fedora), Windows 10, Windows Server 2016, or macOS
- Internet connection

Who this book is for

This book is aimed at system administrators, developers, DevOps engineers, and software engineers who want to get concrete hands-on experience deploying multitier web applications and containerized microservices using Docker. It is meant for anyone who has worked on deploying services in some fashion and wants to take their small-scale setups to the next order of magnitude or wants to learn more about it.

Conventions

In this book, you will find a number of text styles that distinguish between different kinds of information. Here are some examples of these styles and an explanation of their meaning.

Code words in text, folder names, filenames, file extensions, pathnames, dummy URLs, user input, and Twitter handles are shown as follows: "If you go to http://127.0.0.1:8080 in your browser again, you will see that our app works just like before!"

A block of code is set as follows:

```
# Make sure we are fully up to date
RUN apt-get update -q && \
apt-get dist-upgrade -y && \
apt-get clean && \
apt-get autoclean
```

When we wish to draw your attention to a particular part of a code block, the relevant lines or items are set in bold:

```
# Make sure we are fully up to date
RUN apt-get update -q && \
apt-get dist-upgrade -y && \
apt-get clean && \
apt-get autoclean
```

Any command-line input or output is written as follows:

```
$ docker swarm leave --force
Node left the swarm.
```

New terms and **important words** are shown in bold. Words that you see on the screen, for example, in menus or dialog boxes, appear in the text like this: "In order to download new modules, we will go to **Files** | **Settings** | **Project Name** | **Project Interpreter**."

Warnings or important notes appear like this.

Tips and tricks appear like this.

Reader feedback

Feedback from our readers is always welcome. Let us know what you think about this book-what you liked or disliked. Reader feedback is important for us as it helps us develop titles that you will really get the most out of. To send us general feedback, simply email feedback@packtpub.com, and mention the book's title in the subject of your message. If there is a topic that you have expertise in and you are interested in either writing or contributing to a book, see our author guide at www.packtpub.com/authors.

Customer support

Now that you are the proud owner of a Packt book, we have a number of things to help you to get the most from your purchase.

Downloading the example code

You can download the example code files for this book from your account at http://www.packtpub.com. If you purchased this book elsewhere, you can visit http://www.packtpub.com/support and register to have the files emailed directly to you. You can download the code files by following these steps:

1. Log in or register to our website using your email address and password.
2. Hover the mouse pointer on the **SUPPORT** tab at the top.
3. Click on **Code Downloads & Errata**.
4. Enter the name of the book in the **Search** box.
5. Select the book for which you're looking to download the code files.
6. Choose from the drop-down menu where you purchased this book from.
7. Click on **Code Download**.

Once the file is downloaded, please make sure that you unzip or extract the folder using the latest version of:

- WinRAR / 7-Zip for Windows
- Zipeg / iZip / UnRarX for Mac
- 7-Zip / PeaZip for Linux

The code bundle for the book is also hosted on GitHub at `https://github.com/PacktPublishing/Deployment-with-Docker/`. We also have other code bundles from our rich catalog of books and videos available at `https://github.com/PacktPublishing/`. Check them out!

Downloading the color images of this book

We also provide you with a PDF file that has color images of the screenshots/diagrams used in this book. The color images will help you better understand the changes in the output. You can download this file from `https://www.packtpub.com/sites/default/files/downloads/DeploymentwithDocker_ColorImages.pdf`.

Errata

Although we have taken every care to ensure the accuracy of our content, mistakes do happen. If you find a mistake in one of our books-maybe a mistake in the text or the code-we would be grateful if you could report this to us. By doing so, you can save other readers from frustration and help us improve subsequent versions of this book. If you find any errata, please report them by visiting `http://www.packtpub.com/submit-errata`, selecting your book, clicking on the **Errata Submission Form** link, and entering the details of your errata. Once your errata are verified, your submission will be accepted and the errata will be uploaded to our website or added to any list of existing errata under the Errata section of that title. To view the previously submitted errata, go to `https://www.packtpub.com/books/content/support` and enter the name of the book in the search field. The required information will appear under the **Errata** section.

Piracy

Piracy of copyrighted material on the internet is an ongoing problem across all media. At Packt, we take the protection of our copyright and licenses very seriously. If you come across any illegal copies of our works in any form on the internet, please provide us with the location address or website name immediately so that we can pursue a remedy. Please contact us at `copyright@packtpub.com` with a link to the suspected pirated material. We appreciate your help in protecting our authors and our ability to bring you valuable content.

Questions

If you have a problem with any aspect of this book, you can contact us at `questions@packtpub.com`, and we will do our best to address the problem.

1
Containers - Not Just Another Buzzword

In technology, sometimes the jumps in progress are small but, as is the case with containerization, the jumps have been massive and turn the long-held practices and teachings completely upside down. With this book, we will take you from running a tiny service to building elastically scalable systems using containerization with Docker, the cornerstone of this revolution. We will perform a steady but consistent ramp-up through the basic blocks with a focus on the inner workings of Docker, and, as we continue, we will try to spend a majority of the time in the world of complex deployments and their considerations.

Let's take a look at what we will cover in this chapter:

- What are containers and why do we need them?

- Docker's place in the container world

- Thinking with a container mindset

The what and why of containers

We can't start talking about Docker without actually covering the ideas that make it such a powerful tool. A container, at the most basic level, is an isolated user-space environment for a given discrete set of functionality. In other words, it is a way to modularize a system (or a part of one) into pieces that are much easier to manage and maintain while often also being very resilient to failures.

In practice, this net gain is never free and requires some investment in the adoption and implementation of new tooling (such as Docker), but the change pays heavy dividends to the adopters in a drastic reduction of development, maintenance, and scaling costs over its lifetime.

At this point, you might ask this: how exactly are containers able to provide such huge benefits? To understand this, we first need to take a look at deployments before such tooling was available.

In the earlier days of deployments, the process for deploying a service would go something like this:

1. Developer would write some code.
2. Operations would deploy that code.
3. If there were any problems in deployment, the operations team would tell the developer to fix something and we would go back to step 1.

A simplification of this process would look something like this:

```
dev machine => code => ops => bare-metal hosts
```

The developer would have to wait for the whole process to bounce back for them to try to write a fix anytime there was a problem. What is even worse, operations groups would often have to use various arcane forms of magic to ensure that the code that developers gave them can actually run on deployment machines, as differences in library versions, OS patches, and language compilers/interpreters were all high risk for failures and likely to spend a huge amount of time in this long cycle of break-patch-deploy attempts.

The next step in the evolution of deployments came to improve this workflow with the virtualization of bare-metal hosts as manual maintenance of a heterogeneous mix of machines and environments is a complete nightmare even when they were in single-digit counts. Early tools such as chroot came out in the late 70s but were later replaced (though not fully) with hypervisors such as Xen, KVM, Hyper-V, and a few others, which not only reduced the management complexity of larger systems, but also provided Ops and developers both with a deployment environment that was more consistent as well as more computationally dense:

```
dev machine => code => ops => n hosts * VM deployments per host
```

This helped out in the reduction of failures at the end of the pipeline, but the path from the developer to the deployment was still a risk as the VM environments could very easily get out of sync with the developers.

From here, if we really try to figure out how to make this system better, we can already see how Docker and other container technologies are the organic next step. By making the developers' sandbox environment as close as we can get to the one in production, a developer with an adequately functional container system can literally bypass the ops step, be sure that the code will work on the deployment environment, and prevent any lengthy rewrite cycles due to the overhead of multiple group interactions:

```
dev machine => container => n hosts * VM deployments per host
```

With Ops being needed primarily in the early stages of system setup, developers can now be empowered to take their code directly from the idea all the way to the user with the confidence that a majority of issues that they will find will be ones that they will be able to fix.

If you consider this the new model of deploying services, it is very reasonable to understand why we have DevOps roles nowadays, why there is such a buzz around **Platform as a Service** (**PaaS**) setups, and how so many tech giants can apply a change to a service used by millions at a time within 15 minutes with something as simple as `git push origin` by a developer without any other interactions with the system.

But the benefits don't stop there either! If you have many little containers everywhere and if you have increased or decreased demand for a service, you can add or eliminate a portion of your host machines, and if the container orchestration is properly done, there will be zero downtime and zero user-noticeable changes on scaling changes. This comes in extremely handy to providers of services that need to handle variable loads at different times--think of Netflix and their peak viewership times as an example. In most cases, these can also be automated on almost all cloud platforms (that is, AWS Auto Scaling Groups, Google Cluster Autoscaler, and Azure Autoscale) so that if some triggers occur or there are changes in resource consumption, the service will automatically scale up and down the number of hosts to handle the load. By automating all these processes, your PaaS can pretty much be a fire-and-forget flexible layer, on top of which developers can worry about things that really matter and not waste time with things such as trying to figure out whether some system library is installed on deployment hosts.

Now don't get me wrong; making one of these amazing PaaS services is not an easy task by any stretch of imagination, and the road is covered in countless hidden traps but if you want to be able to sleep soundly throughout the night without phone calls from angry customers, bosses, or coworkers, you must strive to be as close as you can to these ideal setups regardless of whether you are a developer or not.

Docker's place

So far, we have talked a lot about containers but haven't mentioned Docker yet. While Docker has been emerging as the de facto standard in containerization, it is currently one of many competing technologies in this space, and what is relevant today may not be tomorrow. For this reason, we will cover a little bit of the container ecosystem so that if you see shifts occurring in this space, don't hesitate to try another solution, as picking the right tool for the job almost always beats out trying to, as the saying goes, fit a square peg in a round hole.

While most people know Docker as the **Command-line Interface** (**CLI**) tool, the Docker platform extends above and beyond that to include tooling to create and manage clusters, handle persistent storage, build and share Docker containers, and many others, but for now, we will focus on the most important part of that ecosystem: the Docker container.

Introduction to Docker containers

Docker containers, in essence, are a grouping of a number of filesystem layers that are stacked on top of each other in a sequence to create the final layout that is then run in an isolated environment by the host machine's kernel. Each layer describes which files have been added, modified, and/or deleted relative to its previous parent layer. For example, you have a base layer with a file `/foo/bar`, and the next layer adds a file `/foo/baz`. When the container starts, it will combine the layers in order and the resulting container will have both `/foo/bar` and `/foo/baz`. This process is repeated for any new layer to end up with a fully composed filesystem to run the specified service or services.

Think of the arrangement of the filesystem layers in an image as the intricate layering of sounds in a symphony: you have the percussion instruments in the back to provide the base for the sound, wind instruments a bit closer to drive the movements, and in the front, the string instruments with the lead melody. Together, it creates a pleasing end result. In the case of Docker, you generally have the base layers set up the main OS layers and configuration, the service infrastructure layers go on top of that (interpreter installation, the compilation of helpers, and so on), and the final image that you run is finally topped with the actual service code. For now, this is all you will need to know, but we will cover this topic in much more detail in the next chapter.

In essence, Docker in its current form is a platform that allows easy and fast development of isolated (or not depending on how the service is configured) Linux and Windows services within containers that are scalable, easily interchangeable, and easily distributable.

The competition

Before we get too deep into Docker itself, let us also cover some of the current competitors in broad strokes and see how they differ from Docker itself. The curious thing about almost all of them is that they are generally a form of abstraction around Linux control groups (`cgroups`) and namespaces that limit the use of Linux host's physical resources and isolate groups of processes from each other, respectively. While almost every tooling mentioned here provides some sort of containerization of resources, it can differ greatly in the depth of isolation, implementation security, and/or the container distribution.

rkt

`rkt`, often written as **Rocket**, is the closest competing application containerization platform from CoreOS that was started as a more secure application container runtime. Over time, Docker has closed a number of its security failings but unlike `rkt`, which runs with limited privileges as a user service, Docker's main service runs as root. This means that if someone manages to break out of the Docker container, they will automatically have full access to the host's root, which is obviously a really bad thing from an operations perspective while with `rkt`, the hacker would also need to escalate their privilege from the limited user. While this comparison here isn't painting Docker in great light from a security standpoint, if its development trajectory is to be extrapolated, it is possible and likely that this issue will be heavily mitigated and/or fixed in the future.

Another interesting difference is that unlike Docker, which is designed to run a single process within the container, `rkt` can run multiple processes within a container. This makes deploying multiple services within a single container much easier. Now, having said that, you actually *can* run multiple processes within a Docker container (we will cover this at a later point in the book) but it is a great pain to set that up properly but I did find in practice that the pressure to keep services and containers based on a single process really pushes the developer to create containers as true microservices instead of treating them as mini VMs so don't consider this necessarily as a problem.

While there are many other smaller reasons to choose Docker over `rkt` and vice versa, one massive thing cannot be ignored: the rate of adoption. While `rkt` is a bit younger, Docker has been adopted by almost all big tech giants, and there doesn't seem to be any sign of stopping the trend. With this in mind, if you need to work on microservices today, the choice is probably very clear but as with any tech field, the ecosystem may look much differently in a year or even just a couple of months.

System-level virtualization

On the opposite side, we have platforms for working with full system images instead of applications like LXD, OpenVZ, KVM, and a few others. They, unlike Docker and rkt, are designed to provide you with full support for all of the virtualized system services but at the cost of much higher resource usage purely by its definition. While having separate system containers on a host is needed for things like better security, isolation, and possibly compatibility, almost the entire use of these containers from personal experience can be moved to an application-level virtualization system with a bit of work to provide better resource use profile and higher modularity at a slight increase of cost in creating the initial infrastructure. A sensible rule to follow here is that if you are writing applications and services, you should probably use application-level virtualization but if you are providing VMs to the end user or want much more isolation between services you should use a system-level virtualization.

Desktop application-level virtualizations

Flatpak, AppImage, Snaps, and other similar technologies also provide isolation and packaging for single-application level containers, but unlike Docker, all of them target the deployment of desktop applications and do not have as precise control over the container life cycle (that is starting, stopping, forced termination, and so on) nor do they generally provide layered images. Instead, most of these tools have nice wrapper **Graphical User Interfaces** (**GUIs**) and provide a significantly better workflow for installing, running, and updating desktop applications. While most have large overlaps with Docker due to the same underlying reliance on mentioned cgroups and namespaces, these application-level virtualization platforms do not traditionally handle server applications (applications that run without UI components) and vice versa. Since this field is still young and the space they all cover is relatively small, you can probably expect consolidations and cross-overs so in this case it would be either for Docker to enter the desktop application delivery space and/or for one or more of these competing technologies to try to support server applications.

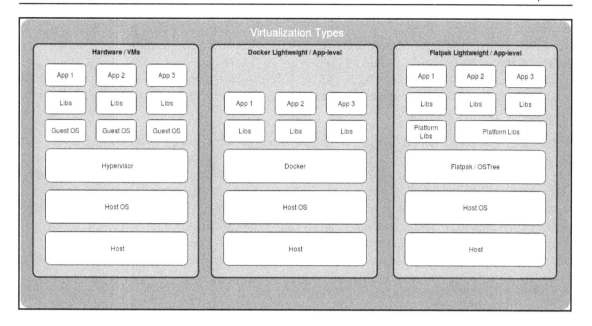

When should containerization be considered?

We've covered a lot of ground so far, but there is an important aspect that we did not cover yet but which is an extremely important thing to evaluate as containers do not make sense in a large array of circumstances as the end deployment target regardless of how much buzz there is around this concept, so we will cover some general use cases where this type of platform should really be considered (or not). While containerization should be the end goal in most cases from an operations perspective and offers huge dividends with minimal effort when injected into the development process, turning deployment machines into a containerized platform is a pretty tricky process, and if you will not gain tangible benefits from it, you might as well dedicate this time to something that will bring real and tangible value to your services.

Let's start this by covering scaling thresholds first. If your services as a whole can completely fit and run well on a relatively small or medium virtual machine or a bare-metal host and you don't anticipate sudden scaling needs, virtualization on the deployment machines will lead you down the path of pain that really isn't warranted in most cases. The high front-loaded costs of setting up even a benign but robust virtualized setup will usually be better spent on developing service features at that level.

If you see increases in demand with a service backed with a VM or bare-metal host, you can always scale up to a larger host (vertical scaling) and refocus your team but for anything less than that, you probably shouldn't go that route. There have been many cases where a business has spent months working to get the container technology implemented since it is so popular, only to lose their customers due to lack of development resources and having to shut their doors.

Now that your system is maxing out the limits of vertical scalability, is it a good time to add things such as Docker clusters to the mix? The real answer is "maybe". If your services are homogeneous and consistent across hosts, such as sharded or clustered databases or simple APIs, in most cases, this still isn't the right time either as you can scale this system easily with host images and some sort of a load balancer. If you're opting for a bit more fanciness, you can use a cloud-based **Database as a Service** (**DBaaS**) such as Amazon RDS, Microsoft DocumentDB, or Google BigQuery and auto-scale service hosts up or down through the same provider (or even a different one) based on the required level of performance.

If there is ample foreshadowing of service variety beyond this, the need for a much shorter pipeline from developer to deployment, rising complexity, or exponential growth, you should consider each of these as triggers to re-evaluate your pros/cons but there is no clear threshold that will be a clear cut-off. A good rule of thumb here, though, is that if you have a slow period for your team it won't hurt to explore the containerization options or to gear up your skills in this space, but be *very* careful to not underestimate the time it would take to properly set up such a platform regardless of how easy the Getting Started instructions look on many of these tools.

With this all, what are the clear signs that you need to get containers into your workflow as soon as you can? There can be many subtle hints here but the following list covers the ones that should immediately bring the containers topic up for discussion if the answer is yes, as the benefits greatly outweigh the time investment into your service platform:

- Do you have more than 10 unique, discrete, and interconnected services in your deployment?
- Do you have three or more programming languages you need to support on the hosts?
- Are your ops resources constantly deploying and upgrading services?
- Do any of your services require "four 9s" (99.99%) or better availability?
- Do you have a recurring pattern of services breaking in deployments because developers are not considerate of the environment that the services will run in?
- Do you have a talented Dev or Ops team that's sitting idle?
- Does your project have a burning hole in the wallet?

Okay, maybe the last one is a bit of a joke but it is in the list to illustrate, in somewhat of a sarcastic tone, that at the time of writing this getting a PaaS platform operational, stable, and secure is neither easy nor cheap regardless of whether your currency is time or money. Many will try to trick you into the idea that you should always use containers and make everything Dockerized, but keep a skeptical mindset and make sure that you evaluate your options with care.

The ideal Docker deployment

Now that we have the real-talk parts done with, let us say that we are truly ready to tackle containers and Docker for an imaginary service. We covered bits and pieces of this earlier in the chapter, but we will here concretely define what our ideal requirements would look like if we had ample time to work on them:

- Developers should be able to deploy a new service without any need for ops resources
- The system can auto-discover new instances of services running
- The system is flexibly scalable both up and down
- On desired code commits, the new code will automatically get deployed without Dev or Ops intervention
- You can seamlessly handle degraded nodes and services without interruption
- You are capable of using the full extent of the resources available on hosts (RAM, CPUs, and so on)
- Nodes should almost never need to be accessed individually by developers

If these are the requirements, you will be happy to know that almost all of them are feasible to a large extent and that we will cover almost all of them in detail in this book. For many of them, we will need to get into Docker *way* deeper and beyond most of the materials you will find elsewhere, but there is no point in teaching you deployments that you cannot take to the field that only print out "Hello World"s.

As we explore each topic in the following chapters, we will be sure to cover any pitfalls as there are many such complex system interactions. Some will be obvious to you, but many probably will not (for example, the PID1 issue), as the tooling in this space is relatively young and many tools critical for the Docker ecosystem are not even version 1.0 or have reached version 1.0 only recently.

Thus, you should consider this technology space to still be in its early stages of development so be realistic, don't expect miracles, and expect a healthy dose of little "gotchas". Keep also in mind that some of the biggest tech giants have been using Docker for a long time now (Red Hat, Microsoft, Google, IBM, and so on), so don't get scared either.

To get started and really begin our journey, we need to first reconsider the way we think about services.

The container mindset

Today, as we have somewhat covered earlier in the chapter, vast majority of services deployed today are a big mess of ad hoc or manually connected and configured pieces that tend to break apart as soon as a single piece is changed or moved. It is easy to imagine this as a tower of cards where the piece that needs changing is often in the middle of it, with risks taking the whole structure down. Small-to-medium projects and talented Dev and Ops team can mostly manage this level of complexity but it is really not a scalable methodology.

The developer workflow

Even if you're not working on a PaaS system, it is good to consider each piece of a service as something that should have a consistent environment between the developer and final deployment hosts, be able to run anywhere with minimal changes, and is modular enough to be swapped out with an API-compatible analogue if needed. For many of these cases, even a local Docker usage can go far in making the deployments easier as you can isolate each component into small pieces that don't change as your development environment changes.

To illustrate this, imagine a practical case where we are writing a simple web service that talks to a database on a system that is based on the latest Ubuntu, but our deployment environment is some iteration of CentOS. In this case, due to their vastly different support cycle lengths coordinating between versions and libraries will be extremely difficult, so as a developer, you can use Docker to provide you with the same version of the database that CentOS would have, and you can test your service in a CentOS-based container to ensure that all the libraries and dependencies can work when it gets deployed. This process will improve the development workflow even if the real deployment hosts have no containerization.

Now we will take this example in a slightly more realistic direction: what if you need to run your service without modifications of code on all currently supported versions of CentOS?

With Docker, you can have a container for each version of the OS that you can test the service against in order to ensure that you are not going to get any surprises. For additional points, you can automate a test suite runner to launch each one of the OS version containers one by one (or even better, in parallel) to run your whole test suite against them automatically on any code changes. With just these few small tweaks, we have taken an ad-hoc service that would constantly break in production to something that you almost never have to worry about as you can be confident that it will work when deployed, which is really powerful tooling to have.

If you extend this process, you can locally create Docker recipes (Dockerfiles), which we will get into in the next chapter in detail, with the exact set of steps needed to get your service running from a vanilla CentOS installation to fully capable of running the service. These steps can be taken with minimal changes by the ops teams as input to their automated configuration management (CM) system, such as Ansible, Salt, Puppet, or Chef, to ensure that the hosts will have the exact baseline that is required for things to run properly. This codified transfer of exact steps needed on the end target written by the service developer is exactly why Docker is such a powerful tool.

As is hopefully becoming apparent, Docker as a tool not only improves your development processes if they're on the deployment machines, but it can also be used throughout the process to standardize your environments and thus increase the efficiency of almost every part of the deployment pipeline. With Docker, you will most likely forget the infamous phrase that instills dread in every Ops person: "it works fine on my machine!". This, by itself, should be enough to make you consider splicing in container-based workflows even if your deployment infrastructure doesn't support containers.

 The bottom line here that we've been dancing around and which you should always consider is that with the current tooling available, turning your whole deployment infrastructure into a container-based one is slightly difficult, but the addition of containers in any other part of your development process is generally not too difficult and can provide exponential workflow improvements to your team.

Summary

In this chapter, we followed along the history of deployments and looked at how containers with Docker bring us closer to this new world of micro-services. Docker was examined with a high-level overview about which parts we are most interested in. We covered the competition and where Docker fits into the ecosystem with some use cases. Lastly, we also covered when you should - and more importantly, when you shouldn't - consider containers in your infrastructure and development workflow.

In the next chapter, we will finally get our hands dirty and look into how to install and run Docker images along with creating our first Docker image, so be sure to stick around.

2
Rolling Up the Sleeves

In the previous chapter, we looked at what containers are, what role they can fill in your infrastructure, and why Docker is the one leading the pack in service deployments. Now that we know what Docker is and isn't, we can get started with the basics. In this chapter, we will cover the following topics:

- Installing Docker
- Extending a container
- Building a container
- Debugging containers

Installing Docker

The installation of Docker varies greatly between operating systems, but for most systems, there are detailed instructions at `https://docs.docker.com/engine/installation/`. Two levels of Docker are generally available: the **Community Edition (CE)** and the **Enterprise Edition (EE)**. While slightly different, for almost everything that we will work on in this book, the Community Edition is perfectly functional and will suffice in every way. Once you reach levels of scale where you need much more advanced features, such as security scans, LDAP, and technical support, the Enterprise Edition might make sense. As would be expected, the Enterprise Edition is not free, and you can take a look at `https://www.docker.com/pricing` to see how these editions differ.

For our examples and any OS-specific commands in this book, from here on, we will be using Ubuntu's **Long Term Support** (**LTS**) version, with Ubuntu being currently the most popular Linux distribution. The latest version of the LTS product available is 16.04, which will be the base for our CLI interactions and examples but by the time you read this book, 18.04 might be available too. Keep in mind that outside of the installation part, most code and examples are very portable and should generally run on other platforms, so even if there are changes needed, they should be minimal. That said, developing Docker services on non-Linux platforms may not be as refined or stable due to the fact that Docker is generally used to deploy Linux-based services on Linux machines even though other niche cases are supported to some extent. Microsoft has been making significant advancements in this space with Docker for Windows since they have been trying to push their own container strategy, so keep an eye on their progress as it may become a pretty competent development platform.

 Some manual networking examples in later chapters may not work fully in macOS due to the different implementation of this subsystem for that platform. For those, using a virtual machine with Ubuntu LTS is advised if you want to follow along.

So, with our clean Ubuntu 16.04 LTS machine, VM, or a compatible OS, let's get Docker installed. While the Docker package is already available on `apt` repositories within the distribution, I would highly discourage installation this way, as these versions are usually much older. While this is not a problem for most software, for fast-moving projects such as Docker, it will put you at a significant disadvantage when it comes to support for the latest features. For this reason, we will install Docker from its own apt repository:

 Warning! There are couple of other ways to install Docker using many of the following tools, but unless absolutely necessary, installation with the `sudo curl -sSL https://somesite.com/ | sh` pattern or anything similar to it is a very dangerous thing to do as you are rooting your own box for a website without checking what the script does. This execution pattern also leaves minimal evidence of what was done behind. Additionally mid-stream exception can corrupt the download but still execute, partially causing damage, and you are only relying on **Transport Layer Security** (**TLS**), for which hundreds of organizations across the world can create fake certificates. In other words, if you care about your machine, you should never, ever try to install software in this way unless, of course, the software vendor is clueless about security and they force you to do this, in which case, you are at their mercy.

```
$ # Install the pre-requisites
$ sudo apt install -y apt-transport-https \
                        curl

$ # Add Docker's signing key into our apt configuration to ensure they are
the only ones that can send us updates. This key should match the one that
the apt repository is using so check the online installation instruction if
you see "NO_PUBKEY <key_id>" errors.
$ apt-key adv --keyserver hkp://p80.pool.sks-keyservers.net:80 \
            --recv-keys 58118E89F3A912897C070ADBF76221572C52609D

$ # Add the repository location to apt. Your URL may be different depending
on if Xenial is your distribution.
$ echo "deb https://apt.dockerproject.org/repo ubuntu-xenial main" | sudo
tee -a /etc/apt/sources.list.d/docker.list

$ # Update the apt listings and install Docker
$ sudo apt update
$ sudo apt install docker-engine
```

By default, Docker will require `sudo` (or `root`) prefixed to all of your commands to run including ones in this book that don't have it explicitly mentioned. Generally, for development machines, this is a big pain to deal with so I might mention, but *strongly* discourage, that you can also add your current user to the `docker` group so that you do not need to prefix every Docker command with `sudo`:

1. Add user to group with `usermod` (for example `$ sudo usermod -aG docker $USER`).

2. Fully log out and log back in (groups are evaluated only on session start).

Keep in mind that this is a *huge* security hole that can allow a local user to escalate to root privileges trivially so never, under any circumstance, do this on any server that will sit on the Internet.

If all of the preceding commands work as expected, you will be able to see whether Docker is installed:

```
$ docker --version
Docker version 17.05.0-ce, build 89658be
```

Having Docker installed without anything to run is pretty useless, so let us see whether we can get an image that we can run locally. Our choices here would be to either make our own image from scratch or use something that's already built. Given that a big reason why Docker has reached such high adoption rates is its ease of sharing of images through Docker Hub (`https://hub.docker.com/`) and we're just starting out, we will delay creating our own image for a little bit to explore this site, a centralized place for publishing and downloading Docker images.

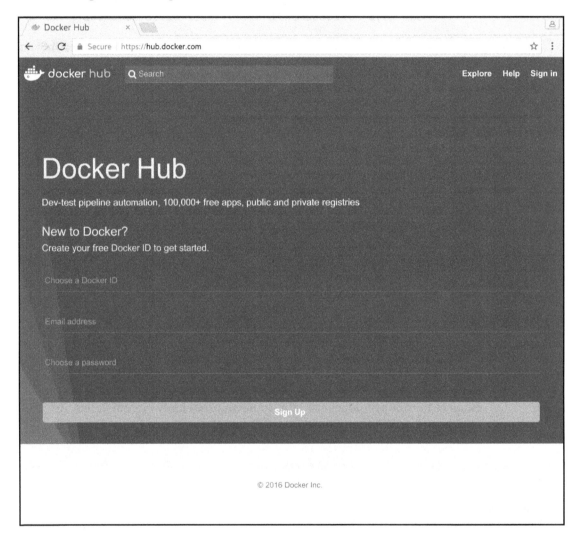

Behind this non-descriptive and bland page is the storage of thousands of Docker images, and since we are not interested in publishing images right now, we can just click on the **Explore** button in the top-right corner of the page to see what images are available:

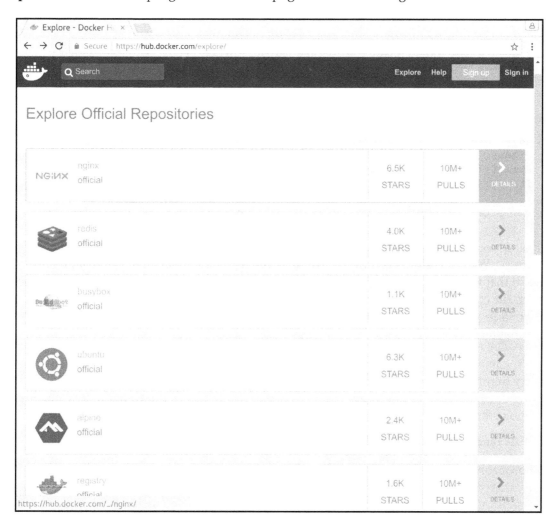

As you can see, this lists the most popular images at the time of writing, but you can look for specific ones through the **Search** box in the upper-left corner as well. For now, as mentioned a while ago, we will not be spending too much time here, but it will be valuable for you to know how to run images from Docker Hub, so we will try to pull and run one of them to show you how it is done.

The top container available here right now seems to be NGINX, so we will try to run that in our Docker environment. If you have not worked with NGINX before, it is a high-performance web server that is used by a large number of websites on the internet. At this stage, we just want to get the feel for running these containers, so let us see how that is done:

```
$ # Pull the image from the server to our local repository
$ docker pull nginx
Using default tag: latest
latest: Pulling from library/nginx
94ed0c431eb5: Pull complete
9406c100a1c3: Pull complete
aa74daafd50c: Pull complete
Digest:
sha256:788fa27763db6d69ad3444e8ba72f947df9e7e163bad7c1f5614f8fd27a311c3
Status: Downloaded newer image for nginx:latest
```

The `pull` command pulls any and all layers that compose this image. In this case, the NGINX image is based on three stacked layers and has a hash of `788fa277..27a311c3`, and since we didn't specify a specific version that we wanted, we got the default tag, which is `latest`. With this single command, we have retrieved the NGINX image from Docker Hub so that we can run it locally. If we wanted to use a different tag or pull from a different server, the command gets the more expressive form similar to `docker pull <hostname_or_ip>:<port>/<tag_name>`, but we will cover these advanced usages in later chapters.

With the image now sitting in our local Docker storage (usually in `/var/lib/docker`), we can try to run it. NGINX has an absolute sea of possible options that you can examine in further detail at `https://hub.docker.com/_/nginx/`, but we are interested in just starting the image for now:

```
$ docker run nginx
```

You probably noticed that nothing is happening, but do not worry as this is expected. Sadly, this command by itself is not enough as NGINX will run in foreground and not be accessible over a socket at all, so we need to cover a few flags and switches to really make it useful. So let's shut the container down by pressing *Ctrl + C* and try again, this time adding some of the necessary flags:

```
$ docker run -d \
            -p 8080:80 \
            nginx
dd1fd1b62d9cf556d96edc3ae7549f469e972267191ba725b0ad6081dda31e74
```

The -d flag runs the container in the background (the detached mode) so that our Terminal isn't held on by NGINX and the -p 8080:80 flag maps our local port 8080 to the container's port 80. Containers often have specific ports that they expose, amd in this case, it is 80 but without the mapping we would have no way of accessing it. The output that the command returns is a unique identifier (container ID) that can be used to track and control this specific container after starting it. Hopefully, you can now see how the port whitelisting approach of Docker adds an extra level of security as only the things you explicitly allow to listen are permitted.

You can now open your browser to http://localhost:8080, and you should see a page similar to this one:

But how exactly did we know that port 80 needs to be listened to? Indeed, we will cover that in just a second, but first, because we started this container in the detached mode, it will still be running in the background and we should probably make sure that we stop it too. To see which containers we have running, let's check our Docker container statuses with docker ps:

```
$ docker ps
CONTAINER ID IMAGE COMMAND CREATED STATUS PORTS NAMES
dd1fd1b62d9c nginx "nginx -g 'daemon ..." 13 minutes ago Up 13 minutes
0.0.0.0:8080->80/tcp dazzling_swanson
```

What we see here is that our NGINX container is still running, that it has mapped localhost interface ports 8080 (including externally accessible ones) with the container's port 80, and that we have been running it for 13 minutes. If we had more containers, they would all be listed here so this command is extremely useful for working with Docker containers and is generally used for debugging and container management.

Since we wanted to shut this container down, we will actually do that now. To shut a container down, we need to know the container ID that is both the value that was returned by docker run and the value that the first column of docker ps shows (dd1fd1b62d9c). Feel free to use either the short or long version of the ID, but for brevity, we will use the former:

```
$ docker stop dd1fd1b62d9c
dd1fd1b62d9c
```

This will gracefully try to stop the container and return the resources used back to the OS and after a specific timeout, kill it forcefully. If the container was really stuck and we knew it, we could replace stop with kill to hard kill the process, but that's rarely needed since stop generally does the same thing if the process is not responding. We will now make sure that our container is gone:

```
$ docker ps
CONTAINER ID IMAGE COMMAND CREATED STATUS PORTS NAMES
```

Yes, things look as we expect them to, but beware that while stopped containers are not visible, they are not completely removed from the filesystem by default:

```
$ docker ps -a
CONTAINER ID IMAGE COMMAND CREATED STATUS PORTS NAMES
dd1fd1b62d9c nginx "nginx -g 'daemon ..." 24 minutes ago Exited (137) 2
minutes ago dazzling_swanson
```

The -a flag is used to show all container statuses, not just the running ones, and you can see that the system still knows about our old container. We can even resume it with docker start!

```
$ docker start dd1fd1b62d9c
dd1fd1b62d9c

$ docker ps
CONTAINER ID IMAGE COMMAND CREATED STATUS PORTS NAMES
dd1fd1b62d9c nginx "nginx -g 'daemon ..." 28 minutes ago Up About a minute
0.0.0.0:8080->80/tcp dazzling_swanson
```

To really remove our container permanently, we need to explicitly get rid of it using `docker rm`, as shown here, or run the `docker run` command with the `--rm` switch (we'll cover this one in the next few pages):

```
$ docker stop dd1fd1b62d9c
dd1fd1b62d9c

$ docker rm dd1fd1b62d9c
dd1fd1b62d9c

$ docker ps -a
CONTAINER ID IMAGE COMMAND CREATED STATUS PORTS NAMES
```

Success!

Now let us get back to the earlier question of how we knew that the container needed to have port 80 mapped to it? We have a couple of options there for finding this information out, and the simplest one is starting the container and checking in `docker ps` to see which ports are unbound:

```
$ docker run -d \
          --rm \
          nginx
f64b35fc42c33f4af2648bf4f1dce316b095b30d31edf703e099b93470ab725a

$ docker ps
CONTAINER ID IMAGE COMMAND CREATED STATUS PORTS NAMES
f64b35fc42c3 nginx "nginx -g 'daemon ..." 4 seconds ago Up 3 seconds 80/tcp
awesome_bell
```

The new flag here that we used with `docker run` is `--rm`, which we just mentioned, and it tells the Docker daemon to remove the container completely after it is stopped so we don't have to do it manually ourselves.

 If you already have a container that you want to check the mapped ports on, you can use `docker port <container_id>` command but we are omitting it here since it cannot be used on images, but just containers.

While this is the quickest way to see what ports will be needed, the general way to inspect an image outside of reading its Dockerfile and documentation is through `docker inspect`:

```
$ # Inspect NGINX image info and after you match our query, return also
next two lines
$ docker inspect nginx | grep -A2 "ExposedPorts"
"ExposedPorts": {
```

```
    "80/tcp": {}
},
```

Additionally, `docker inspect` can show all kinds of other interesting information, such as the following:

- The ID of the image
- The tag name
- The image creation date
- Hardcoded environment variables
- The command that the container runs on start
- The size of the container
- Image layers IDs
- Volumes specified

Feel free to run the inspect command on any container or image and see what gems you might find there. Majority of the time, this output is mainly used for debugging, but in cases where the image documentation is lacking, it can be an invaluable tool to get you running in a minimal amount of time.

Debugging containers

Often in general work with containers, you will likely have to figure out what is going on with a container that is running, but `docker ps` is not good enough to provide you with all the information you need to figure things out. For these cases, the first command to use is `docker logs`. This command displays any output that the container has emitted, including both `stdout` and `stderr` streams. For the following logs, I started the same NGINX container from before and accessed its hosted page on `localhost`:

```
$ docker run -d \
           -p 8080:80 \
           nginx
06ebb46f64817329d360bb897bda824f932b9bcf380ed871709c2033af069118

$ # Access the page http://localhost:8080 with your browser

$ docker logs 06ebb46f
172.17.0.1 - - [02/Aug/2017:01:39:51 +0000] "GET / HTTP/1.1" 200 612 "-"
"Mozilla/5.0 (Windows NT 6.3; rv:36.0) Gecko/20100101 Firefox/36.01" "-"
2017/08/02 01:39:51 [error] 6#6: *1 open()
"/usr/share/nginx/html/favicon.ico" failed (2: No such file or directory),
```

```
client: 172.17.0.1, server: localhost, request: "GET /favicon.ico
HTTP/1.1", host: "localhost:8080"
172.17.0.1 - - [02/Aug/2017:01:39:51 +0000] "GET /favicon.ico HTTP/1.1" 404
169 "-" "Mozilla/5.0 (Windows NT 6.3; rv:36.0) Gecko/20100101
Firefox/36.01" "-"
172.17.0.1 - - [02/Aug/2017:01:39:52 +0000] "GET / HTTP/1.1" 200 612 "-"
"Mozilla/5.0 (Windows NT 6.3; rv:36.0) Gecko/20100101 Firefox/36.01" "-"
```

You can see here that NGINX records all access and the associated response codes that are invaluable to debugging a web server. In general, the output can vary from very useful to garbage depending on what is running the service, but it is usually a good place to start your search. You can also add the `-f` flag if you want to follow the logs as they are being written, which is very helpful when logs are large and you are trying to filter noise from specific things you are looking for.

Seeing what the container sees

When logs aren't really enough to figure things out, the command to use is `docker exec` in order to execute a command on the running container that can include access to a full-blown shell:

```
$ docker run -d \
            -p 8080:80 \
            nginx
06ebb46f64817329d360bb897bda824f932b9bcf380ed871709c2033af069118

$ docker exec 06ebb46f ls -la /etc/nginx/conf.d/
total 12
drwxr-xr-x 2 root root 4096 Jul 26 07:33 .
drwxr-xr-x 3 root root 4096 Jul 26 07:33 ..
-rw-r--r-- 1 root root 1093 Jul 11 13:06 default.conf
```

In this case, we used `docker exec` to run the `ls` command in the container, but as-is that is not really a powerful debugging tool. What if we try to get that full shell within the container and examine it that way?

```
$ docker exec -it \
            06ebb46f /bin/bash
root@06ebb46f6481:/# ls -la /etc/nginx/conf.d/
total 12
drwxr-xr-x 2 root root 4096 Jul 26 07:33 .
drwxr-xr-x 3 root root 4096 Jul 26 07:33 ..
-rw-r--r-- 1 root root 1093 Jul 11 13:06 default.conf
root@06ebb46f6481:/# exit
exit
```

```
$ # Back to host shell
```

This time, we used `-it`, which is shorthand for `-i` and `-t` flags that combine to set up the interactive Terminal needed for a full shell access and then we use `/bin/bash` to run Bash within the container. The shell within the container is a much more useful tool here, but we are at the mercy of the container itself in terms of installed tooling since many images trim out any unnecessary packages from the image--in this case, the NGINX container doesn't have `ps`, which is an extremely valuable utility for finding causes of problems. Since containers are isolated throwaway components generally, sometimes it might be fine to add your debugging tools to the container in order to find out what is causing problems (though we will cover a much better way of doing this with `pid` namespaces joining in later chapters):

```
$ docker exec -it 06ebb46f /bin/bash

root@06ebb46f6481:/# ps  # No ps on system
bash: ps: command not found

root@06ebb46f6481:/# apt-get update -q
Hit:1 http://security.debian.org stretch/updates InRelease
Get:3 http://nginx.org/packages/mainline/debian stretch InRelease [2854 B]
Ign:2 http://cdn-fastly.deb.debian.org/debian stretch InRelease
Hit:4 http://cdn-fastly.deb.debian.org/debian stretch-updates InRelease
Hit:5 http://cdn-fastly.deb.debian.org/debian stretch Release
Fetched 2854 B in 0s (2860 B/s)
Reading package lists...

root@06ebb46f6481:/# apt-get install -y procps
<snip>
The following NEW packages will be installed:
libgpm2 libncurses5 libprocps6 procps psmisc
0 upgraded, 5 newly installed, 0 to remove and 0 not upgraded.
Need to get 558 kB of archives.
After this operation, 1785 kB of additional disk space will be used.
<snip>

root@06ebb46f6481:/# ps
PID TTY TIME CMD
31 ? 00:00:00 bash
595 ? 00:00:00 ps

root@06ebb46f6481:/#
```

As you can see, adding any debug tooling to the container from its upstream distribution is easy, but be aware that once you find your issue, you should start a new container and remove the old one to clean up the leftover junk since it is wasting space and a new container will start from the image that did not have your newly-installed debugging tools added (in our case `procps`).

Another thing to keep in mind is that sometimes, the images prevent the installation of additional packages, so for those cases we will need to wait until later chapters to see how we can use namespaces to work in such constrained settings.

Sometimes, the container is locked into a limited user shell, and because of it, you will be unable to access or modify other parts of the system of the container. In such configurations, you can add the `-u 0` flag to run the `docker exec` command as `root` (`user 0`). You can also specify any other username or user ID instead, but generally if you need a secondary user to work with on a container, `root` is what you want.

Our first Dockerfile

Now that we know a little bit about how to get around containers, this is a good place to try out creating our own container. To start building a container, the first thing that we need to know is that the default filename that Docker looks for when building images is `Dockerfile`. While you can use different names for this main configuration file, it is highly discouraged though in some rare cases, you might not be able to avoid it - if, for example, you need a test suite image and the main image build files in the same folder. For now, we will assume you just have a single build configuration, and with that in mind, how about we see what one of these basic `Dockerfile` looks like. Create a test folder somewhere on your filesystem and put this into a file named `Dockerfile`:

```
FROM ubuntu:latest

RUN apt-get update -q && \
    apt-get install -qy iputils-ping

CMD ["ping", "google.com"]
```

Let's examine this file line by line. First, we have the `FROM ubuntu:latest` line in there. This line indicates that we want to use the latest Ubuntu Docker image as our base on which we will layer our own service. This image will be automatically pulled from Docker Hub, but this image can also be from a custom repository, your own local image, and could be based on any other image as long as it provides a good base for your service (that is, NGINX, Apline Linux, Jenkins, and so on) if we wanted to.

The next line is very important as the base Ubuntu image does not come with almost anything out of the box, so we need to install the package that provides the ping utility (`iputils-ping`) through its package manager `apt` , just like we would on the command line by using the `RUN` directive to Docker. Before we install it, though, we also need to make sure that our update indexes are up-to-date, and we use `apt-get update` for that. In a bit, we will cover in detail why we used `&&` to chain the `update` and `install` commands, but for now, we will magically ignore it so that we don't derail our example too much.

The `CMD` directive instructs Docker that by default, Docker will run `"ping" "google.com"` every time the container is started without further arguments. This directive is used to start the service within the container, and it ties the life cycle of the container to that process, so if our `ping` fails, our container terminates, and vice versa. You can only have one `CMD` line in your Dockerfile, so be especially careful what you use it for.

Now that we have the whole container configured, let's build it:

```
$ # Build using Dockerfile from current directory and tag our resulting
image as "test_container"
$ docker build -t test_container .

Sending build context to Docker daemon 1.716MB
Step 1/3 : FROM ubuntu:latest
---> 14f60031763d
Step 2/3 : RUN apt-get update -q && apt-get install -qy iputils-ping
---> Running in ad1ea6a6d4fc
Get:1 http://security.ubuntu.com/ubuntu xenial-security InRelease [102 kB]
<snip>
The following NEW packages will be installed:
iputils-ping libffi6 libgmp10 libgnutls-openssl27 libgnutls30 libhogweed4
libidn11 libnettle6 libp11-kit0 libtasn1-6
0 upgraded, 10 newly installed, 0 to remove and 8 not upgraded.
Need to get 1304 kB of archives.
<snip>
Setting up iputils-ping (3:20121221-5ubuntu2) ...
Processing triggers for libc-bin (2.23-0ubuntu9) ...
---> eab9729248d9
Removing intermediate container ad1ea6a6d4fc
Step 3/3 : CMD ping google.com
```

```
---> Running in 44fbc308e790
---> a719d8db1c35
Removing intermediate container 44fbc308e790
Successfully built a719d8db1c35
Successfully tagged test_container:latest
```

As the comment on it implies, what we did here with `docker build -t test_container` . is that we built the container (using the default Dockerfile configuration name) in our current directory and tagged it with the name `test_container`. Since we didn't specify the version at the end of `test_container`, Docker assigned us one called `latest`, as we can see from the end of the output. If we carefully examine the output, we can also see that each change to the base image creates a new layer and that layer's ID is then used as the input into the next directive, each layer creating its own filesystem diff onto the image. If, for example, we run the build again, Docker is smart enough to know that nothing has changed and it will use the cached version of those layers again. Compare the final container ID (`a719d8db1c35`) with the one from the previous run:

```
$ docker build -t test_container .

Sending build context to Docker daemon 1.716MB
Step 1/3 : FROM ubuntu:latest
---> 14f60031763d
Step 2/3 : RUN apt-get update -q && apt-get install -qy iputils-ping
---> Using cache
---> eab9729248d9
Step 3/3 : CMD ping google.com
---> Using cache
---> a719d8db1c35
Successfully built a719d8db1c35
Successfully tagged test_container:latest
```

If any change is detected in the directives of the Dockerfile, Docker will rebuild that layer and any subsequent ones to ensure consistency. This functionality and selective "cache busting" will also be covered later and it has a very important role in managing your repository and image sizes.

With the container built, let's see whether it actually works (to exit its loop, press *Ctrl + C*):

```
$ # Run the image tagged "test_container"
$ docker run test_container

PING google.com (216.58.216.78) 56(84) bytes of data.
64 bytes from ord30s21-in-f14.1e100.net (216.58.216.78): icmp_seq=1 ttl=52
time=45.9 ms
64 bytes from ord30s21-in-f14.1e100.net (216.58.216.78): icmp_seq=2 ttl=52
```

```
time=41.9 ms
64 bytes from ord30s21-in-f14.1e100.net (216.58.216.78): icmp_seq=3 ttl=52
time=249 ms
^C
--- google.com ping statistics ---
3 packets transmitted, 3 received, 0% packet loss, time 2002ms
rtt min/avg/max/mdev = 41.963/112.460/249.470/96.894 ms
```

Another success! You wrote your first running Docker container!

Breaking the cache

In the container we just wrote, we somewhat glanced over the line RUN apt-get update -q && apt-get install -qy iputils-ping since it requires a bit of a deeper discussion here. In most Linux distributions, packages rotate in versions all the time, but the listing of these indexes that tell us where to find these is baked into the original Docker image when it gets created (ubuntu:latest in this case). Before we can install a package, in most cases, our index files have been stale for too long (if they haven't been completely removed), so we need to update them. Splitting this && joined line into two separate ones would work for that first build:

```
RUN apt-get update -q
RUN apt-get install -qy iputils-ping
```

But what happens when you add another package to that second line later, as shown in the following line?

```
RUN apt-get install -qy curl iputils-ping
```

In this case, Docker is not very smart and will consider the update line to be unchanged and will not run the update command again, so it will use the state from the cache for the update layer and then continue on to the next one that tries to install curl (since that one did change since the last build), which is likely to fail if enough versions have been rotated in the repositories as the indexes will be stale again. To prevent this from occurring, we join the update and the install commands with && so they are treated as one directive and create one layer, in which case, changing any part of either of the two joined commands will break the cache and run the update correctly. Sadly, as you get more involved with scalable Docker components, using odd tricks such as these to manage the cache and do selective cache busting will become a large part of your work.

A container more practical

This is probably where we start diverging from other Docker materials out there that practically assume that with just this basic knowledge, the rest of the work is a cakewalk when it is really nothing like that. It is not rocket science, but these simple examples really do not do enough to get us where we need to be, so we will use a practical example based a bit on our previous work with NGINX and create a container that uses this web server image to provide and serve up content that we will bake into the image.

 This example and all the other ones in this book are also available on GitHub at `https://github.com/sgnn7/deploying_with_docker`. You can use either `git` or their web interface to follow along with the examples, but all examples of code that we will use will be directly included in the book too.

To begin creating our web server, we need to create a directory to put all of our files in:

```
$ mkdir ~/advanced_nginx
$ cd ~/advanced_nginx
```

The first file we need to create is our dummy text file that we will try to serve up in the image:

```
$ echo "Just a test file" > test.txt
```

The next file we will need is the required NGINX configuration. Put the following text into a file called `nginx_main_site.conf`:

```
server {
  listen 80;
  server_name _;
  root /srv/www/html;

  # Deny access to any files prefixed with '.'
  location ~/\. {
    deny all;
  }

  # Serve up the root path at <host>/
  location / {
    index index.html;
    autoindex on;
  }
}
```

If you've never worked with NGINX, let's check out what this file does. In the first block, we are creating a `server` that listens on port `80` rooted in `/srv/www/html` on the image. The second block, while not strictly needed and would require changing for bigger websites, should be muscle memory for anyone working on NGINX since it prevents the downloading of hidden files like `.htaccess`, `.htpasswd`, and many others that should not be available publicly. The last block just makes sure that any path starting with `/` will be read from `root` and if the index file is not provided, it will use `index.html`. If no such file is available and we are in a directory, `autoindex` ensures that it can show you a human-readable listing of a directory.

 While this NGINX configuration is functional, there are many things that it is not including (SSL configuration, logging, error files, file lookup matching, and so on), but that is mostly because this is a book is trying to focus on Docker itself and not NGINX. If you would like to learn more about how to fully and properly configure NGINX, you can visit `https://nginx.org/en/docs/` for more information.

With the configuration written, we can now create our Dockerfile, which will take our test file, our configuration file, and the NGINX image and turn it all into a Docker image that runs a web server and serves up our test file:

```
FROM nginx:latest

# Make sure we are fully up to date
RUN apt-get update -q && \
    apt-get dist-upgrade -y

# Remove the default configuration
RUN rm /etc/nginx/conf.d/default.conf

# Create our website's directory and make sure
# that the webserver process can read it
RUN mkdir -p /srv/www/html && \
    chown nginx:nginx /srv/www/html

# Put our custom server configuration in
COPY nginx_main_site.conf /etc/nginx/conf.d/

# Copy our test file in the location that is
# being served up
COPY test.txt /srv/www/html/
```

This Dockerfile probably looks a lot different from the first one, so we will spend some time diving into what we are doing here.

Extending another container with FROM

Similar to our last container, our `FROM nginx:latest` line ensures that we are using the latest version of a base image, but instead of Ubuntu, here, we will use NGINX as our base. The `latest` ensures that we get the image with the latest features and often patches too at a slight risk of breakages and API incompatibility in the future.

When writing your Docker containers, you will often have to make these trade-off decisions based on your situation and stability requirements, but the NGINX API has been very stable for years now, so in this specific case, we do not need the stability that the named tags provide. If we wanted one of those tagged versions here, `latest` would just change to the version we wanted that is offered on Docker Hub, which we can find at `https://hub.docker.com/_/nginx/`, so something like `FROM nginx:1.13` would have been perfectly fine too.

Ensuring the latest patches are included

Our next steps, `apt-get upgrade` and `apt-get dist-upgrade`, are a bit controversial in the current Docker world, but I think they are a good addition, and I'll explain why. On a regular `deb` package-based Linux distribution (that is, Debian, Ubuntu, and so on), these two commands ensure that your system is fully up to date with the currently released packages for your version of the system. This means that any package that isn't the newest version will be upgraded and any obsolete packages will be replaced with newer ones. Since the general maxim of Docker is that the containers are more or less disposable, updating your container this way seems to be somewhat frowned upon, but it's not without its faults.

Since most Docker images on Docker Hub are only built when the base source files or Dockerfile itself changes, many of these images have older and/or unpatched system libraries, so when the service uses them as a dynamic library, it may be vulnerable to any bugs that have since been fixed. To ensure that we are not behind on this security hardening, we make sure that we update the system before we do anything else. While there is a small risk of the service breaking due to the system API possibly changing and there is an increase in image size due to the additional changes applied, the trade-off is, in my opinion, not good enough to leave the service unprotected, but feel free to use your best judgment here.

Applying our custom NGINX configuration

Our directive after the system update (RUN rm /etc/nginx/conf.d/default.conf) is one that removes the default web server configuration from the container. You can find out more about the NGINX configuration with the link from our last tip, but for now, it will suffice to say that by default, all the individual site configuration files are stored in /etc/nginx/conf.d and NGINX Docker image comes out of the box with a simple example file called default.conf, which we absolutely do not want to use.

While we could overwrite the mentioned file, we would be stuck with the name default, which isn't very descriptive, so for our configuration, we will delete this one and add ours with a better filename.

Next, we need to make sure that the folder we will be serving files from is available and readable by the web server process. The first command using mkdir -p creates all the relevant directories, but since NGINX doesn't run as the root, we need to know what user the process will be reading the files we want to serve up or otherwise our server will not be able to display anything. We can find what the original configuration has there as the default user by showing the first few lines of the system-wide NGINX configuration included in the image at /etc/nginx/nginx.conf:

```
$ # Print top 2 lines of main config file in NGINX image
$ docker run --rm \
            nginx /bin/head -2 /etc/nginx/nginx.conf

user nginx;
```

Perfect! Well, now that the user that needs to be able to read this directory is nginx, we will change the owner of our target folder with chown nginx:nginx /srv/www/html, but what is going on with that new style of run Docker command we just used when trying to find this out? If you include a command after specifying the image name instead of the CMD directive in the image, Docker will substitute it with this new command. In the preceding command, we are running the /bin/head executable, passing in arguments to tell it that we only want the top two lines from the /etc/nginx/nginx.conf file. Since this command exits as soon as it is done, the container stops and is fully removed because we used the --rm flag.

With the default configuration gone and our directories created, we can now copy our main configuration for NGINX in place with COPY nginx_main_site.conf /etc/nginx/conf.d/. The COPY argument does pretty much the obvious thing of copying a file from the current build directory into the image at a specified location.

Be very careful with how you end the COPY directive argument, as leaving the slash off will put the source into a file at the destination even if the destination is a directory. To ensure that this doesn't happen, always end your target directory paths with a slash.

Adding our main test.txt file that we want hosted is the last part, and it follows along the same lines as the other COPY directive, but we will make sure that we put this one in the folder that our NGINX configuration is referencing. Since we turned on the autoindex flag for this endpoint, there are no additional steps to be taken as the folder itself will be browsable.

Building and running

Now that we went over the whole build configuration, we can create our image and see what we just made:

```
$ docker build -t web_server .

Sending build context to Docker daemon 17.41kB
Step 1/6 : FROM nginx:latest
 ---> b8efb18f159b
Step 2/6 : RUN apt-get update -q && apt-get dist-upgrade -yq
 ---> Running in 5cd9ae3712da
Get:1 http://nginx.org/packages/mainline/debian stretch InRelease [2854 B]
Get:2 http://security.debian.org stretch/updates InRelease [62.9 kB]
Get:3 http://nginx.org/packages/mainline/debian stretch/nginx amd64
Packages [11.1 kB]
Get:5 http://security.debian.org stretch/updates/main amd64 Packages [156
kB]
Ign:4 http://cdn-fastly.deb.debian.org/debian stretch InRelease
Get:6 http://cdn-fastly.deb.debian.org/debian stretch-updates InRelease
[88.5 kB]
Get:7 http://cdn-fastly.deb.debian.org/debian stretch Release [118 kB]
Get:8 http://cdn-fastly.deb.debian.org/debian stretch Release.gpg [2373 B]
Get:9 http://cdn-fastly.deb.debian.org/debian stretch/main amd64 Packages
[9497 kB]
Fetched 9939 kB in 40s (246 kB/s)
Reading package lists...
Reading package lists...
Building dependency tree...
Reading state information...
Calculating upgrade...
0 upgraded, 0 newly installed, 0 to remove and 0 not upgraded.
 ---> 4bbd446af380
Removing intermediate container 5cd9ae3712da
```

```
Step 3/6 : RUN rm /etc/nginx/conf.d/default.conf
 ---> Running in 39ad3da8979a
 ---> 7678bc9abdf2
Removing intermediate container 39ad3da8979a
Step 4/6 : RUN mkdir -p /srv/www/html && chown nginx:nginx /srv/www/html
 ---> Running in e6e50483e207
 ---> 5565de1d2ec8
Removing intermediate container e6e50483e207
Step 5/6 : COPY nginx_main_site.conf /etc/nginx/conf.d/
 ---> 624833d750f9
Removing intermediate container a2591854ff1a
Step 6/6 : COPY test.txt /srv/www/html/
 ---> 59668a8f45dd
Removing intermediate container f96dccae7b5b
Successfully built 59668a8f45dd
Successfully tagged web_server:latest
```

Seems like the container build is just fine; let's run it:

```
$ docker run -d \
           -p 8080:80 \
           --rm \
           web_server
bc457d0c2fb0b5706b4ca51b37ca2c7b8cdecefa2e5ba95123aee4458e472377

$ docker ps
CONTAINER ID IMAGE COMMAND CREATED STATUS PORTS NAMES
bc457d0c2fb0 web_server "nginx -g 'daemon ..." 30 seconds ago Up 29 seconds
0.0.0.0:8080->80/tcp goofy_barti
```

So far, so good, as it seems to be running fine. Now we will access the container with our browser at `http://localhost:8080`.

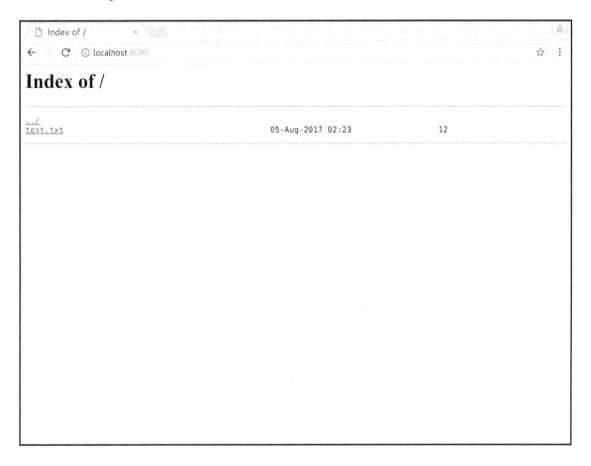

As we were hoping, our server is working and showing us the content of /srv/www/html, but let's click on test.txt to make sure it is working too:

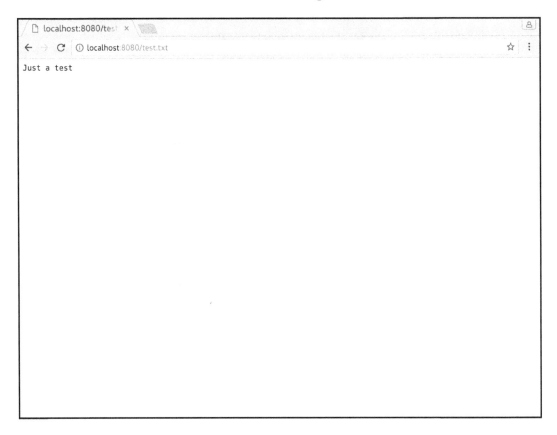

Great, it looks like our plan worked and we have created a high-performance static website hosting server container! Sure, there are many other things we can add to this, but our main goal of extending a sample image to do something useful is a success!

Service from scratch

Our last example was decently comprehensive but it left out some important Docker commands that we should also know, so we will use another example, albeit reworking the web server solution in a slightly less optimal way, to both show them used and to explain what they do. In the process, we will go a bit deeper and see whether we can make as many parts of the service on our own.

We will start this example with creating a clean directory and creating the same test file we used earlier:

```
$ mkdir ~/python_webserver
$ cd ~/python_webserver

$ echo "Just a test file" > test.txt
```

Now we will create our bit-more-complex Python-based web server container by putting the following content in the `Dockerfile`:

```
FROM python:3

# Add some labels for cache busting and annotating
LABEL version="1.0"
LABEL org.sgnn7.name="python-webserver"

# Set a variable that we will keep reusing to prevent typos
ENV SRV_PATH=/srv/www/html

# Make sure we are fully up to date
RUN apt-get update -q && \
    apt-get dist-upgrade -y

# Let Docker know that the exposed port we will use is 8000
EXPOSE 8000

# Create our website's directory, then create a limited user
# and group
RUN mkdir -p $SRV_PATH && \
    groupadd -r -g 350 pythonsrv && \
    useradd -r -m -u 350 -g 350 pythonsrv

# Define ./external as an externally-mounted directory
VOLUME $SRV_PATH/external

# To serve things up with Python, we need to be in that
# same directory
WORKDIR $SRV_PATH

# Copy our test file
COPY test.txt $SRV_PATH/

# Add a URL-hosted content into the image
ADD https://raw.githubusercontent.com/moby/moby/master/README.md \
    $SRV_PATH/

# Make sure that we can read all of these files as a
```

```
# limited user
RUN chown -R pythonsrv:pythonsrv $SRV_PATH

# From here on out, use the limited user
USER pythonsrv

# Run the simple http python server to serve up the content
CMD [ "python3", "-m", "http.server" ]
```

 Using Python's built-in web server is highly discouraged in almost all cases, as it is neither scalable nor configurable in any significant way, but it serves as a good example of a service that could be hosted through Docker and is available on almost all systems with Python. Do not use this in real production services unless you really know what you are doing.

Barring the note about using python's web server module in production, this is still a good example of all of the other major Dockerfile directives that we didn't cover and that you will now learn how to use.

Labels

Our first new directive here is LABEL:

```
LABEL version="1.0"
LABEL org.sgnn7.name="python-webserver"
```

LABEL <key>=<value> or LABEL <key> <value> is used to add metadata about the image that is being built, which can later be examined and filtered by docker ps and docker images using something like docker images --filter "<key>=<value>". Keys are generally all lowercase in the reverse-dns notation, but you can use anything you want here and version should be present on every image, so we use the top-level version key name. However, the version here is not only there so that we can filter images but also to break Docker's cache if we change it. Without cache-busting of this sort or through the manually set flag during builds (docker build --no-cache), Docker will keep reusing the cache all the way up to the most recently changed directive or files so there is a high probability that your container will stay stuck in a frozen package configuration. This condition may or may not be what you want, but just in case you have automated build tooling, adding a version layer that can break the cache whenever you change it makes the container very easy to update.

Setting environment variables with ENV

ENV, unlike some of these other commands, should be mostly self-explanatory: it sets the environmental variables both in the Dockerfile and the container. Since we would need to keep re-typing /srv/www/html in our Dockerfile, in order to prevent typos and to ensure easy changes to our final server directory target, we set the SRV_PATH variable that we keep reusing with $SRV_PATH later. Generally for Docker containers, almost all the configurations to containers are done through environmental variables such as these, so expect to see this directive more in the later chapters.

 Even though we don't use it in this example, you need to watch out when using environment variables in the CMD directive directly as it does not get expanded but runs directly. You can ensure that your variable gets expanded in CMD by using it as part of a shell command structure similar to this: CMD ["sh", " c", "echo", "$SRV_PATH"].

Exposing ports

Our next new directive here is EXPOSE 8000. Remember how we used docker info to find out what port the NGINX container was using? This directive filled in that information in the metadata and is used by the Docker orchestration tooling to map incoming ports into the right ingress port on the container. Since Python's HTTP server starts its service on port 8000 by default, we use EXPOSE to inform Docker that whoever uses this container should make sure that they map this port on the host. You can also list multiple ports here with this directive but since our service is using only one, we will not need to use that right now.

Container security layering with limited users

The following novel block of code in our Dockerfile is probably a little bit of a convoluted puzzle, but we will go through it together:

```
RUN mkdir -p $SRV_PATH && \
    groupadd -r -g 350 pythonsrv && \
    useradd -r -m -u 350 -g 350 pythonsrv
```

This is something we need to expand on multiple levels, but the first thing you need to know is that by default, Dockerfile directives are executed as `root`, and if at any point later you do not specify a different `USER`, your service will run with `root` credentials, which is a massive hole from a security perspective that we are trying to patch up by running our service as a limited user only. However, without the user and group defined, we cannot switch our context away from the `root`, so we create both a `pythonsrv` group first and then we follow it up by creating the `pythonsrv` user attached to the said group. The `-r` flags mark the user and group a system-level entity and is a good practice for groups and users that will not be directly logged into.

Speaking of users and groups, if you mount a volume from the host to the Docker container that is running as a limited user, if neither the host nor the container perfectly agree on the user and group IDs (`uid` and `gid`, respectively), you cannot read or write files from volumes. To avoid this situation, we use a stable UID and GID of `350` that is easy to remember and is not normally in the regular UID/GID tables on most host systems. This number is mostly arbitrary, but as long as it is in the service range for your host OS and doesn't clash with the users or groups on the host either, it should be fine.

The last flag that wasn't covered so far is `-m`, and what it does is create the home directory skeleton files for the user. Most of the time, you will not need this, but if any subsequent operations try to use `$HOME` (such as `npm` or a large swathe of other services), there will be no such directory unless you specify this flag and your build will fail so we make sure we do not hit this condition by creating `$HOME` for the `pythonsrv` user.

To round this off, we chained all of these `RUN` commands together to ensure that we use as few layers as we can. Each layer creates additional metadata and increases the size of your image, so just like the Docker best practices document states, we try to reduce them by stacking these commands together. While it is not the best thing to do in all cases as debugging this style of configuration is pretty difficult, it does usually trim the container size significantly.

VOLUMEs and data that lives outside of the container

But what if we want to add files that live outside of the container that might need to persist even when the container dies? That is where the `VOLUME` directive comes into play. With `VOLUME`s, any time you start the container, this path is actually assumed to be mounted from outside of the container, and if none is provided, one will be created and attached for you automatically.

Here, we are assigning our `/srv/www/html/external` path to this unnamed volume, but we will reserve majority of our detailed discussion about volumes for later chapters.

Setting the working directory

Since the Python HTTP server can only serve files from the current directory that it runs in, without explicitly configuring this correctly our container would show files out of the `/` directory. To work around this, we include `WORKDIR $SRV_ROOT` into the `Dockerfile` which changes our working directory to the one that will contain the files we want to serve up. A thing to note about this command is that you can reuse it as many times as you want and it applies to any subsequent commands in the Dockerfile (such as `RUN` or `CMD`).

Adding files from the internet

What about trying to add files to your container that are not hosted locally and/or due to licensing you cannot include them in your repository where the `Dockerfile` lives? For this specific purpose, there is the `ADD` directive. This command downloads the file from the URI provided and puts it in the container. If the file is local compressed archive, such as a `.tgz` or a `.zip` file and the target path ends with a slash, it will get expanded into that directory, making this a very useful option as opposed to `COPY`. In the example that we're writing here, we will take a semi-random file from GitHub and put it in the directory to be included with the following:

```
ADD https://raw.githubusercontent.com/moby/moby/master/README.md \
  $SRV_PATH/
```

Changing the current user

We have explained why we need to run our service as a limited user and how we created the user for it, but now is the time to permanently switch the context to `pythonsrv`. Using `USER pythonsrv`, any further commands will be executed as `pythonsrv` user, including the container's `CMD` executable command, which is exactly what we want. Just like `WORKDIR`, this directive can be used multiple times in a `Dockerfile`, but for our purposes, there is no need to do the rest of the configuration as non-`root`. Generally, it is a good practice to keep this layer statement as high as possible in the `Dockerfile` since it is very unlikely that it will change and would be unlikely to break cache. However, for this example, we can't move it higher as our previous command uses `chown`, which requires `root` privileges.

Putting it all together

We're nearly done! The last thing we need to do is start Python's built-in HTTP server module when our container starts:

```
CMD [ "python3", "-m", "http.server" ]
```

With everything in place, we can build and start our new container:

```
$ docker build -t python_server .
Sending build context to Docker daemon 16.9kB
Step 1/14 : FROM python:3
 ---> 968120d8cbe8
<snip>
Step 14/14 : CMD python3 -m http.server
 ---> Running in 55262476f342
 ---> 38fab9dca6cd
Removing intermediate container 55262476f342
Successfully built 38fab9dca6cd
Successfully tagged python_server:latest

$ docker run -d \
            -p 8000:8000 \
            --rm \
            python_server
d19e9bf7fe70793d7fce49f3bd268917015167c51bd35d7a476feaac629c32b8
```

We can cross our fingers and check what we have built by accessing
`http://localhost:8000`:

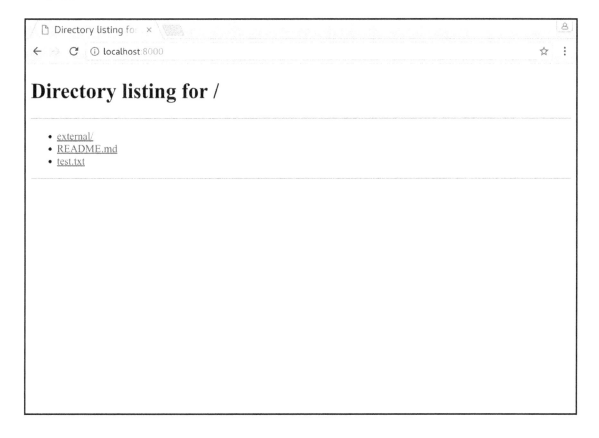

It works! Clicking on the `test.txt` shows the correct `Just a test` string and `README.md` that we fetched from GitHub downloads just fine when clicked. With all of the functionality there, what is in the `external/` directory?

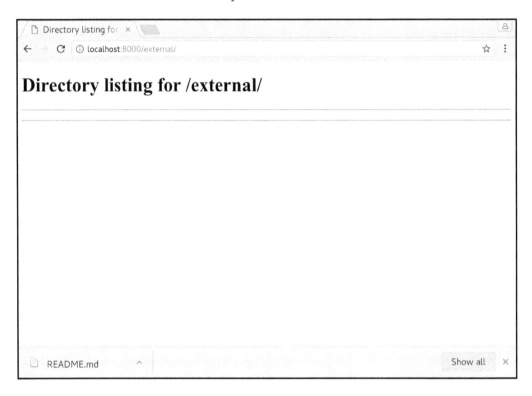

If the volume is empty, it is really no surprise that our directory here is empty too. How about we see whether we can mount some files from our host into this directory:

```
$ # Kill our old container that is still running
$ docker kill d19e9bf7
d19e9bf7

$ # Run our image but mount our current folder to container's
$ # /srv/www/html/external folder
$ docker run -d \
            -p 8000:8000 \
            --rm \
            -v $(pwd):/srv/www/html/external \
            python_server
9756b456074f167d698326aa4cbe5245648e5487be51b37b00fee36067464b0e
```

Here, we are mounting our current directory (`$(pwd)`) to our `/srv/www/html/external` target with our `-v` flag. So what does `http://localhost:8000/external` look like now? Do we have our files visible?

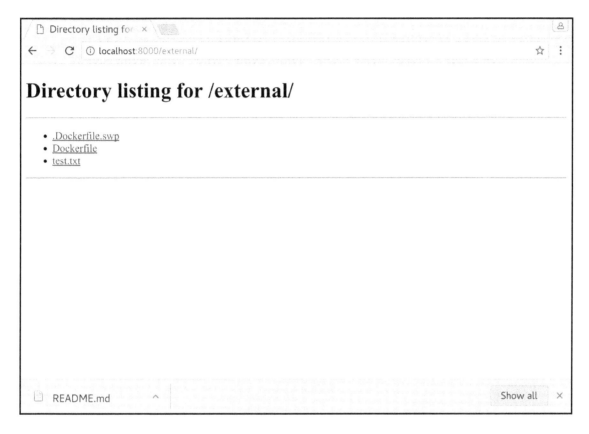

Indeed we do - our service works exactly as we expect it to! A real service written from scratch!

With a working service under our belt, we should now be able to continue our journey into Docker in the next chapter by scaling our containers.

Summary

In this chapter, we covered everything from the basic Docker container to extending an existing container, all the way to creating our own service from scratch. Along the way, we covered the most important Docker and Dockerfile commands and how to use them and, even more importantly, *where* and *why* to use them. While this was not the most in-depth coverage of the topic, it is just the right amount of depth we need in order to start working on scaling containers in our next chapter.

3
Service Decomposition

This chapter will cover how to take the knowledge from the previous chapter and use it to create and build an addition of a database and an application server container, since real-world services are usually composed in such a way. Once we get them all built up, we will see what is needed in order to group them together into a more usable service and cover even of more Docker under the hood.

In this chapter, we will cover the following topics:

- A quick review of Docker commands
- Writing a real service with:
    - A web server service
    - An application service
    - A database
- Introducing volumes
- Security considerations for credential passing

A quick review

Before we start, let's review the Docker and Dockerfile commands we covered previously in a single section in two lists that you can use as a reference later.

Docker commands

Here are all of the commands we covered for Docker with a few others added, which you might use if you build containers frequently:

 For more in-depth information about parameters required for each, or to see commands that we have not covered yet, type `docker help` in the Terminal or the command by itself into the Terminal. You can also visit `https://docs.docker.com/` and explore the documentation if the information provided by the CLI output is not good enough, and it may contain more recent data.

```
docker attach - Attach the shell's input/output/error stream to the
container
docker build - Build a Docker image based on a provided Dockerfile
docker cp - Copy files between container and host
docker exec - Execute a command in a running container
docker images - List image available to your installation of docker
docker info - Display information about the system
docker inspect - Display information about Docker layers, containers,
images, etc
docker kill - Forcefully terminate a container
docker logs - Display logs from a container since it last started
docker pause - Pause all processes within a container
docker ps - List information about containers and their resource usage
docker pull - Pull an image from a remote repository into the local
registry
docker push - Push an image from the local registry into a remote
repository
docker rm - Remove a container
docker rmi - Remove an image from the local repository
docker run - Start a new container and run it
docker search - Search DockerHub for images
docker start - Start a stopped container
docker stop - Stop a running container nicely (wait for container to shut
down)
docker tag - Create a tag for an image
docker top - Show running processes of a container
docker unpause - Resume all processes in a paused container
docker version - Show the Docker version
```

Recently, Docker commands have begun to be isolated into their own docker CLI sections like `docker container`, to separate them from other cluster management commands. To use this newer syntax, just prepend any command with the container (that is, `docker stop` turns into `docker container stop`). You can feel free to use either version, though keep an eye out as you can probably expect the older style to be deprecated at some point even though the new style is overly verbose for most Docker usage.

Dockerfile commands

The following list is a similar one, but this time, we are covering the commands you can use in a Dockerfile, and we've arranged it in an order similar to the one you would use when working within the Dockerfile:

`FROM <image_name>[:<tag>]`: Base the current image on `<image_name>`

`LABEL <key>=<value> [<key>=value>...]`: Add metadata to the image

`EXPOSE <port>`: Indicate which port should be mapped into the container

`WORKDIR <path>`: Set the current directory for the following commands

`RUN <command> [ && <command>... ]`: Execute one or more shell commands

`ENV <name>=<value>`: Set an environment variable to a specific value

`VOLUME <path>`: Indicates that the <path> should be externally mounted volume

`COPY <src> <dest>`: Copy a local file, a group of files, or a folder into the container

`ADD <src> <dest>`: The same as `COPY` but can handle URIs and local archives

`USER <user | uid>`: Set the runtime context to `<user>` or `<uid>` for commands after this one

`CMD ["<path>", "<arg1>", ...]`: Define the command to run when the container is started

 Since almost all containers you would want to build can be constructed with this set, this list is not the whole superset of Docker commands, and a few of them have been intentionally left out. If you get curious about things such as `ENTRYPOINT`, `ARG`, `HEALTHCHECK`, or others, you can check out the complete documentation at `https://docs.docker.com/engine/reference/builder/`.

Writing a real service

So far, we have spent time making fake or mock container services that helped us build Docker skills, but we have not had a chance to work on something that resembles a real-world service. In general, most of the simpler services that get utilized out there will look something similar to what is shown in this high-level diagram:

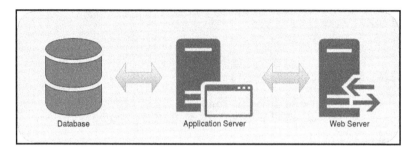

An overview

Here we will discuss each service in detail.

Web servers:

The rightmost piece in the image we just looked at is a web server. Web servers act as high-speed HTTP request processing handlers and are generally used in this context as follows:

- Reverse-proxy endpoints for resources within the clusters, **Virtual Private Cloud** (**VPC**), and/or **Virtual Private Network** (**VPN**)
- Hardened gatekeepers to limit resource access and/or prevent abuse
- Analytics collection points
- Load balancers
- Static content delivery servers
- Reducers of application server logic utilization
- SSL termination endpoints
- Caches of remote data
- Data diodes (allow either ingress or egress of data but not both)
- Local or federated account AAA handlers

This particular piece of our imaginary service is not always strictly required if the need for security is extremely low, the services are internal, and processing power is abundant, but in almost all other cases where any of these conditions are not present, the addition of a web server is practically mandatory. A good analogy to a web server is your home router. While it is not strictly necessary for you to use the Internet, a dedicated router enables better sharing of your network and serves as a dedicated security appliance between you and the Internet. While we have spent much of the previous chapter using NGINX, many others can be used (Apache, Microsoft IIS, lighttpd, and so on) and are generally functionally interchangeable, but beware of significantly different configuration setups.

Application servers:

So if the web server is doing all this for us, what does the application server do? The application server is actually your main service logic, generally wrapped up in some web-accessible endpoints or a queue-consuming daemon. This piece could be used as follows:

- The main website framework
- Data manipulation API logic
- Some sort of data transformation layer
- Data aggregation framework

The main distinction between an application server versus a web server is that the web server generally operates on static data and makes generally rigid decisions in a flow, while the application server does almost all of the dynamic data processing in a non-linear fashion. Things that fall under this category are generally frameworks such as Node.js, Ruby on Rails, JBoss, Tornado, and others for running specific programming language applications which can process requests. Try not to think of needing a big framework as a requirement here since even the right Bash script or a C file could do the job just as well and still qualify as an application server.

The reason why we defer as much of the work as we can to the web server instead of the application server is that due to the framework overhead, an application server is generally extremely slow and thus unsuitable to do simple, small, and repetitive tasks that a web server could chew through without breaking a sweat. For reference, an average specialized web server will be about an order of magnitude more efficient at serving up static pages than a full blown application server and, by inference, that much faster than most application servers. As mentioned earlier, you can probably handle low loads on an application server on its own or with some tuning medium ones, but anything above that is something that deserves a dedicated reverse proxy.

The database: Once we have this logic and static file processing down, they are sadly mostly useless without the actual data to transform and pass around. As with any software that uses data, this is done with a backing database. Since we want to be able to scale any piece of the system and isolate discrete components, the database gets its own section. In the pre-container world, though, we were dependent on big, monolithic databases that provided us with **Atomicity**, **Consistency**, **Isolation**, **and Durability** (**ACID**) properties, and they did their job well. However, in the container world, we absolutely do not want this type of architecture as it is neither as resilient nor as horizontally scalable as databases that are shardable and able to be clustered.

With these new-style databases, though, you generally do not get the same assurance that your data is treated in the same manner as the old-style ones, and it is an important distinction to have. What you get with most container-friendly databases instead of ACID is **Basically Available**, **Soft state**, **Eventual consistency** (**BASE**), which pretty much means that data will eventually be correct, but between the update initially being sent and the final state, the data may be in various states of intermediate values.

What we are going to build

We want to make a service that will be able to serve as a good example but not be too complicated, to show what a real-word example of a service might probably look like. For this use case, we will make a container grouping that can do two things behind basic HTTP authentication:

- Save a string entered in a form on the landing page to a database.
- When we land on the homepage, show the list of all strings saved so far.

Here, we will try to cover as many things as we can while also building a generally realistic prototype of a container-backed web service. Keep in mind that with the available tooling, even making a service as simple as this is not very easy so we will attempt to reduce the complexity where we can though the difficulty of our content does ramp up from here.

The implementation

As we covered the three major pieces that we need in general service architectures already, we will split our project into the same discrete parts with a web server, application server, and a database container, and we will outline the steps needed to build them here. As mentioned earlier, you can use Git to check out all of the code easily from GitHub at `https://github.com/sgnn7/deploying_with_docker` if you do not want to retype the code from these examples.

Web server

We can choose any web server software here, but since we have already worked with NGINX earlier, it makes sense that we would try to reuse bits and pieces of this component--it is practically what the container architecture is all about! The web server component will provide some basic authentication, cache data, and act as a reverse-proxy for the application server behind it. Our basic setup that we worked on earlier can be used here, but we will modify it a bit so that instead of serving files directly, it acts as a proxy and then use authentication based on a credentials file we will create in our `Dockerfile`. Let's create a new folder named `web_server` and add these files to it:

`nginx_main_site.conf`:

```
server {
  listen  80;
  server_name     _;

  root /srv/www/html;

  location ~/\. {
    deny all;
  }

  location / {
    auth_basic           "Authentication required";
    auth_basic_user_file /srv/www/html/.htpasswd;

    proxy_pass           http://172.17.0.1:8000;
  }
}
```

There are three interesting parts about this configuration here. The first one is the inclusion of `auth_basic_` commands that enable HTTP Basic authentication on all endpoints provided by this configuration. The second, if you were observant enough of the new `.`-prefixed credentials file, is the fact that our denial of fetching all files starting with a `.` is needed now since we added `.htpasswd`. The third and the final interesting thing here is the use of `proxy_pass`, which allows the server to route all traffic that is authenticated to the backend application server. Why we use `http://172.17.0.1:8000` as the destination is beginning to open the proverbial Pandora's box of Docker networking, so we will explain why we used it later as we will derail our service building if we cover it now.

Warning! In most cases, using basic authentication is a practical joke of security without HTTPS as we use it here since anyone on the network can sniff out your credentials in plaintext with the simplest of tools. In your services, at the very least, mandate the HTTPS protocol is you use basic auth or rely on stronger forms of credentials-passing before deploying services to anything with direct Internet access.

We can now add our new `Dockerfile` in that same directory, which will look like this:

```
FROM nginx:latest
# Make sure we are fully up to date
RUN apt-get update -q && \
    apt-get dist-upgrade -y && \
    apt-get install openssl && \
    apt-get clean && \
    apt-get autoclean

# Setup any variables we need
ENV SRV_PATH /srv/www/html

# Get a variable defined for our password
ARG PASSWORD=test

# Remove default configuration
RUN rm /etc/nginx/conf.d/default.conf

# Change ownership of copied files
RUN mkdir -p $SRV_PATH && \
    chown nginx:nginx $SRV_PATH

# Setup authentication file
RUN printf "user:$(openssl passwd -1 $PASSWORD)\n" >> $SRV_PATH/.htpasswd

# Add our own configuration in
COPY nginx_main_site.conf /etc/nginx/conf.d/
```

As you can see, we've made a couple of changes here from our original work in the previous chapter. The initial thing that should stick out is the new way to write the RUN apt-get line, which we've annotated here briefly:

```
RUN apt-get update -q && \        # Update our repository information
    apt-get dist-upgrade -y && \   # Upgrade any packages we already have
    apt-get install openssl && \   # Install dependency (openssl)
    apt-get clean && \             # Remove cached package files
    apt-get autoclean              # Remove any packages that are no longer
needed on the system
```

Unlike in previous images, here, we install the openssl package since we will need it to create NGINX-encrypted passwords for authentication, but the clean and autoclean lines are here to make sure we remove any cached apt packages on the system and remove orphaned packages, giving us a smaller image which is something we should always strive for. Just like before, we combine all of the lines in a similar manner early on so that the filesystem difference between the previous and current layer will only be the required changes and nothing else, making it a very compact change. When writing your own images, if you find yourself needing even more fat trimming, many more things can be removed (such as removing documentation files, /var directories, unnecessary optional packages, and so on), but these two should be the ones to use in most cases as they're simple to do and work pretty well on Debian-based systems.

Authentication

Without proper authentication, our server is wide open to anyone accessing it so we add a username/password combo to act as a gatekeeper to our service:

```
ARG PASSWORD=test
...
RUN printf "user:$(openssl passwd -1 $PASSWORD)\n" >> $SRV_PATH/.htpasswd
```

ARG acts as a build-time substitute for an ENV directive and allows the password to be passed in as a build argument with --build-arg <arg>. If the build is not provided with one, it should default to the argument after the equals sign, which is a very insecure test in this case. We will use this variable a bit lower in the Dockerfile to create the .htpasswd file with a specific password for our user.

The second line uses openssl, which we installed earlier, to take this build arg and create the .htpasswd file with encrypted credentials in a format that NGINX and most other web servers can understand (<username>:<hashed_password>).

Warning! Keep in mind that the `-1` algorithm is less secure than the **Salted SHA** (SSHA) method of creating `.htpasswd` passwords, but to create them in this way would have involved more complicated commands that would have distracted from our main purpose here, but you can visit `https://nginx.org/en/docs/http/ngx_http_auth_basic_module.html#auth_basic_user_file` for more details. Also be aware that you should never use online password generators as they can (and often do) steal your entered information.

If you haven't worked with Bash sub-shells before, `$(openssl ...)` is run in a separate shell and the output is substituted as a string variable before the rest is evaluated so the `>>` append operation will only see the encrypted password after `username:` and nothing related to `openssl`. As it should be somewhat apparent from these things, if we don't provide any build arguments, the container will have a single username `user` with a password set to `test`.

Warning! This type of credential passing to the image is used here as an example and is very nonsecure since anyone can run `docker history` and see what this variable was set to or start the image and echo the `PASSWORD` variable. In general, preferred ways of passing this type of sensitive data are through environment variables when you launch the container, mounting the credentials file as a volume onto the container, using `docker secret`, or an external credentials sharing service. We may cover some of these in later chapters, but for now, you should just keep in mind not to use this particular way of passing credentials in production due to security concerns.

With the `web_server` piece finished up, we can move to the next piece: the database.

The database

While SQL databases have come a long way in their ability to be sharded and clustered and generally provide good performance, many of cluster-friendly solutions have been based on NoSQL and in most cases use a key/value storage; plus, they have been gaining ground versus the entrenched SQL players in the ecosystem with each passing year. To get our feet wet quickest and with least amount of effort, we'll choose MongoDB here, which is a breeze to get working, and because it is NoSQL, we don't have to set up any kind of schema either, massively reducing our need for tricky configurations!

Warning! The default setup for MongoDB is very easy to do, but it does not enable any security by default, so anyone with network access to that container can read and write data to any database. In a private cloud, this might be somewhat acceptable, but in any other situation, it is not something that should be done, so keep in mind that if you plan on deploying MongoDB and make sure it is set up at least with some sort of isolation and/or authentication.

Our whole setup for the database here will be really simple, and if we didn't need to harden it with package updates, we wouldn't even have a custom one:

```
FROM mongo:3

# Make sure we are fully up to date
RUN apt-get update -q && \
    apt-get dist-upgrade -y && \
    apt-get clean && \
    apt-get autoclean
```

The only thing we should consider when we run it is to make sure that the database storage volume from the container (`/var/lib/mongodb`) is mounted from the host into the container so that we preserve it if the container stops, but we can worry about that once we start launching the container group.

The application server

For this component, we will pick a framework with a minimal amount of boilerplate needed to get a service up and operational, which most people would say today is Node.js with Express. Since Node.js is based on JavaScript, which was originally based on a Java-like syntax, most people who worked on HTML should be able to figure out what the application code is be doing, but before we get there, we need to define our Node package and our dependencies, so create a new `application_server` directory on the same level as `web_server` and add the following to a file called `package.json`:

```
{
  "name": "application-server",
  "version": "0.0.1",
  "scripts": {
    "start": "node index.js"
  },
  "dependencies": {
    "express": "^4.15.4"
  }
}
```

There's nothing really magical here; we're just using a Node package definition file to declare that we need Express as a dependency and that our `npm start` command should run `node index.js`.

Let's also make our Dockerfile now:

```
FROM node:8

# Make sure we are fully up to date
RUN apt-get update -q && \
    apt-get dist-upgrade -y && \
    apt-get clean && \
    apt-get autoclean

# Container port that should get exposed
EXPOSE 8000

# Setup any variables we need
ENV SRV_PATH /usr/local/share/word_test

# Make our directory
RUN mkdir -p $SRV_PATH && \
    chown node:node $SRV_PATH

WORKDIR $SRV_PATH

USER node

COPY . $SRV_PATH/

RUN npm install

CMD ["npm", "start"]
```

Many of these things should be very familiar here, especially with people familiar with Node. We are starting with the `node:8` image, adding our application code, installing the dependencies we defined in `package.json` (with `npm install`), and then finally making sure that the app starts when run from the `docker` CLI.

The order here is pretty important to both avoid cache breaking and ensure proper permissions. We place things that we don't expect to change much (`USER`, `WORKDIR`, `EXPOSE`, `mkdir`, and `chown`) above `COPY` since they are much less likely to change as opposed to the application code and since they're mostly interchangeable, we arrange them in the ascending order of what we think are the least likely to change in the future in order to prevent rebuilding of layers and wasted computing power.

Here is also a Node.js-specific image optimization trick: since `npm install` is usually the most time and CPU intensive part of dealing with code changes to a Node application, you can even further optimize this Dockerfile by copying only `package.json`, running `npm install`, and then copying the rest of the files to the container. Creating the container in this manner will only do the pricey `npm install` if `package.json` changes and will generally improve build times by a large margin, but this was excluded from this example in order to not derail our main conversation with framework-specific optimizations.

So far, we haven't really defined any application code, so let's see what that looks like too. First, we need an HTML view to be our landing page, and we can throw one together pretty quickly using a `pug` (formerly also known as `jade`) template. Create a `views/` folder and put this in a file named `index.pug` located in that folder:

```
html
  head
    title Docker words
  body
    h1 Saved Words

    form(method='POST' action='/new')
        input.form-control(type='text', placeholder='New word' name='word')
        button(type='submit') Save

    ul
        for word in words
            li= word
```

You don't have to know much about this templating style except that it is a simple HTML page on which we will display all items from the `words` array passed into it during rendering, and if a new word is put in, there will be a form submitted as a `POST` request to the `/new` endpoint.

The main application logic

There is no easy way around this, but our main application logic file, `index.js`, won't be as simple as the other configuration files have been:

```
'use strict'

// Load our dependencies
const bodyParser = require('body-parser')
const express = require('express');
```

```
const mongo = require('mongodb')

// Setup database and server constants
const DB_NAME = 'word_database';
const DB_HOST = process.env.DB_HOST || 'localhost:27017';
const COLLECTION_NAME = 'words';
const SERVER_PORT = 8000;

// Create our app, database clients, and the word list array
const app = express();
const client = mongo.MongoClient();
const dbUri = `mongodb://${DB_HOST}/${DB_NAME}`;
const words = [];

// Setup our templating engine and form data parser
app.set('view engine', 'pug')
app.use(bodyParser.urlencoded({ extended: false }))

// Load all words that are in the database
function loadWordsFromDatabase() {
    return client.connect(dbUri).then((db) => {
        return db.collection(COLLECTION_NAME).find({}).toArray();
    })
    .then((docs) => {
        words.push.apply(words, docs.map(doc => doc.word));
        return words;
    });
}

// Our main landing page handler
app.get('/', (req, res) => {
    res.render('index', { words: words });
});

// Handler for POSTing a new word
app.post('/new', (req, res) => {
    const word = req.body.word;

    console.info(`Got word: ${word}`);
    if (word) {
        client.connect(dbUri).then((db) => {
            db.collection(COLLECTION_NAME).insertOne({ word }, () => {
                db.close();
                words.push(word);
            });
        });
    }
```

```
    res.redirect('/');
});

// Start everything by loading words and then starting the server
loadWordsFromDatabase().then((words) => {
    console.info(`Data loaded from database (${words.length} words)`);
    app.listen(SERVER_PORT, () => {
        console.info("Server started on port %d...", SERVER_PORT);
    });
});
```

This file may seem daunting at first, but this is possibly the smallest API service that you can make from scratch that is also fully functional.

 If you would like to learn more about either Node, Express, or the MongoDB driver, you can visit https://nodejs.org/en/, https://expressjs.com/, and https://github.com/mongodb/node-mongodb-native. If you don't feel like typing, you can also copy and paste this file from https://github.com/sgnn7/deploying_with_docker/.

The basic operation of this app is as follows:

- Load any existing words from the MongoDB database
- Keep a copy of that list in a variable so that we only need to fetch things from the database once
- Open a port 8000 and listen for requests
- If we receive a GET request on /, return the rendered index.html template and fill it in with the word list array
- If we receive a POST to /new:
    - Save the value in the database
    - Update our word list
    - Send us back to /

One part here, however, needs special attention:

```
const DB_HOST = process.env.DB_HOST || 'localhost:27017';
```

Remember when we previously mentioned that much of image configuration should be done through environment variables before? That is exactly what we are doing here! If an environment variable DB_HOST is set (as we expect it to be when running as a container), we will use it as the hostname, but if none is provided (as we expect it when running locally), it will assume that the database is running locally on the standard MongoDB port. This provides the flexibility of being configurable as a container and being able to be tested locally by a developer outside of Docker.

With the main logic file in place, our service should now be arranged in a similar filesystem layout as this:

```
$ tree ./
./
├── Dockerfile
├── index.js
├── package.json
└── views
    └── index.pug

1 directory, 4 files
```

Since this is really the only easy part to test out of the three, let's install MongoDB locally and see what the service does. You can visit https://docs.mongodb.com/manual/installation/ for information on how to install it for other platforms, but I've included the following steps to do this manually on Ubuntu 16.04:

```
$ # Install MongoDB
$ sudo apt-key adv --keyserver hkp://keyserver.ubuntu.com:80 --recv
0C49F3730359A14518585931BC711F9BA15703C6
$ echo "deb [ arch=amd64,arm64 ] http://repo.mongodb.org/apt/ubuntu
xenial/mongodb-org/3.4 multiverse" | sudo tee
/etc/apt/sources.list.d/mongodb-org-3.4.list

$ sudo apt-get update
$ sudo apt-get install -y mongodb-org
$ sudo systemctl start mongodb

$ # Install our service dependencies
$ npm install
application-server@0.0.1
/home/sg/checkout/deploying_with_docker/chapter_3/prototype_service/applica
tion_server
<snip>
npm WARN application-server@0.0.1 No license field.

$ # Run the service</strong>
```

```
$ npm start
> application-server@0.0.1 start
/home/sg/checkout/deploying_with_docker/chapter_3/prototype_service/applica
tion_server
> node index.js

Data loaded from database (10 words)
Server started on port 8000...
```

It seems to work: let's check out the browser by going to `http://localhost:8000`!

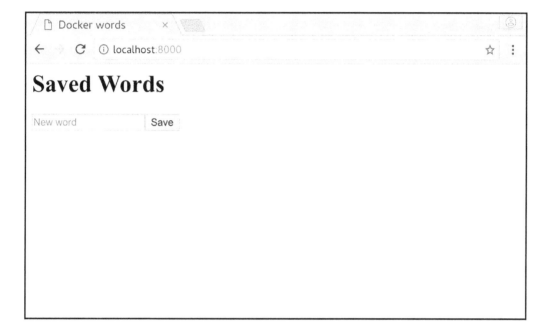

Let's put a few words in it and see what happens:

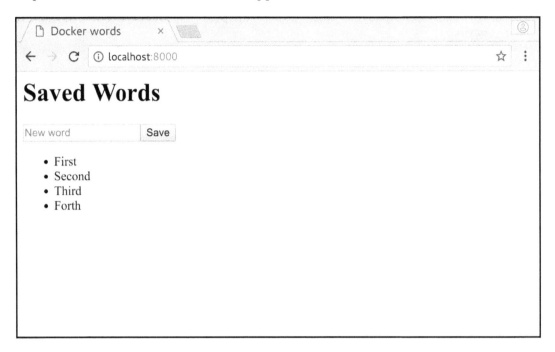

So far, so good! The final test is restarting the service and making sure that we see the same list. Press *Ctrl* + *C* out of our Node process and run `npm start`. You should see the same list again, which means that it is working as expected!

Running it all together

So, we have our `web_server`, `application_server`, and `database` containers all figured out. Let's verify that you have all the files matching these before moving on:

```
$ tree .
.
├── application_server
│   ├── Dockerfile
│   ├── index.js
│   ├── package.json
│   └── views
│       └── index.pug
├── database
│   └── Dockerfile
└── web_server
```

```
├──── Dockerfile
└──── nginx_main_site.conf

4 directories, 7 files
```

The next step for us is to build all the containers:

```
$ # Build the app server image
$ cd application_server
$ docker build -t application_server .
Sending build context to Docker daemon 34.3kB
Step 1/10 : FROM node:8
<snip>
Successfully built f04778cb3778
Successfully tagged application_server:latest

$ # Build the database image
$ cd ../database
$ docker build -t database .
Sending build context to Docker daemon 2.048kB
Step 1/2 : FROM mongo:3
<snip>
Successfully built 7c0f9399a152
Successfully tagged database:latest

$ # Build the web server image
$ cd ../web_server
$ docker build -t web_server .
Sending build context to Docker daemon 3.584kB
Step 1/8 : FROM nginx:latest
<snip>
Successfully built 738c17ddeca8
Successfully tagged web_server:latest
```

This sequential building is great for showing what needs to be done in each step, but always think about automation and how manual processes can be improved. In this particular case, this whole block of statements and execution could have also been done from the parent directory with this single line: `for dir in *; do cd $dir; docker build -t $dir .; cd ..; done`

Launching

With the three relevant containers made, we can now launch them. Some care needs to be taken that they are launched in order as our application tries to read the data from the database as soon as it is started and we don't want the web server up if the application isn't there, so we will launch them in this order: database -> application_server -> web_server:

```
$ docker run --rm \
            -d \
            -p 27000:27017 \
            database
3baec5d1ceb6ec277a87c46bcf32f3600084ca47e0edf26209ca94c974694009

$ docker run --rm \
            -d \
            -e DB_HOST=172.17.0.1:27000 \
            -p 8000:8000 \
            application_server
dad98a02ab6fff63a2f4096f4e285f350f084b844ddb5d10ea3c8f5b7d1cb24b

$ docker run --rm \
            -d \
            -p 8080:80 \
            web_server
3ba3d1c2a25f26273592a9446fc6ee2a876904d0773aea295a06ed3d664eca5d

$ # Verify that all containers are running
$ docker ps --format "table {{.Image}}\t{{.Status}}\t{{.ID}}\t{{.Ports}}"
IMAGE                   STATUS          CONTAINER ID        PORTS
web_server              Up 11 seconds   3ba3d1c2a25f
0.0.0.0:8080->80/tcp
application_server      Up 26 seconds   dad98a02ab6f
0.0.0.0:8000->8000/tcp
database                Up 45 seconds   3baec5d1ceb6
0.0.0.0:27000->27017/tcp
```

A few things to note here:

- We mapped local port 27000 to database 27017 intentionally so that we wouldn't have the conflict with the MongoDB database already running on the host.
- We passed in the magic 172.17.0.1 IP as the host and port 27000 to our application server to use as the database host.
- We started the web server on port 8080 instead of 80 for the web server in order to make sure that we don't need root permissions*.

If you do not see three containers running, check the logs with `docker logs <container id>`. The most likely culprit will probably be the mismatch between the IP/port on a container and the destination, so just fix and restart the container that is failing until you have all three running. If you have a lot of problems, do not hesitate to start the containers in the non-daemon mode by removing the `-d` flag from the commands we used.

* - On *nix systems, ports below `1024` are called registered or privileged ports that govern many important aspects of communications for a system. To prevent malicious use of these system ports, root-level access is required on almost all such platforms. Since we don't really care which port we will be using for this testing, we will avoid this issue altogether by selecting port 8080.

The flow of information in this setup is approximated to this:

```
Browser <=> localhost:8080 <=> web_server:80 <=> 172.17.0.1:8000 (Docker
"localhost") <=> app_server <=> 172.17.0.1:27000 (Docker "localhost") <=>
database:27017
```

Testing

We have all the pieces running, so let's give it a whirl at `http://localhost:8080`!

Nice; our authentication is working! Let's put in our super-secret credentials (User: `user`, Password: `test`).

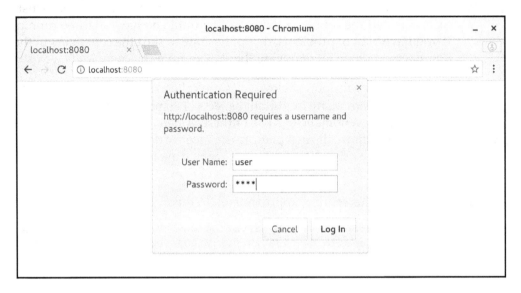

Once we log in, we should be able to see our application server take the processing of the request over and give us the form to enter the words we want to save:

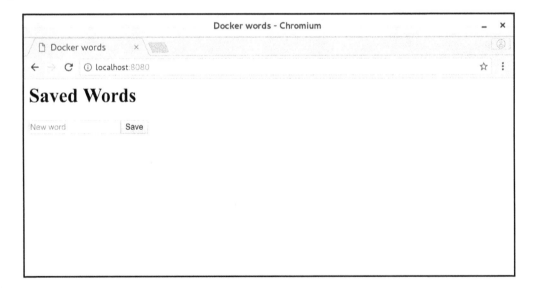

Just as we wanted, the application server is handling requests once we authenticate! Enter a few words and see what happens:

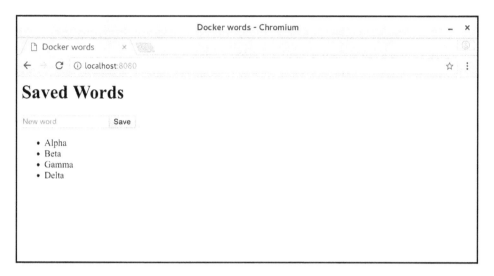

Congratulations! You have made your first containerized service!

Limitations and issues with our implementation

We should take a minute here to consider what parts of our service might need improving if you are to use it in a real system and what the most optimal/practical mitigations might be. As the critical part of working with containers and the cloud is evaluating the pros and cons of larger architectures, this is something you should always try to do when developing a new system or changing an existing one.

From a cursory look, these are the obvious things that could be improved, what the impact is, and what might be the possible mitigations:

- The database has no authentication
    - **Class**: Security, very high impact
    - **Mitigation**: Private cloud or use authentication
- Database data is stored within Docker container (data lost if the container is lost)
    - **Class**: Stability, critical impact
    - **Mitigation**: Mounted volume and/or sharding and clustering

- Hardcoded endpoints
  - **Class**: Ops, very high impact
  - **Mitigation**: Service discovery (we will cover this in later chapters)
- Application server assumes it is the only one changing the word list
  - **Class**: Scaling, very high impact
  - **Mitigation**: Refresh data on each page load
- Application server requires database on container start
  - **Class**: Scaling/Ops, medium impact
  - **Mitigation**: Defer loading until the page is hit and/or show message that the database is not available
- Web server authentication is baked into the image
  - **Class**: Security, critical impact
  - **Mitigation**: Add credentials at runtime
- Web server authentication is over HTTP
  - **Class**: Security, very high impact
  - **Mitigation**: Use HTTPS and/or OAuth

Fixing the critical issues

Since we are pretty early in our Docker journey, we will only cover a few workarounds for the most critical issues for now, which are as follows:

- Database data is stored within the Docker container (data is lost if the container is lost).
- Web server authentication is baked into the image.

Using a local volume

The first issue is a very serious problem because all of our data is currently tied to our container, so if the database app stops, you have to restart the same container to get your data back. In this situation, if the container is run with the `--rm` flag and stops or is otherwise terminated, all the data associated with it would disappear, which is definitely not something we want. While large-scale solutions for this problem are done with sharding, clustering, and/or persistent volumes for our level, we should be fine by just mounting the data volume where we want to keep our data into the container directly. This should keep the data on the host filesystem if anything happens to the container and can be further backed up or moved somewhere else if needed.

This process of mounting (sometimes called mapping) a directory into the container is actually relatively easy to do when we start it if our volume is a named volume stored within Docker internals:

```
$ docker run --rm -d -v local_storage:/data/db -p 27000:27017 database
```

What this will do is create a named volume in Docker's local storage called local_storage, which will be seamlessly mounted on /data/db in the container (the place where the MongoDB image stores its data in the images from Docker Hub). If the container dies or anything happens to it, you can mount this volume onto a different container and retain the data.

-v , --volume , and using a named volume are not the only ways to create volumes for Docker containers. We will cover the reasons why we use this syntax as opposed to other options (that is, --mount) in more detail in Chapter 5, *Keeping the Data Persistent,* which specifically deals with volumes.

Let us see this in action (this may require a MongoDB client CLI on your host machine):

```
$ # Start our container
$ docker run --rm \
            -d \
            -v local_storage:/data/db \
            -p 27000:27017 \
            database
16c72859da1b6f5fbe75aa735b539303c5c14442d8b64b733eca257dc31a2722

$ # Insert a test record in test_db/coll1 as { "item": "value" }
$ mongo localhost:27000
MongoDB shell version: 2.6.10
connecting to: localhost:27000/test

> use test_db
switched to db test_db

> db.createCollection("coll1")
{ "ok" : 1 }

> db.coll1.insert({"item": "value"})
WriteResult({ "nInserted" : 1 })

> exit
bye

$ # Stop the container. The --rm flag will remove it.
```

```
$ docker stop 16c72859
16c72859

$ # See what volumes we have
$ docker volume ls
DRIVER               VOLUME NAME
local                local_storage

$ # Run a new container with the volume we saved data onto
$ docker run --rm \
          -d \
          -v local_storage:/data/db \
          -p 27000:27017 \
          database
a5ef005ab9426614d044cc224258fe3f8d63228dd71dee65c188f1a10594b356

$ # Check if we have our records saved
$ mongo localhost:27000
MongoDB shell version: 2.6.10
connecting to: localhost:27000/test

> use test_db
switched to db test_db

> db.coll1.find()
{ "_id" : ObjectId("599cc7010a367b3ad1668078"), "item" : "value" }

> exit

$ # Cleanup
$ docker stop a5ef005a
a5ef005a
```

As you can see, our record persisted through the original container's destruction, which is exactly what we want! We will cover how to handle volumes in other ways in later chapters, but this should be enough to get us where we want with this critical issue in our little service.

Generating the credentials at runtime

Unlike the database problem, this particular issue is not as easy to deal with, mostly because credentials are a tough problem to deal with from a security perspective. If you include a build argument or a baked-in environment variable, anyone with access to the image can read it. Also, if you pass in the credentials through an environment variable during container creation, anyone that has docker CLI access can read it so you're mostly left with mounting of volumes with credentials to the container.

There are a few other ways of passing credentials securely, though they are a bit outside of the scope of this exercise such as env variables that contain hashed passwords, using a broker secrets-sharing service, using cloud-specific roles mechanisms (that is, AWS, IAM Role, `user-data`), and a few others, but the important part for this section is to understand which things you should try not to do when handling authentication data.

To work around this, we will generate our own credentials file locally on the host machine and mount it to the container when it starts. Substitute `user123` with whatever username you want and `password123` with an alphanumeric password:

```
$ printf "user123:$(openssl passwd -1 password123)\n" >> ~/test_htpasswd

$ # Start the web_server with our password as the credentials source
$ docker run --rm \
            -v $HOME/test_htpasswd:/srv/www/html/.htpasswd \
            -p 8080:80 web_server
1b96c35269dadb1ac98ea711eec4ea670ad7878a933745678f4385d57e96224a
```

With this small change, your web server will now be secured with the new username and the new password and the configuration won't be available to people able to run docker commands either. You can access `http://127.0.0.1:8080` to see that the new username and password are the only credentials that work.

Introducing Docker networking

At an earlier point, we have somewhat glanced over our use of IP `172.17.0.1` in the `web_server` code, and it is something that is not well covered in other materials, but it is a *very* important thing to understand if you want to have a solid grasp on Docker. When the Docker service is started on a machine, a number of networking `iptables` rules are added to your machine in order to allow the container to connect to the world through forwarding and vice versa. Effectively, your machine becomes an Internet router for all containers started. On top of this, each new container is assigned a virtual address (most likely in the range of `172.17.0.2+`) and any communication it does will be normally invisible to the other containers unless a software-defined network is created, so connecting multiple container on the same machine is actually a really tricky task to do manually without helper software that is in the Docker infrastructure called **Service Discovery**.

Since we didn't want the overhead of this Service Discovery for now (which we will cover later in more depth), and we couldn't use `localhost/127.0.0.1/::1`, which would not have worked at all, we needed to give it the Docker virtual router IP (almost always `172.17.0.1`) so that it would find our actual machine where other container ports have been bound.

 Please note that large parts of this next section do not work on macOS nor Windows machines due to the way their networking stack is implemented for Docker. For those systems, I would suggest that you use an Ubuntu virtual machine to follow along.

If you would like to verify this, we can use a few commands outside and inside of Docker in order to really see what is happening:

```
$ # Host's iptables. If you have running containers, DOCKER chain wouldn't
be empty.
$ sudo iptables -L
<snip>
Chain FORWARD (policy DROP)
target       prot opt source                destination
DOCKER-ISOLATION  all  --  anywhere                 anywhere
ACCEPT       all  --  anywhere             anywhere            ctstate
RELATED,ESTABLISHED
DOCKER       all  --  anywhere             anywhere
ACCEPT       all  --  anywhere             anywhere
ACCEPT       all  --  anywhere             anywhere
<snip>
Chain DOCKER (1 references)
target       prot opt source                destination

Chain DOCKER-ISOLATION (1 references)
target       prot opt source                destination
RETURN       all  --  anywhere             anywhere
<snip>

$ # Host's network addresses is 172.17.0.1
$ ip addr
<snip>
5: docker0: <BROADCAST,MULTICAST,UP,LOWER_UP> mtu 1500 qdisc noqueue state
UP group default
    link/ether 02:42:3c:3a:77:c1 brd ff:ff:ff:ff:ff:ff
    inet 172.17.0.1/16 scope global docker0
       valid_lft forever preferred_lft forever
    inet6 fe80::42:3cff:fe3a:77c1/64 scope link
       valid_lft forever preferred_lft forever
<snip>
```

```
$ # Get container's network addresses
$ docker run --rm \
            -it \
            web_server /bin/bash

root@08b6521702ef:/# # Install pre-requisite (iproute2) package
root@08b6521702ef:/# apt-get update && apt-get install -y iproute2
<snip>

root@08b6521702ef:/# # Check the container internal address (172.17.0.2)
root@08b6521702ef:/# ip addr
1: lo: <LOOPBACK,UP,LOWER_UP> mtu 65536 qdisc noqueue state UNKNOWN group
default qlen 1000
    link/loopback 00:00:00:00:00:00 brd 00:00:00:00:00:00
    inet 127.0.0.1/8 scope host lo
        valid_lft forever preferred_lft forever
722: eth0@if723: <BROADCAST,MULTICAST,UP,LOWER_UP> mtu 1500 qdisc noqueue
state UP group default
    link/ether 02:42:ac:11:00:02 brd ff:ff:ff:ff:ff:ff link-netnsid 0
    inet 172.17.0.2/16 scope global eth0
        valid_lft forever preferred_lft forever

root@08b6521702ef:/# # Verify that our main route is through our host at
172.17.0.1
root@08b6521702ef:/# ip route
default via 172.17.0.1 dev eth0
172.17.0.0/16 dev eth0 proto kernel scope link src 172.17.0.2

root@08b6521702ef:/# exit
```

As you can see, this system is a bit odd, but it works pretty well. Generally when building bigger systems, service discovery is practically mandatory, so you wouldn't have to worry about such low-level details in the field.

Summary

In this chapter, we covered how to build multiple containers to make a basic service composed of a web server, application server, and the database, launch multiple containers together, and tie them together with networking. We also worked through what the most common issues might be when connecting services and what the common pitfalls with these basic building blocks are. Some hints about future topics were also given (volumes, service discovery, credentials passing, and so on), but we will cover those in later chapters in depth. In the next chapter, we will be turning our little service into a robust service with horizontally scaled components.

4
Scaling the Containers

In this chapter, we will be taking our service and trying to scale it horizontally with multiple instances of the same container. We will cover the following topics in this chapter:

- Orchestration options and their pros/cons
- Service discovery
- State reconciliation
- The deployment of your own Docker Swarm cluster
- Deploying our word service from the previous chapter onto that cluster

Service discovery

Before we get any further, we really need to get deeply familiar with the conceptual Docker container connectivity, which is, unsurprisingly, in some ways very similar to building high-availability services with servers in a non-containerized world. Because of this, covering this topic in some depth will not only expand your understanding of Docker networking, but also help in generally building out resilient services.

A recap of Docker networking

In the previous chapter, we covered a bit of the Docker networking layout, so we will cover the main points here:

- By default, Docker containers run on an isolated virtual network on the host
- Each container has its own network address in that network
- By default, `localhost` for a container is *not* the host machine's `localhost`
- There is high overhead of manual work in order to connect containers manually
- Manual networking connections between containers are inherently fragile

In the parallel world of setting up a local server network, the base experience of Docker connectivity is very much akin to hooking up your whole network with static IPs. While this approach is not very difficult to get working, maintaining it is extremely hard and laborious, which is why we need something better than that.

Service Discovery in depth

Since we don't want to deal with this fragile system of keeping and maintaining hardcoded IP addresses, we need to figure out a way so our connections are flexible and require no adjustments from the client if the target service dies or a new one is created. It would also be nice if each connection to the same service is equally balanced between all instances of the same service. Ideally, our services would look something like this:

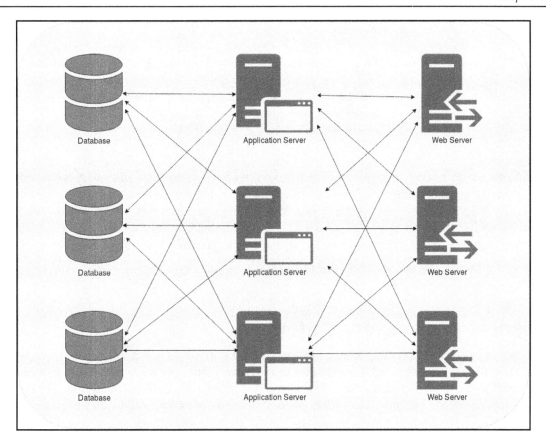

For this exact use case for the Internet, DNS was created so that clients would have a way to find servers even if the IP address or network changes from anywhere in the world. As an added benefit, we have target addresses that are easier to remember (DNS names such as `https://google.com` instead of something such as `https://123.45.67.89`) and the ability to distribute the processing to as many handling services as we want.

If you have not worked with DNS in depth, the main principles are reduced to these basic steps:

1. The user (or app) wants to connect to a server (that is, `google.com`).
2. The local machine either uses its own cached DNS answer or goes out to the DNS system and searches for this name.
3. The local machine gets back the IP address (`123.45.67.89`) that it should use as the target.
4. The local machine connects to the IP address.

The DNS system is much more complicated than the single sentences mentioned here. While DNS is a really good thing to know about in any server-oriented tech position, here, it was sufficient just to know that the input to the DNS system is a hostname and the output is the real target (IP). If you would like to know more about how the DNS system actually works, I recommend that you visit `https://en.wikipedia.org/wiki/Domain_Name_System` at your leisure.

If we coerce the DNS handling that is implemented in almost all clients already as a way to automatically discover services, we could make ourselves the service discovery mechanism that we have been looking for! If we make it smart enough, it can tell us where the running container is, load balance between all instances of the same container, and provide us with a static name to use as our target. As one may expect, almost all container service discovery systems have this exact pattern of functionality; it just generally differs if it is done as either a client-side discovery pattern, server-side discovery pattern, or some sort of a hybrid system.

Client-side discovery pattern

This type of pattern isn't used often, but it pretty much involves using a service-aware client to discover other services and to load balance between them. The advantage here is that the client can make intelligent decisions about where to connect to and in which manner, but the downside is that this decision making is distributed onto each service and hard to maintain but it is not dependent on a single source of truth (single service registry) that could take down a whole cluster if it fails.

The architecture generally looks something similar to this:

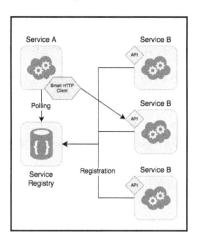

Server-side discovery pattern

The more common service discovery pattern is a centralized server-side discovery pattern where the DNS system is used to direct the clients to the container. In this particular way of finding services, a container registers and de-registers itself from the service registry, which holds the state of the system. This state, in turn, is used to populate the DNS entries that the client then contacts to find the target(s) that it is trying to connect to. While this system is generally pretty stable and flexible, it sometimes suffers from really tricky issues that generally hamper DNS systems elsewhere, such as DNS caching, which uses stale IP addresses until the **time-to-live** (**TTL**) expires or when the app itself caches the DNS entry regardless of updates (NGINX and Java apps are notorious for this).

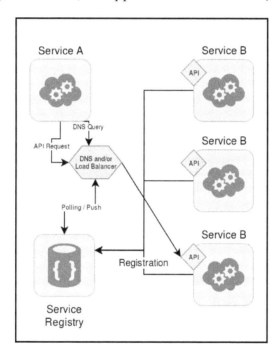

Hybrid systems

This grouping includes all other combinations that we haven't covered yet, but it covers the class of largest deployments that use a tool, HAProxy, which we will cover in some detail later. What it basically does is tie a specific port on the host (that is, `<host>:10101`) to a load-balanced target somewhere else in the cluster.

From the client perspective, they are connecting to a single and stable location and the HAProxy then tunnels it seamlessly to the right target.

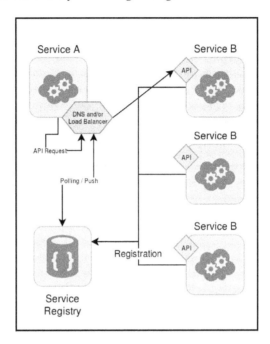

This setup supports both pull and push refreshing of methods and is very resilient, but we will take a deep dive into this type of setup in later chapters.

Picking the (un)available options

With all of these types of service discoveries available, we should be able to handle any container scaling that we want, but we need to keep something very important in mind: almost all service discovery tooling is intimately bound to the system used for deploying and managing the containers (also known as container orchestration) due to the fact that updates to container endpoints are generally just an orchestration system implementation detail. Because of this, service discovery systems usually aren't as portable as one might like, so the choice of this infrastructure piece usually gets decided by your orchestration tooling (with a few exceptions here and there).

Container orchestration

As we somewhat hinted earlier, service discovery is a critical part of deploying a container-based system in any capacity. Without something like that, you might as well just use bare-metal servers as the majority of advantages gained using containers have been lost. To have an effective service discovery system, you are pretty much mandated to use some sort of container orchestration platform, and luckily (or maybe un-luckily?), options for container orchestration have been sprouting at an almost alarming rate! In general terms, though, at the time of writing this book (and in my humble opinion), the popular and stable choices come down to mainly these:

- Docker Swarm
- Kubernetes
- Apache Mesos/Marathon
- Cloud-based offerings (Amazon ECS, Google Container Engine, Azure Container Service, and so on)

Each one has its own vocabulary and the way in which the infrastructure pieces connect, so before we go any further, we need to cover the pertinent vocabulary in regard to orchestration services that will mostly be reusable between all of them:

- **Node**: An instance of Docker Engine. Generally used only when talking about cluster-connected instances.
- **Service**: A functionality grouping that is composed of one or more running instances of the same Docker image.
- **Task**: A specific and unique instance of a running service. This is usually a single running Docker container.
- **Scaling**: The count of tasks specified for a service to run. This usually determines how much throughput a service can support.
- **Manager node**: A node in charge of management and orchestration duties of the cluster.
- **Worker node**: A node designated as a task runner.

State reconciliation

Besides our just-learned dictionary, we also need to understand the underlying algorithm of almost all orchestration frameworks, state reconciliation, which deserves its own little section here. The basic principle that this works on is a very simple three-step process, as follows:

- The user setting the desired count(s) of each service or a service disappearing.
- The orchestration framework seeing what is needed in order to change the current state to the desired state (delta evaluation).
- Executing whatever is needed to take the cluster to that state (known as state reconciliation).

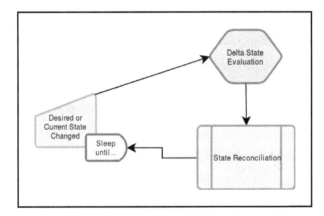

For example, if we currently have five running tasks for a service in the cluster and change the desired state to only three tasks, our management/orchestration system will see that the difference is −2 and thus pick two random tasks and kill them seamlessly. Conversely, if we have three tasks running and we want five instead, the management/orchestration system will see that the desired delta is +2 so it will pick two places with available resources for it and start two new tasks. A short explanation of two state transitions should also help clarify this process:

```
Initial State: Service #1 (3 tasks), Service #2 (2 tasks)
Desired State: Service #1 (1 task),  Service #2 (4 tasks)

Reconciliation:
 - Kill 2 random Service #1 tasks
 - Start 2 Service #2 tasks on available nodes

New Initial State: Service #1 (1 tasks), Service #2 (4 tasks)
```

```
New Desired State: Service #1 (2 tasks), Service #2 (0 tasks)

Reconciliation:
  - Start 1 tasks of Service #1 on available node
  - Kill all 4 running tasks of Service #2

Final State: Service #1 (2 tasks), Service #2 (0 tasks)
```

Using this very simple but powerful logic, we can dynamically scale up and down our services without worrying about the intermediate stages (to a degree). Internally, keeping and maintaining states is such a difficult task that most orchestration frameworks use a special, high-speed key-value store component to do this for them (that is, `etcd`, `ZooKeeper`, and `Consul`).

Since our system only cares about where our current state is and where it needs to be, this algorithm also doubles as the system for building resilience as a dead node, or the container will reduce the current task count for applications and will trigger a state transition back to the desired counts automatically. As long as services are mostly stateless and you have the resources to run the new services, these clusters are resilient to almost any type of failure and now you can hopefully see how a few simple concepts tie together to create such a robust infrastructure.

With our new understanding of management and orchestration framework basics, we will now take a brief look at each one of our available options (Docker Swarm, Kubernetes, Marathon) and see how they compare with each other.

Docker Swarm

Out of the box, Docker contains an orchestration framework and a management platform very architecturally similar to the one covered just a second ago, called Docker Swarm. Swarm allows a pretty quick and simple way to get scaling integrated with your platform with minimal ramp-up time and given that it is already a part of Docker itself, you really don't need much else to deploy a simple set of services in a clustered environment. As an added benefit, it contains a pretty solid service discovery framework, has multi-host networking capability, and uses TLS for communication between nodes.

Multi-host networking capability is the ability of a system to create a virtual network across multiple physical machines that are transparent from the point of view of the container. Using one of these, your containers can communicate with each other as if they were on the same physical network, simplifying the connectivity logic and reducing operational costs. We will look into this aspect of clustering in depth a bit later.

The cluster configuration for Docker Swarm can be a simple YAML file, but the downside is that GUI tools are, at the time of writing this, somewhat lacking, though Portainer (`https:/ /portainer.io`) and Shipyard (`https://shipyard-project.com`) are getting to be pretty decent, so this might not be a problem for too long. Additionally, some large-scale ops tooling is missing and it seems that generally, features of Swarm are heavily evolving and thus in a state of flux, so my personal recommendation would be to use this type of orchestration if you need to get something up and running quickly on small-to-largish scales. As this product gets more and more mature (and since Docker Inc. is placing a lot of development resources behind this), it will probably improve significantly, and I expect it to match Kubernetes features in many respect so keep an eye out for its feature news.

Kubernetes

Kubernetes is Google's cloud platform and orchestration engine that currently provides a bit more in terms of features than does Swarm. The setup of Kubernetes is much more difficult as you need: a master, a node (the worker according to our earlier dictionary), and pods (grouping of one or more containers). Pods are always co-located and co-scheduled, so handling their dependencies is a bit easier to deal with but you do not get the same isolation. The interesting thing to keep in mind here is that all containers within the pod share the same IP address/ports, share volumes, and are generally within the same isolation group. It is almost better to think of a pod as a small virtual machine running many services than many containers running in parallel.

Kubernetes has been gaining a massive amount of community traction lately and is probably the most deployed cluster orchestration and management system in use, though to be fair, finding exact figures is tricky, with a majority of them being deployed in private clouds. Given that Google has been using this system for a while and on such a large scale, it has a pretty proven track record and I would probably recommended it for medium-to-large scales. If you don't mind the overhead of setting everything up, I think even smaller scales would be acceptable, but in that space, Docker Swarm is so easy to use that using Kubernetes for it is generally impractical.

At the time of writing this book, both Mesos and Docker EE have included capabilities to support Kubernetes so if you would want to bet on an orchestration engine, this would probably be it.

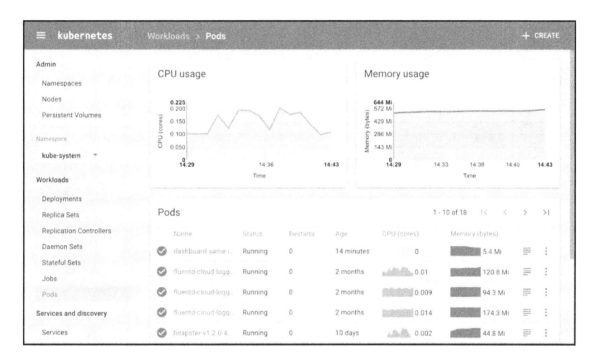

Apache Mesos/Marathon

When you really need to dial up the scaling to levels of Twitter and Airbnb, you probably need something even more powerful than Swarm or Kubernetes, which is where Mesos and Marathon come into play. Apache Mesos was not actually built with Docker in mind but as a general cluster-management tooling that provides resource management in a consistent way for applications that run on top of it with APIs. You can run anything from scripts, actual applications, and multiple platforms (such as HDFS and Hadoop) with relative ease. For container-based orchestration and scheduling on this platform these days, Marathon is the general go-to here.

 As mentioned a little bit earlier, Kubernetes support has been now available again for Mesos after being in a broken state for a while so the suggestion of Marathon may change by the time you read this text.

Marathon runs as an application (in a very loose sense of the word) on top of Mesos as the container orchestration platform and provides all kind of niceties, such as a great UI (though Kubernetes has one too), metrics, constraints, persistent volumes (experimental at the time of writing this), and many others. As a platform, Mesos and Marathon are probably the most powerful combo for handling clusters in the tens-of-thousands-of-nodes range, but to get everything pieced together, unless you use the pre-packaged DC/OS solution (`https://dcos.io/`), it is in my experience really, really tricky to get up and running compared to the other two. If you need to cover the range of medium-to-largest of scales with added flexibility in order to run other platforms (such as Chronos) on it too, currently, I would strongly recommend this combo.

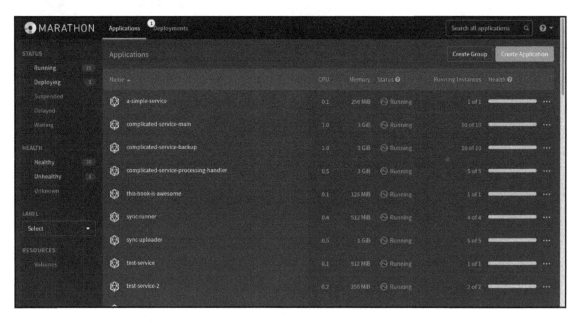

Cloud-based offerings

If all of this seems too much trouble and you don't mind paying a hefty premium every month for it, all the big cloud players have some sort of container-based service offering. Since these vary wildly both in functionality and feature set, anything that would get put onto this page in that regard will probably be outdated by the time it gets published, and we are more interested in deploying services on our own, so I will leave you links to the appropriate offerings that will have up-to-date information if you choose this route:

- **Amazon ECS**: `https://aws.amazon.com/ecs/`
- **Google Container Engine**: `https://cloud.google.com/container-engine/`

- **Microsoft Azure** (**Azure Container Service**): `https://azure.microsoft.com/en-us/services/container-service/`
- **Oracle Container Cloud Service**: `https://cloud.oracle.com/container`
- **Docker Cloud**: `https://cloud.docker.com/`
- Probably many others that I have missed

Personally, I would recommend this approach for small-to-medium deployments due to ease of use and tested environments. If your needs expand past these scales, implementing your service on scalable groups of virtual machines on **Virtual Private Clouds** (**VPCs**) with the same cloud service provider is generally one of the ways to go as you can tailor your infrastructure in the exact way that your needs expand, though the upfront DevOps costs are not small, so decide accordingly. A good rule of thumb to remember with pretty much any cloud offering is that with easy tooling already provided you get much quicker deployments counterbalanced by increased costs (usually hidden) and lack of flexibility/customizability.

Implementing orchestration

With our newly-gained understanding of the orchestration and management offerings out there, it is time to try this out ourselves. In our next exercise, we will first try to use Docker Swarm to create and play a bit with a local cluster and then we will try to deploy our service from the previous chapter onto it.

Setting up a Docker Swarm cluster

Since all the functionality to set up a Docker Swarm cluster is already included in the Docker installation, this is actually a really easy thing to do. Let's see what commands we have available to us:

```
$ docker swarm
<snip>
Commands:
  init        Initialize a swarm
  join        Join a swarm as a node and/or manager
  join-token  Manage join tokens
  leave       Leave the swarm
  unlock      Unlock swarm
  unlock-key  Manage the unlock key
  update      Update the swarm
```

A few things to note here--some more apparent than others:

- You create a swarm with `docker swarm init`
- You join a cluster with `docker swarm join` and the machine can be a worker node, a manager node, or both
- Authentication is managed using tokens (unique strings that need to match)
- If something happens to a manager node, such as a restart or power cycle, and you have set up auto-locking of the swarm, you will need an unlock key to unlock the TLS keys

So far, so good, so let's see whether we can set up a swarm with our machine serving both as a manager and a worker to see how this works.

Initializing a Docker Swarm cluster

To create our swarm, we first need to instantiate it:

```
$ docker swarm init

Swarm initialized: current node (osb7tritzhtlux1o9unlu2vd0) is now a
manager.

To add a worker to this swarm, run the following command:

    docker swarm join \
    --token
SWMTKN-1-4atg39hw64uagiqk3i6s3zlv5mforrzj0kk1aeae22tpsat2jj-2zn0ak0ldxo58d1
q7347t4rd5 \
    192.168.4.128:2377

To add a manager to this swarm, run 'docker swarm join-token manager' and
follow the instructions.

$ # Make sure that our node is operational
$ docker node ls
ID                           HOSTNAME  STATUS  AVAILABILITY  MANAGER STATUS
osb7tritzhtlux1o9unlu2vd0 *  feather2  Ready   Active        Leader
```

We have created a swarm with that command and we are automatically enrolled as a manager node. If you take a look at the output, the command for adding worker nodes is just `docker swarm join --token <token> <ip>`, but we are interested in a single-node deployment for now, so we won't need to worry about it. Given that our manager node is also a worker node, we can just use it as-is to throw a few services on it.

Deploying services

Most of the commands we will initially need are accessible through the `docker services` command:

```
$ docker service
<snip>
Commands:
  create      Create a new service
  inspect     Display detailed information on one or more services
  logs        Fetch the logs of a service or task
  ls          List services
  ps          List the tasks of one or more services
  rm          Remove one or more services
  scale       Scale one or multiple replicated services
  update      Update a service
```

 As you might be suspecting, given how similar these commands are to some of the ones for managing containers, once you move to an orchestration platform as opposed to fiddling with containers directly, the ideal management of your services would be done through the orchestration itself. I would probably expand this and go as far as to say that if you are working with containers too much while having an orchestration platform, you did not set something up or you did not set it up correctly.

We will now try to get some sort of service running on our Swarm, but since we are just exploring how all this works, we can use a very slimmed down (and a very insecure) version of our Python web server from Chapter 2, *Rolling Up the Sleeves*. Create a new folder and add this to a new `Dockerfile`:

```
FROM python:3

ENV SRV_PATH=/srv/www/html

EXPOSE 8000

RUN mkdir -p $SRV_PATH && \
```

```
groupadd -r -g 350 pythonsrv && \
useradd -r -m -u 350 -g 350 pythonsrv && \
echo "Test file content" > $SRV_PATH/test.txt && \
chown -R pythonsrv:pythonsrv $SRV_PATH

WORKDIR $SRV_PATH

CMD [ "python3", "-m", "http.server" ]
```

Let's build it so that our local registry has an image to pull from when we define our service:

```
$ docker build -t simple_server .
```

With the image in place, let's deploy it on our swarm:

```
$ docker service create --detach=true \
                        --name simple-server \
                        -p 8000:8000 \
                        simple_server
image simple_server could not be accessed on a registry to record
its digest. Each node will access simple_server independently,
possibly leading to different nodes running different
versions of the image.

z0z90wgylcpf11xxbm8knks9m

$ docker service ls
ID              NAME            MODE        REPLICAS IMAGE          PORTS
z0z90wgylcpf simple-server replicated 1/1        simple_server
*:8000->8000/tcp
```

 The warning shown is actually very important: our service is only available on our local machine's Docker registry when we built it, so using a Swarm service that is spread between multiple nodes will have issues since other machines will not be able to load the same image. For this reason, having the image registry available from a single source to all of the nodes is mandatory for cluster deployments. We will cover this issue in more detail as we progress through this and following chapters.

If we check out `http://127.0.0.1:8000`, we can see that our service is running! Let's see this:

If we scale this service to three instances, we can see how our orchestration tool is handling the state transitions:

```
$ docker service scale simple-server=3

image simple_server could not be accessed on a registry to record
its digest. Each node will access simple_server independently,
possibly leading to different nodes running different
versions of the image.

simple-server scaled to 3

$ docker service ls
ID              NAME            MODE         REPLICAS IMAGE          PORTS
z0z90wgylcpf simple-server replicated 2/3      simple_server
*:8000->8000/tcp

$ # After waiting a bit, let's see if we have 3 instances now
$ docker service ls
ID              NAME            MODE         REPLICAS IMAGE          PORTS
z0z90wgylcpf simple-server replicated 3/3      simple_server
*:8000->8000/tcp
```

```
$ # You can even use regular container commands to see it
$ docker ps --format 'table {{.ID}}   {{.Image}}   {{.Ports}}'
CONTAINER ID   IMAGE   PORTS
0c9fdf88634f   simple_server:latest   8000/tcp
98d158f82132   simple_server:latest   8000/tcp
9242a969632f   simple_server:latest   8000/tcp
```

You can see how this is adjusting the container instances to fit our specified parameters. What if we now add something in the mix that will happen in real life-a container death:

```
$ docker ps --format 'table {{.ID}}   {{.Image}}   {{.Ports}}'
CONTAINER ID   IMAGE   PORTS
0c9fdf88634f   simple_server:latest   8000/tcp
98d158f82132   simple_server:latest   8000/tcp
9242a969632f   simple_server:latest   8000/tcp

$ docker kill 0c9fdf88634f
0c9fdf88634f

$ # We should only now have 2 containers
$ docker ps --format 'table {{.ID}}   {{.Image}}   {{.Ports}}'
CONTAINER ID   IMAGE   PORTS
98d158f82132   simple_server:latest   8000/tcp
9242a969632f   simple_server:latest   8000/tcp

$ # Wait a few seconds and try again
$ docker ps --format 'table {{.ID}}   {{.Image}}   {{.Ports}}'
CONTAINER ID   IMAGE   PORTS
d98622eaabe5   simple_server:latest   8000/tcp
98d158f82132   simple_server:latest   8000/tcp
9242a969632f   simple_server:latest   8000/tcp

$ docker service ls
ID              NAME           MODE        REPLICAS IMAGE          PORTS
z0z90wgylcpf simple-server replicated 3/3      simple_server
*:8000->8000/tcp
```

As you can see, the swarm will bounce back up like nothing happened, and this is exactly why containerization is so powerful: not only can we spread processing tasks among many machines and flexibly scale the throughput, but with identical services we don't really care very much if some (hopefully small) percentage of services dies, as the framework will make it completely seamless for the client. With the built-in service discovery of Docker Swarm, the load balancer will shift the connection to whatever container is running/available so anyone trying to connect to our server should not see much of a difference.

Cleaning up

As with any service that we are finished with, we need to make sure that we clean up any resources we have used up so far. In the case of Swarm, we should probably remove our service and destroy our cluster until we need it again. You can do both of those things using `docker service rm` and `docker swarm leave`:

```
$ docker service ls
ID              NAME          MODE        REPLICAS IMAGE           PORTS
z0z90wgylcpf simple-server replicated 3/3        simple_server
*:8000->8000/tcp

$ docker service rm simple-server
simple-server

$ docker service ls
ID              NAME          MODE        REPLICAS IMAGE           PORTS

$ docker swarm leave --force
Node left the swarm.
```

> The reason why we had to use the `--force` flag here is due to the fact that we are a manager node and we are the last one in the cluster, so by default, Docker will prevent this action without it. In a multi-node setup, you will not generally need this flag.

With this action, we are now back at where we started and are ready to do this with a real service.

Using Swarm to orchestrate our words service

In the previous chapter, we built a simple service that can be used to add and list words entered on a form. But if you remember, we heavily used somewhat of an implementation detail to connect the services together, making it extremely fragile if not downright hacked-up together. With our new-found knowledge of service discovery and our understanding of Docker Swarm orchestration, we can try to get our old code ready for real cluster deployment and move away from the fragile setup we had earlier.

The application server

Copy the old application server folder from `Chapter 3`, *Service Decomposition*, to a new folder and we will change our main handler code (`index.js`) since we have to accommodate the fact that we will not be the only instance reading from and writing to the database anymore.

As always, all code can also be found at `https://github.com/sgnn7/deploying_with_docker`. This particular implementation can be found in `chapter_4/clustered_application`.

Warning! As you start thinking about similar containers running in parallel, you have to start being extra careful about data changes that can and will occur outside of the container's realm of control. For this reason, keeping or caching the state in any form in a running container is usually a recipe for disaster and data inconsistencies. To avoid this issue, in general, you should try to make sure that you re-read the information from your upstream sources (that is, the database) before doing any transformation or passing of the data like we do here.

index.js

This file is pretty much the same one from the last chapter but we will be making a few changes to eliminate caching:

```
'use strict'

const bodyParser = require('body-parser')
const express = require('express');
const mongo = require('mongodb')

const DB_NAME = 'word_database';
const DB_HOST = process.env.DB_HOST || 'localhost:27017';
const COLLECTION_NAME = 'words';
const SERVER_PORT = 8000;

const app = express();
const client = mongo.MongoClient();
const dbUri = `mongodb://${DB_HOST}/${DB_NAME}`;

app.set('view engine', 'pug')
app.use(bodyParser.urlencoded({ extended: false }))

function loadWordsFromDatabase() {
```

```
        return client.connect(dbUri).then((db) => {
            return db.collection(COLLECTION_NAME).find({}).toArray();
        })
        .then((docs) => {
            return docs.map(doc => doc.word);
        });
    }

    app.get('/', (req, res) => {
        console.info("Loading data from database...");
        loadWordsFromDatabase().then(words => {
            console.info("Data loaded, showing the result...");
            res.render('index', { words: words });
        });
    });

    app.post('/new', (req, res) => {
        const word = req.body.word;

        console.info(`Got word: ${word}`);
        if (word) {
            client.connect(dbUri).then((db) => {
                db.collection(COLLECTION_NAME).insertOne({ word }, () => {
                    db.close();
                });
            });
        }

        res.redirect('/');
    });

    app.listen(SERVER_PORT, () => {
        console.info("Server started on port %d...", SERVER_PORT);
    });
```

If may have noticed, many things are similar, but there are fundamental changes too:

- We don't pre-load the words on start as the list might change from the time the service initializes and the user requests data.
- We load the saved words on each GET request in order to make sure we always get fresh data.
- When we save the word, we just insert it into the database and don't preserve it in the application as we will get new data on GET re-display.

Using this approach, any changes done to the data in the database by any app instances will immediately be reflected in all of them. Additionally, if a database administrator changed any of the data, we will also see those changes within the application. Since our service also uses an environment variable for the database host, we should not need to change it to the support service discovery.

 Caution! Be aware that because we read the database on each GET request, our changes to support clustering are not free and come with an increase in database queries, which can become a real bottleneck when the networking, cache invalidation, or disk transfers become overly saturated by these requests. Additionally, since we read the database before we display the data, slowdowns in the backend processing of our database find() will be user-visible, possibly causing undesired user experience, so keep these things in mind as you develop container-friendly services.

The web server

Our web server changes will be a bit trickier due to a quirk/feature of the NGINX configuration processing that may also impact you if you do Java-based DNS resolution. Essentially, NGINX caches DNS entries so hard that effectively, once it reads the configuration files, any new DNS resolution within that configuration will not actually take place at all unless some extra flags (resolver) are specified. With the Docker service being constantly mutable and relocatable, this is a serious issue that must be worked around to function properly on the Swarm. Here, you have a couple of options:

- Run a DNS forwarder (such as dnsmasq) in parallel with NGINX and use that as the resolver. This requires running both dnsmasq and NGINX in the same container.
- Populate the NGINX configuration container start with the same resolvers from the system using something such as envsubst: this requires all containers to be in the same user-defined network.
- Hardcode the DNS resolver IP (127.0.0.11): this also requires all containers to be in the same user-defined network.

For robustness, we will use the second option, so copy the web server from the previous chapter into a new folder and rename it to `nginx_main_site.conf.template`. We will then add a resolver configuration to it and a variable `$APP_NAME` for our proxy host endpoint:

```
server {
  listen          8080;
  server_name     _;

  resolver $DNS_RESOLVERS;

  root /srv/www/html;

  location ~/\. {
    deny all;
  }

  location / {
    auth_basic            "Authentication required";
    auth_basic_user_file /srv/www/html/.htpasswd;

    proxy_pass            http://$APP_NAME:8000;
  }
}
```

Since NGINX does not handle environment variable substitution in the configuration files, we will write a wrapper script around it. Add a new file called `start_nginx.sh` and include the following content in it that takes the host's resolvers and generates the new main_site config:

```
#!/bin/bash -e

export DNS_RESOLVERS=$(cat /etc/resolv.conf | grep 'nameserver' | awk '{
print $2 }' | xargs echo)

cat /etc/nginx/conf.d/nginx_main_site.conf.template | envsubst
'$DNS_RESOLVERS $APP_NAME' > /etc/nginx/conf.d/nginx_main_site.conf

nginx -g 'daemon off;'
```

To get this to run, we finally need to make sure we start NGINX with this script instead of the one built in, so we need to modify our `Dockerfile` as well.

Open up our Dockerfile and make sure that it has the following:

```
FROM nginx:latest

RUN apt-get update -q && \
    apt-get dist-upgrade -y && \
    apt-get install openssl && \
    apt-get clean && \
    apt-get autoclean

EXPOSE 8080

ENV SRV_PATH /srv/www/html

ARG PASSWORD=test

RUN rm /etc/nginx/conf.d/default.conf

COPY start_nginx.sh /usr/local/bin/

RUN mkdir -p $SRV_PATH && \
    chown nginx:nginx $SRV_PATH && \
    printf "user:$(openssl passwd -crypt $PASSWORD)\n" >>
$SRV_PATH/.htpasswd && \
    chmod +x /usr/local/bin/start_nginx.sh

COPY nginx_main_site.conf.template /etc/nginx/conf.d/

CMD ["/usr/local/bin/start_nginx.sh"]
```

Here, the main change is the start up script CMD override and turning the configuration into a template with the rest pretty much left alone.

Database

Unlike the other two containers, we will leave the database in one container due to a combination of things:

- MongoDB can scale to high GB/low TB dataset sizes easily with vertical scaling.
- Databases are extremely difficult to scale up without in-depth knowledge of volumes (covered in the next chapter).
- Sharding and replica sets of databases are generally complicated enough for whole books to be written on this topic alone.

We may cover this topic in a later chapter, but here, it would derail us from our general goal of learning how to deploy services so we will just have our single database instance that we used in the previous chapter for now.

Deploying it all

As we did for our simple web server, we will begin by creating another Swarm cluster:

```
$ docker swarm init
Swarm initialized: current node (1y1h7rgpxbsfqryvrxa04rvcp) is now a
manager.

To add a worker to this swarm, run the following command:

    docker swarm join \
    --token SWMTKN-1-36flmf9vnika6x5mbxx7vf9kldqaw6bq8lxtkeyaj4r5s4611n-
aiqlw49iufv3s6po4z2fytos1 \
    192.168.4.128:2377
```

Then, we need to create our overlay network for the service-discovery hostname resolution to work. You don't need to know much about this other than it creates an isolated network that we will add all the services to:

```
$ docker network create --driver overlay service_network
44cyg4vsitbx81p208vslp0rx
```

Finally, we will build and launch our containers:

```
$ cd ../database
$ docker build . -t local_database
$ docker service create -d --replicas 1 \
                            --name local-database \
                            --network service_network \
                            --mount
type=volume,source=database_volume,destination=/data/db \
                            local_database
<snip>
pilssv8du68rg0oztm6gdsqse

$ cd ../application_server
$ docker build -t application_server .
$ docker service create -d -e DB_HOST=local-database \
                            --replicas 3 \
                            --network service_network \
                            --name application-server \
                            application_server
```

```
<snip>
pue2ant1lg2u8ejocbsovsxy3

$ cd ../web_server
$ docker build -t web_server .
$ docker service create -d --name web-server \
                        --network service_network \
                        --replicas 3 \
                        -e APP_NAME=application-server \
                        -p 8080:8080 \
                        web_server
<snip>
swi95q7z38i2wepmdzoiuudv7

$ # Sanity checks
$ docker service ls
ID              NAME                MODE        REPLICAS  IMAGE
PORTS
pilssv8du68r local-database      replicated 1/1       local_database
pue2ant1lg2u application-server replicated 3/3       application_server
swi95q7z38i2 web-server         replicated 3/3       web_server
*:8080->8080/tcp

$ docker ps --format 'table {{.ID}}   {{.Image}}\t   {{.Ports}}'
CONTAINER ID  IMAGE                      PORTS
8cdbec233de7  application_server:latest  8000/tcp
372c0b3195cd  application_server:latest  8000/tcp
6be2d6e9ce77  web_server:latest          80/tcp, 8080/tcp
7aca0c1564f0  web_server:latest          80/tcp, 8080/tcp
3d621c697ed0  web_server:latest          80/tcp, 8080/tcp
d3dad64c4837  application_server:latest  8000/tcp
aab4b2e62952  local_database:latest      27017/tcp
```

If you are having trouble with getting these services up and running, you can check the logs with `docker service logs <service_name>` in order to figure out what went wrong. You can also use `docker logs <container_id>` if a specific container is having trouble.

With these in place, we can now check whether our code works at
`http://127.0.0.1:8080` (username: `user`, password: `test`):

Looks like it is working! Once we put in our credentials, we should be redirected to the main application page:

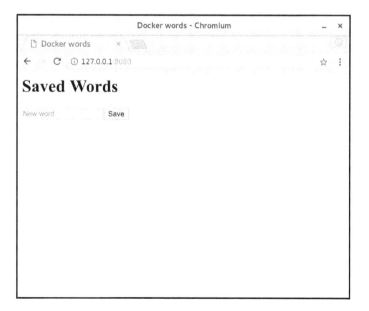

Does the database work if we put in some words?

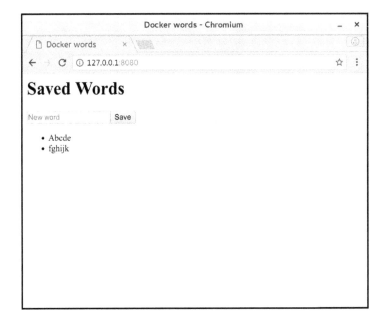

Indeed! We have really created a 1-node swarm-backed service, and it is scalable plus load balanced!

The Docker stack

As it was pretty obvious from just a few paragraphs before, a manual setup of these services seems somewhat of a pain, so here we introduce a new tool that can help us do this much easier: Docker Stack. This tool uses a YAML file to get things to deploy all the services easily and repeatedly.

First we will clean up our old exercise before trying to use Docker stack configuration:

```
$ docker service ls -q | xargs docker service rm
pilssv8du68r
pue2ant1lg2u
swi95q7z38i2

$ docker network rm service_network
service_network
```

Now we can write our YAML configuration file--you can easily notice the parallels that the CLI has to this configuration file:

You can find more information about all the available options usable in Docker stack YAML files by visiting https://docs.docker.com/docker-cloud/apps/stack-yaml-reference/. Generally, anything you can set with the CLI commands, you can do the same with the YAML configuration.

```yaml
version: "3"
services:
  local-database:
    image: local_database
    networks:
      - service_network
    deploy:
      replicas: 1
      restart_policy:
        condition: on-failure
    volumes:
      - database_volume:/data/db

  application-server:
    image: application_server
    networks:
      - service_network
    depends_on:
      - local-database
    environment:
      - DB_HOST=local-database
    deploy:
      replicas: 3
      restart_policy:
        condition: on-failure

  web-server:
    image: web_server
    networks:
      - service_network
    ports:
      - 8080:8080
    depends_on:
      - application-server
    environment:
      - APP_NAME=application-server
    deploy:
      replicas: 3
```

```
        restart_policy:
          condition: on-failure

  networks:
    service_network:

  volumes:
    database_volume:
```

What about starting our stack? That's easy too! Stack has almost the same commands as `docker services`:

```
$ docker stack deploy --compose-file swarm_application.yml swarm_test
Creating network swarm_test_service_network
Creating service swarm_test_local-database
Creating service swarm_test_application-server
Creating service swarm_test_web-server

$ # Sanity checks
$ docker stack ls
NAME           SERVICES
swarm_test   3

$ docker stack services swarm_test
ID              NAME                            MODE        REPLICAS
IMAGE                     PORTS
n5qnthc6031k swarm_test_application-server replicated 3/3
application_server
v9ho17uniwc4 swarm_test_web-server           replicated 3/3
web_server               *:8080->8080/tcp
vu06jxakqn6o swarm_test_local-database        replicated 1/1
local_database

$ docker ps --format 'table {{.ID}}   {{.Image}}\t   {{.Ports}}'
CONTAINER ID  IMAGE                           PORTS
afb936897b0d  application_server:latest       8000/tcp
d9c6bab2453a  web_server:latest               80/tcp, 8080/tcp
5e6591ee608b  web_server:latest               80/tcp, 8080/tcp
c8a8dc620023  web_server:latest               80/tcp, 8080/tcp
5db03c196fda  application_server:latest       8000/tcp
d2bf613ecae0  application_server:latest       8000/tcp
369c86b73ae1  local_database:latest           27017/tcp
```

If you go to `http://127.0.0.1:8080` in your browser again, you will see that our app works just like before! We have managed to deploy our whole cluster worth of images with a single file on a Docker Swarm cluster!

Clean up

We are not the kind to leave useless services around, so we will remove our stack and stop our Swarm cluster as we prepare for the next chapter:

```
$ docker stack rm swarm_test
Removing service swarm_test_application-server
Removing service swarm_test_web-server
Removing service swarm_test_local-database
Removing network swarm_test_service_network

$ docker swarm leave --force
Node left the swarm.
```

We won't need to clean up the network or running containers as they will automatically get removed by Docker once our stack is gone. With this part done, we can now move on to the next chapter about volumes with a clean slate.

Summary

In this chapter, we covered a multitude of things like: what service discovery is and why we need it, container orchestration basics and state reconciliation principles, as well as some major players in the orchestration world. With that knowledge in hand, we went on to implement a single-node full cluster using Docker Swarm to show how something like this can be done and near the end we used Docker stack to manage groups of services together, hopefully showing you how this can all be turned from theory to practice.

In the next chapter, we will start exploring the intricate world of Docker volumes and data persistence, so stick with us.

5
Keeping the Data Persistent

In this chapter, we will cover how to keep your important data persistent, safe, and independent of your containers by covering everything about Docker volumes. We will go through various topics, including the following:

- Docker image internals
- Deploying your own instance of a repository
- Transient storage
- Persistent storage
    - Bind-mounts
    - Named volumes
    - Relocatable volumes
- User and group ID handling

While we won't cover all the available storage options, especially ones that are specific to orchestration tooling, this chapter should give you a better understanding of how Docker handles data and what you can do to make sure it is kept in exactly the way you want it.

Docker image internals

To understand even better why we need persistent data, we first need to understand in detail how Docker handles container layers. We covered this topic in some detail in previous chapters, but here, we will spend some time to understand what is going on under the covers. We will first discuss what Docker currently does for handling the written data within containers.

How images are layered

As we covered earlier, Docker stores data that composes the images in a set of discrete, read-only filesystem layers that are stacked on top of each other when you build your image. Any changes done to the filesystem are stacked like transparent slides on top of each other to create the full tree, and any files that have newer content (including being completely removed) will mask the old ones with each new layer. Our former depth of understanding here would probably be sufficient for the basic handling of containers, but for advanced usage, we need to know the full internals on how the data gets handled.

When you start multiple containers with the same base image, all of them are given the same set of filesystem layers as the original image so they start from the exact same filesystem history (barring any mounted volumes or variables), as we'd expect. However, during the start up process, an extra writable layer is added to the top of the image, which persists any data written within that specific container:

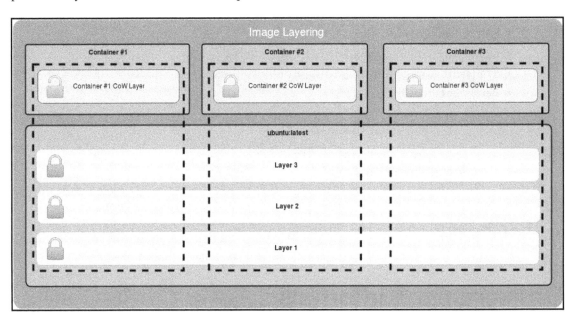

As you would expect, any new files are written to this top layer, but this layer is actually not the same type as the other ones but a special **copy-on-write** (**CoW**) type. If a file that you are writing to in a container is already part of one of the underlying layers, Docker will make a copy of it in the new layer, masking the old one and from that point forward if you read or write to that file, the CoW layer will return its content.

If you destroy this container without trying to save this new CoW layer or without using volumes, as we have experienced this earlier but in a different context, this writable layer will get deleted and all the data written to the filesystem by that container will be effectively lost. In fact, if you generally think of containers as just images with a thin and writable CoW layer, you can see how simple yet effective this layering system is.

Persisting the writable CoW layer(s)

At some point or another, you might want to save the writable container layer to use as a regular image later. While this type of image splicing is highly discouraged, and I would tend to mostly agree, you may find times where it could provides you with an invaluable debugging tooling when you are unable to investigate the container code in other ways. To create an image from an existing container, there is the docker commit command:

```
$ docker commit --help

Usage:  docker commit [OPTIONS] CONTAINER [REPOSITORY[:TAG]]

Create a new image from a container's changes

Options:
  -a, --author string    Author (e.g., "John Hannibal Smith <hannibal@a-
team.com>")
  -c, --change list      Apply Dockerfile instruction to the created image
      --help             Print usage
  -m, --message string   Commit message
  -p, --pause            Pause container during commit (default true)
```

As you can see, we just need some basic information, and Docker will take care of the rest. How about we try this out on our own:

```
$ # Run a new NGINX container and add a new file to it
$ docker run -d nginx:latest
2020a3b1c0fdb83c1f70c13c192eae25e78ca8288c441d753d5b42461727fa78
$ docker exec -it \
          2020a3b1 \
          /bin/bash -c "/bin/echo test > /root/testfile"

$ # Make sure that the file is in /root
$ docker exec -it \
          2020a3b1 \
          /bin/ls /root
testfile

$ # Check what this container's base image is so that we can see changes
```

```
$ docker inspect 2020a3b1 | grep Image
        "Image":
"sha256:b8efb18f159bd948486f18bd8940b56fd2298b438229f5bd2bcf4cedcf037448",
            "Image": "nginx:latest",

$ # Commit our changes to a new image called "new_nginx_image"
$ docker commit -a "Author Name <author@site.com>" \
                -m "Added a test file" \
                2020a3b1 new_nginx_image
sha256:fda147bfb46277e55d9edf090c5a4afa76bc4ca348e446ca980795ad4160fc11

$ # Clean up our original container
$ docker stop 2020a3b1 && docker rm 2020a3b1
2020a3b1
2020a3b1

$ # Run this new image that includes the custom file
$ docker run -d new_nginx_image
16c5835eef14090e058524c18c9cb55f489976605f3d8c41c505babba660952d

$ # Verify that the file is there
$ docker exec -it \
            16c5835e \
            /bin/ls /root
testfile

$ # What about the content?
$ docker exec -it \
            16c5835e \
            /bin/cat /root/testfile
test

$ See what the new container's image is recorded as
$ docker inspect 16c5835e | grep Image
        "Image":
"sha256:fda147bfb46277e55d9edf090c5a4afa76bc4ca348e446ca980795ad4160fc11",
            "Image": "new_nginx_image",

$ # Clean up
$ docker stop 16c5835e && docker rm 16c5835e
16c5835e
16c5835e
```

The `docker commit -c` switch is very useful and adds a command to the image just like the Dockerfile would and accepts the same directives that the Dockerfile does, but since this form is so rarely used, we have decided to skip it. If you would like to know more about this particular form and/or more about `docker commit`, feel free to explore `https://docs.docker.com/engine/reference/commandline/commit/#commit-a-container-with-new-configurations` at leisure.

Running your own image registry

In our previous chapter, during Swarm deploys, we were getting warnings about not using a registry for our images and for a good reason. All the work we did was based on our images being available only to our local Docker Engine so multiple nodes could not have been able to use any of the images that we built. For absolutely bare-bones setups, you can use Docker Hub (`https://hub.docker.com/`) as an option to host your public images, but since practically every **Virtual Private Cloud (VPC)** cluster uses their own internal instance of a private registry for security, speed, and privacy, we will leave Docker Hub as an exercise for you if you want to explore it and we will cover how to run our own registry here.

 Docker has recently come out with a service called Docker Cloud (`https://cloud.docker.com/`), which has private registry hosting and continuous integration and may cover a decent amount of use cases for small-scale deployments, though the service is not free past a single private repository at this time. Generally, though, the most preferred way of setting up scalable Docker-based clusters is a privately hosted registry, so we will focus on that approach, but keep an eye on Docker Cloud's developing feature set as it may fill some operational gaps in your clusters that you can defer as you build other parts of your infrastructure.

To host a registry locally, Docker has provided a Docker Registry image (`registry:2`) that you can run as a regular container with various backends, including the following:

- `inmemory`: A temporary image storage with a local in-memory map. This is only recommended for testing.
- `filesystem`: Stores images using a regular filesystem tree.
- `s3`, `azure`, `swift`, `oss`, `gcs`: Cloud vendor-specific implementations of storage backends.

Let us deploy a registry with a local filesystem backend and see how it can be used.

Warning! The following section does not use TLS-secured or authenticated registry configuration. While this configuration might be acceptable in some rare circumstances in isolated VPCs, generally, you would want to both secure the transport layer with TLS certificates and add some sort of authentication. Luckily, since the API is HTTP-based, you can do most of this with an unsecured registry with a reverse-proxied web server in front of it, like we did earlier with NGINX. Since the certificates need to be "valid" as evaluated by your Docker client and this procedure is different for pretty much every operating system out there, doing the work here would generally not be portable in most configurations, which is why we are skipping it.

```
$ # Make our registry storage folder
$ mkdir registry_storage

$ # Start our registry, mounting the data volume in the container
$ # at the expected location. Use standard port 5000 for it.
$ docker run -d \
            -p 5000:5000 \
            -v $(pwd)/registry_storage:/var/lib/registry \
            --restart=always \
            --name registry \
            registry:2
19e4edf1acec031a34f8e902198e6615fda1e12fb1862a35442ac9d92b32a637


$ # Pull a test image into our local Docker storage
$ docker pull ubuntu:latest
latest: Pulling from library/ubuntu
<snip>
Digest:
sha256:2b9285d3e340ae9d4297f83fed6a9563493945935fc787e98cc32a69f5687641
Status: Downloaded newer image for ubuntu:latest


$ # "Tag our image" by marking it as something that is linked to our local
registry
$ # we just started
$ docker tag ubuntu:latest localhost:5000/local-ubuntu-image


$ # Push our ubuntu:latest image into our local registry under "local-
ubuntu-image" name
$ docker push localhost:5000/local-ubuntu-image
The push refers to a repository [localhost:5000/local-ubuntu-image]
<snip>
latest: digest:
sha256:4b56d10000d71c595e1d4230317b0a18b3c0443b54ac65b9dcd3cac9104dfad2
size: 1357
```

```
$ # Verify that our image is in the right location in registry container
$ ls registry_storage/docker/registry/v2/repositories/
local-ubuntu-image

$ # Remove our images from our main Docker storage
$ docker rmi ubuntu:latest localhost:5000/local-ubuntu-image
Untagged: ubuntu:latest
Untagged: localhost:5000/local-ubuntu-image:latest
<snip>

$ # Verify that our Docker Engine doesn't have either our new image
$ # nor ubuntu:latest
$ docker images
REPOSITORY                      TAG             IMAGE ID          CREATED
SIZE

$ # Pull the image from our registry container to verify that our registry
works
$ docker pull localhost:5000/local-ubuntu-image
Using default tag: latest
latest: Pulling from local-ubuntu-image
<snip>
Digest:
sha256:4b56d10000d71c595e1d4230317b0a18b3c0443b54ac65b9dcd3cac9104dfad2
Status: Downloaded newer image for localhost:5000/local-ubuntu-image:latest

$ # Great! Verify that we have the image.
$ docker images
REPOSITORY                          TAG             IMAGE ID
CREATED             SIZE
localhost:5000/local-ubuntu-image   latest          8b72bba4485f
23 hours ago        120MB
```

As you can see, using the local registry actually seems to be pretty easy! The only new thing introduced here that might need a bit of coverage outside of the registry itself is `--restart=always`, which makes sure that the containers automatically restarts if it exits unexpectedly. The tagging is required to associate an image with the registry, so with doing `docker tag [<source_registry>/]<original_tag_or_id> [<target_registry>/]<new_tag>`, we can effectively assign a new tag to either an existing image tag, or we can create a new tag. As indicated in this small code snippet, both the source and the target can be prefixed with an optional repository location that defaults to `docker.io` (Docker Hub) if not specified.

Sadly, from personal experience, even though this example has made things look real easy, real deployments of the registry are definitely not easy since appearances can be deceiving and there are a few things you need to keep in mind when using it:

- If you use an insecure registry, to access it from a different machine, you must add `"insecure-registries" : ["<ip_or_dns_name>:<port>"]` to `/etc/docker/daemon.json` to every Docker Engine that will be using this registry's images.
  - Note: This configuration is not recommended for a vast number of security reasons.
- If you use an invalid HTTPS certificate, you have to also mark it as an insecure registry on all clients.
  - This configuration is also not recommended as it is only marginally better than the unsecured registry due to possible transport downgrade **Man-in-the-Middle (MITM)** attacks

The final word of advice that I would give you regarding the registry is that the cloud provider backend documentation for the registry has been, in my experience, notoriously and persistently (dare I say intentionally?) incorrect. I would highly recommend that you go through the source code if the registry rejects your settings since setting the right variables is pretty unintuitive. You can also use a mounted file to configure the registry, but if you don't want to build a new image when your cluster is just starting up, environmental variables are the way to go. The environment variables are all-capital names with "_" segment-joined names and match up to the hierarchy of the available options:

```
parent
 └── child_option
     └── some_setting
```

This field for the registry would then be set with `-e PARENT_CHILD_OPTION_SOME_SETTING=<value>`.

> For a complete list of the available registry options, you can visit `https://github.com/docker/docker-registry/blob/master/config/config_sample.yml` and see which ones you would need to run your registry. As mentioned earlier, I have found the main documentation on `docs.docker.com` and a large percentage of documentation on the code repository itself extremely unreliable for configurations, so don't be afraid to read the source code in order to find out what the registry is actually expecting.

To help people who will deploy the registry with the most likely backing storage outside of `filesystem`, which is `s3`, I will leave you a working (at the time of writing this) configuration:

```
$ docker run -d \
          -p 5000:5000 \
          -v $(pwd)/registry_storage:/var/lib/registry \
          -e REGISTRY_STORAGE=s3 \
          -e REGISTRY_STORAGE_CACHE_BLOBDESCRIPTOR=inmemory \
          -e REGISTRY_STORAGE_S3_ACCESSKEY=<aws_key_id> \
          -e REGISTRY_STORAGE_S3_BUCKET=<bucket> \
          -e REGISTRY_STORAGE_S3_REGION=<s3_region> \
          -e REGISTRY_STORAGE_S3_SECRETKEY=<aws_key_secret> \
          --restart=always \
          --name registry \
          registry:2
```

Underlying storage driver

 This section may be a bit too advanced for some readers and does not strictly require reading, but in the interest of fully understanding how Docker handles images and what issues you might encounter on large-scale deployments, I would encourage everyone to at least skim through it as the identification of backing-storage driver issues may be of use. Also, be aware that issues mentioned here may not age gracefully as the Docker code base evolves, so check out their website for up-to-date information.

Unlike what you might have expected from the Docker daemon, the handling of the image layers locally is actually done in a very modular way so that almost any layering filesystem driver can be plugged into the daemon. The storage driver controls how images are stored and retrieved on your docker host(s), and while there may not be any difference from the client's perspective, each one is unique in many aspects.

To start, all of the available storage drivers we will mention are provided by the underlying containerization technology used by Docker, called `containerd`. While knowing anything beyond that last sentence about it is generally overkill for most Docker usages, suffice it to say that it is just one of underlying modules that Docker uses as the image handling API. `containerd` provides a stable API for storing and retrieving images and their designated layers so that any software built on top of it (such as Docker and Kubernetes) can worry about just tying it all together.

You may see references in code and/or documentation about things called graphdrivers, which is pedantically the high-level API that interacts with storage drivers, but in most cases, when it is written, it is used to describe a storage driver that implements the graphdriver API; for example, when a new type of storage driver is talked about, you will often see it referred to as a new graphdriver.

To see which backing filesystem you are using, you can type `docker info` and look for the `Storage Driver` section:

```
$ docker info
<snip>
Storage Driver: overlay2
 Backing Filesystem: extfs
 Supports d_type: true
 Native Overlay Diff: true
<snip>
```

Warning! Changing the storage driver will, in most cases, remove access to any and all images and layers from your machine that were stored by the old driver, so proceed with care! Also, I believe that by changing the storage driver without manually cleaning images and containers either through CLI and/or by deleting things from `/var/lib/docker/` will leave those images and containers dangling, so make sure to clean things up if you consider these changes.

If you would like to change your storage driver to any of the options we will discuss here, you can edit (or create if missing) `/etc/docker/daemon.json` and add the following to it, after which you should restart the docker service:

```
{
  "storage-driver": "driver_name"
}
```

If `daemon.json` does not work, you can also try changing `/etc/default/docker` by adding a `-s` flag to `DOCKER_OPTS` and restarting the service:

```
DOCKER_OPTS="-s driver_name"
```

In general, Docker is transitioning from `/etc/default/docker` (the path dependent on distribution) to `/etc/docker/daemon.json` as its configuration file, so if you see somewhere on the Internet or other documentation that the former file is referenced, see whether you can find the equivalent configuration for `daemon.json` as I believe that it will fully replace the other one at some point in the future (as with all books, probably under a week after this book gets released).

So now that we know what storage drivers are and how to change them, what our the options that we can use here?

aufs

`aufs` (also known as `unionfs`) is the oldest but probably the most mature and stable layered filesystem available for Docker. This storage driver is generally fast to start and efficient in terms of storage and memory overhead. If your kernel has been built with support for this driver, Docker will default to it, but generally, outside of Ubuntu and only with the `linux-image-extra-$(uname -r)` package installed, most distributions do not add that driver to their kernels, nor do they have it available, so most likely your machine will not be able to run it. You could download the kernel source and recompile it with `aufs` support, but generally, this is such a nightmare of a maintenance that you might as well choose a different storage driver if it is not readily available. You can use `grep aufs /proc/filesystems` to check whether your machine has the `aufs` kernel module enabled and available.

Note that the `aufs` driver can only be used on `ext4` and `xfs` filesystems.

btrfs / zfs

These are conceptually less of drivers than actual filesystems that you mount under `/var/lib/docker` and each comes with its own set of pros and cons. Generally, they both have performance impacts as opposed to some of the other options and have a high memory overhead but may provide you with easier management tooling and/or higher density storage. Since these drivers currently have marginal support and I have heard of many critical bugs still affecting them, I would not advise using them in production unless you have very good reasons to do so. If the system has the appropriate drive mounted at `/var/lib/docker` and the related kernel modules are available, Docker will pick these next after `aufs`.

Note that the order of preference here doesn't mean that these two storage drivers are more desirable than the other ones mentioned in this section but purely that if the drive is mounted with the appropriate (and uncommon) filesystem is at the expected Docker location, Docker will assume that this is the configuration that the user wanted.

overlay and overlay2

These particular storage drivers are slowly becoming a favorite for Docker installations. They are very similar to `aufs` but are much faster and simpler implementation. Like `aufs`, both `overlay` and `overlay2` require a kernel overlay module included and loaded, which in general should be available on kernels 3.18 and higher. Also, both can run only on top of `ext4` or `xfs` filesystems. The difference between `overlay` and `overlay2` is that the newer version has improvements that were added in kernel 4.0 to reduce `inode` usage, but the older one has a longer track record in the field. If you have any doubt, `overlay2` is a rock-solid choice in almost any circumstance.

If you have not worked with inodes before, note that they contain the metadata about each individual file on the filesystem and the maximum count allowed is in most cases hardcoded when the filesystem is created. While this hardcoded maximum is fine for most general usages, there are edge cases where you may run out of them, in which case the filesystem will give you errors on any new file creation even though you will have available space to store the file. If you want to learn more about these structures, you can visit `http://www.linfo.org/inode.html` for more information.

Both `overlay` and `overlay2` backing storage driver have been known to cause heavy inode usage due to how they handle file copies internally. While `overlay2` is advertised not to have these issues, I have personally run into inode problems numerous times, with large Docker volumes built with default inode maximums. If you ever use these drivers and notice that the disk is full with messages but you still have space on the device, check your inodes for exhaustion with `df -i` to ensure it is not the docker storage that is causing issues.

devicemapper

Instead of working on file-level devices, this driver operates directly on the block device where your Docker instance is. While the default setup generally sets up a loopback device and is mostly fine for local testing, this particular setup is extremely not suggested for production systems due to the sparse files it creates in the loopback device. For production systems, you are encouraged to combine it with `direct-lvm`, but that kind of intricate setup requires a configuration that is particularly tricky and slower than the `overlay` storage driver, so I would generally not recommend its use unless you are unable to use `aufs` or `overlay`/`overlay2`.

Cleanup of Docker storage

If you work with Docker images and containers, you will notice that, in general, Docker will chew through any storage you give it relatively quickly, so proper maintenance is recommended every now and then to ensure that you do not end up with useless garbage on your hosts or run out of inodes for some storage drivers.

Manual cleanup

First up is the cleanup of all containers that you have run but have forgotten to use `--rm` by using `docker rm`:

```
$ docker rm $(docker ps -aq)
86604ed7bb17
<snip>
7f7178567aba
```

This command effectively finds all containers (`docker ps`), even the ones that you stopped (the `-a` flag), and only returns their IDs (the `-q` flag). This is then passed on to `docker rm`, which will try to remove them one by one. If any containers are still running, it will give you a warning and skip them. Generally, this is just a good thing to do as often as you want if your containers are stateless or have a state stored outside of the container itself.

The next thing up, though potentially much more destructive and more space-saving, is deleting Docker images you have accumulated. If your space issues are frequent, manual removal can be pretty effective. A good rule of thumb is that any images with <none> as their tag (also called dangling) can usually be removed using docker rmi as they, in most cases, indicate that this image was superseded by a newer build of a Dockerfile:

```
$ docker images --filter "dangling=true"
REPOSITORY              TAG                 IMAGE ID            CREATED
SIZE
<none>                  <none>              873473f192c8        7 days ago
129MB
<snip>
registry                <none>              751f286bc25e        7 weeks ago
33.2MB

$ # Use those image IDs and delete them
$ docker rmi $(docker images -q --filter "dangling=true")

Deleted:
sha256:873473f192c8977716fcf658c1fe0df0429d4faf9c833b7c24ef269cacd140ff
<snip>
Deleted:
sha256:2aee30e0a82b1a6b6b36b93800633da378832d623e215be8b4140e8705c4101f
```

Automatic cleanup

All of the things we have just done seem pretty painful to do and are hard to remember so Docker recently added docker image prune to help out in this aspect. By using docker image prune, all dangling images will be removed with a single command:

```
$ docker image prune

WARNING! This will remove all dangling images.
Are you sure you want to continue? [y/N] y

Deleted Images:
untagged:
ubuntu@sha256:2b9285d3e340ae9d4297f83fed6a9563493945935fc787e98cc32a69f5687
641
deleted:
sha256:8b72bba4485f1004e8378bc6bc42775f8d4fb851c750c6c0329d3770b3a09086
<snip>
deleted:
sha256:f4744c6e9f1f2c5e4cfa52bab35e67231a76ede42889ab12f7b04a908f058551

Total reclaimed space: 188MB
```

If you are intent on cleaning any and all images not tied to containers, you can also run `docker image prune -a`. Given that this command is pretty destructive I would not recommend it in most cases other than maybe running it on Docker slave nodes in clusters on a nighty/weekly timer to reduce space usage.

Something to note here, as you might have noticed, deleting all references to an image layer also cascades onto child layers.

Last but not least is volume clean-up, which can be managed with the `docker volume` command. I would recommend that you exercise extreme caution when doing this in order to avoid deleting data that you might need and only use manual volume selection or `prune`:

```
$ docker volume ls
DRIVER                  VOLUME NAME
local                   database_volume
local                   local_storage
local                   swarm_test_database_volume

$ docker volume prune

WARNING! This will remove all volumes not used by at least one container.
Are you sure you want to continue? [y/N] y

Deleted Volumes:
local_storage
swarm_test_database_volume
database_volume

Total reclaimed space: 630.5MB
```

As a reference, I have been running Docker rather lightly the week I wrote this chapter and the removal of stale containers, images, and volumes has reduced my filesystem usage by about 3 GB. While that number is mostly anecdotal and may not seem much, on cloud nodes with small instance hard disks and on clusters with continuous integration added, leaving these things around will get you out of disk space faster than you might realize, so expect to spend some time either doing this manually or automating this process for your nodes in something such as `systemd` timers or `crontab`.

Persistent storage

Since we have covered transient local storage, we can now consider what other options we have for keeping data safe when the container dies or is moved. As we talked about previously, without being able to save data from the container in some fashion to an outside source if a node or the container unexpectedly dies while it is serving up something (such as your database), you will most likely lose some or all your data contained on it, which is definitively something we would like to avoid. Using some form of container-external storage for your data, like we did in earlier chapters with mounted volumes, we can begin to make the cluster really resilient and containers that run on it stateless.

By making containers stateless, you gain confidence to not worry much about exactly what container is running on which Docker Engine as long as they can pull the right image and run it with the right parameters. If you think about it for a minute, you may even notice how this approach has a huge number of similarities with threading, but on steroids. You can imagine Docker Engine like a virtual CPU core, each service as a process, and each task as a thread. With this in mind, if everything is stateless in your system then your cluster is effectively stateless too, and by inference, you must utilize some form of data storage outside of the containers to keep your data safe.

Caution! Lately, I have noticed a number of sources online that have been recommending that you should keep data through massive replication of services with sharding and clustering of backing databases without persisting data on disk, relying on the cloud provider's distributed availability zones and trusting **Service Level Agreements** (**SLA**) to provide you with resilience and self-healing properties for your cluster. While I would agree that these clusters are somewhat resilient, without some type of permanent physical representation of your data on some type of a volume, you may hit cascade outages on your clusters that will chain before the data is replicated fully and risk losing data with no way to restore it. As a personal advice here, I would highly recommend that at least one node in your stateful services uses storage that is on physical media that is not liable to be wiped when issues arise (e.g. NAS, AWS EBS storage, and so on).

Node-local storage

This type of storage that is external to the container is specifically geared toward keeping data separate from your container instances, as we would expect, but is limited to usability only within containers deployed to the same node. Such storage allows a stateless container setup and has many development-geared uses, such as isolated builds and reading of configuration files, but for clustered deployments it is severely limited, as containers that run on other nodes will not have any access to data created on the original node. In either case, we will cover all of these node-local storage types here since most large clusters use some combination of node-local storage and relocatable storage.

Bind mounts

We have seen these earlier, but maybe we did not know what they are. Bind mounts take a specific file or folder and mount it within the container sandbox at a specified location, separated by `:`. The general syntax that we have used so far for this should look similar to the following:

```
$ docker run <run_params> \
            -v /path/on/host:/path/on/container \
            <image>...
```

Newer Docker syntax for this functionality is making its way into becoming a standard where the `-v` and `--volume` is now being replaced with `--mount`, so you should get used to that syntax too. In fact, from here on out, we will use both as much as we can so that you are comfortable with either style, but at the time of writing this book, `--mount` is not yet as fully functional as the alternative so expect some interchanging depending on what works and what does not.

> In particular here, at this time, a simple bind mount volume with an absolute path source just does not work with `--mount` style which is almost all the examples we have used so far which is why we have not introduced this form earlier.

With all that said and out of the way, unlike `--volume`, `--mount` is a `<key>=<value>` comma-separated list of parameters:

- `type`: The type of the mount, which can be `bind`, `volume`, or `tmpfs`.
- `source`: The source for the mount.
- `target`: The path to the location in the container where the source will be mounted.

- `readonly`: Causes the mount to be mounted as read-only.
- `volume-opt`: Extra options for the volume. May be entered more than once.

This is a comparative version to the one we used for `--volume`:

```
$ docker run <run_params> \
            --mount source=/path/on/host,target=/path/on/container \
            <image>...
```

Read-only bind mounts

Another type of a bind mount that we did not really cover earlier is a read-only bind mount. This configuration is used when the data mounted into the container needs to remain read-only, which is very useful when passing configuration files into multiple containers from the host. This form of mounting a volume looks a bit like this for both of the two syntax styles:

```
$ # Old-style
$ docker run <run_params> \
            -v /path/on/host:/path/on/container:ro \
            <image>...

$ # New-style
$ docker run <run_params> \
            --mount
source=/path/on/host,target=/path/on/container,readonly \
            <image>...
```

As mentioned a bit earlier, something that a read-only volume can provide us as opposed to a regular mount is passing configuration files to the containers from the host. This is generally used when the Docker Engine host has something in their configuration that impacts the containers running code (that is, path prefixes for storing or fetching data, which host we're running on, what DNS resolvers the machine is using from `/etc/resolv.conf`, and many others) so in big deployments, it is used extensively and expect to see it often.

 As a good rule of thumb, unless you explicitly need to write data to a volume, always mount it as read-only to the container. This will prevent the inadvertent opening of security holes from a compromised container spreading onto the other containers and the host itself.

Named volumes

Another form of volume mounting is using named volumes. Unlike bind-mounts, named data volumes (often referred to as data volume containers) provide a more portable way to refer to volumes as they do not depend on knowing anything about the host. Under the covers, they work almost exactly the same way as bind-mounts, but they are much easier to handle due to their simpler usage. Also, they have an added benefit of being able to be easily shared among containers and even be managed by host-independent solutions or a completely separate backend.

 Caution! If the named data volume is created by simply running the container, unlike bind-mounts that literally replace all content the container had at that mounted path, the named data volume will copy the content that the container image had at that location into the named data volume when the container launches. This difference is very subtle but can cause serious issues, as you might end up with unexpected content in the volume if you forget about this detail or assume that it behaves the same way as bind-mounts.

Now that we know what named data volumes are, let us create one by using the early-configuration approach (as opposed to creating one by directly running a container):

```
$ # Create our volume
$ docker volume create mongodb_data
mongodb_data

$ docker volume inspect mongodb_data
[
    {
        "Driver": "local",
        "Labels": {},
        "Mountpoint": "/var/lib/docker/volumes/mongodb_data/_data",
        "Name": "mongodb_data",
        "Options": {},
        "Scope": "local"
    }
]

$ # We can start our container now
$ # XXX: For non-bind-mounts, the new "--mount" option
$ #      works fine so we will use it here
$ docker run -d \
          --mount source=mongodb_data,target=/data/db \
          mongo:latest
888a8402d809174d25ac14ba77445c17ab5ed371483c1f38c918a22f3478f25a
```

```
$ # Did it work?
$ docker exec -it 888a8402 ls -la /data/db
total 200
drwxr-xr-x 4 mongodb mongodb  4096 Sep 16 14:10 .
drwxr-xr-x 4 root    root     4096 Sep 13 21:18 ..
-rw-r--r-- 1 mongodb mongodb    49 Sep 16 14:08 WiredTiger
<snip>
-rw-r--r-- 1 mongodb mongodb    95 Sep 16 14:08 storage.bson


$ # Stop the container
$ docker stop 888a8402 && docker rm 888a8402
888a8402
888a8402


$ # What does our host's FS have in the
$ # volume storage? (path used is from docker inspect output)
$ sudo ls -la /var/lib/docker/volumes/mongodb_data/_data
total 72
drwxr-xr-x 4  999 docker 4096 Sep 16 09:08 .
drwxr-xr-x 3 root root   4096 Sep 16 09:03 ..
-rw-r--r-- 1  999 docker 4096 Sep 16 09:08
collection-0-6180071043564974707.wt
<snip>
-rw-r--r-- 1  999 docker 4096 Sep 16 09:08 WiredTiger.wt


$ # Remove the new volume
$ docker volume rm mongodb_data
mongodb_data
```

Manually creating the volume before you use it (using docker volume create) is generally unnecessary but was done here to demonstrate the long-form of doing it but we could have just launched our container as the first step and Docker would have created the volume on its own:

```
$ # Verify that we don't have any volumes
$ docker volume ls
DRIVER           VOLUME NAME

$ # Run our MongoDB without creating the volume beforehand
$ docker run -d \
          --mount source=mongodb_data,target=/data/db \
          mongo:latest
f73a90585d972407fc21eb841d657e5795d45adc22d7ad27a75f7d5b0bf86f69


$ # Stop and remove our container
$ docker stop f73a9058 && docker rm f73a9058
f73a9058
f73a9058
```

```
$ # Check our volumes
$ docker volume ls
DRIVER                  VOLUME NAME
local
4182af67f0d2445e8e2289a4c427d0725335b732522989087579677cf937eb53
local                   mongodb_data

$ # Remove our new volumes
$ docker volume rm mongodb_data
4182af67f0d2445e8e2289a4c427d0725335b732522989087579677cf937eb53
mongodb_data
4182af67f0d2445e8e2289a4c427d0725335b732522989087579677cf937eb53
```

You may have noticed here, though, we ended up with two volumes instead of just our expected `mongodb_data` and if you followed the previous example with this one, you might actually have three (one named, two with random names). This is because every container launched will create all the local volumes defined in the `Dockerfile` regardless of whether you name them or not, and our MongoDB image actually defines two volumes:

```
$ # See what volumes Mongo image defines
$ docker inspect mongo:latest | grep -A 3 Volumes
<snip>
            "Volumes": {
                "/data/configdb": {},
                "/data/db": {}
            },
```

We only gave a name to the first one so the `/data/configdb` volume received a random one. Be aware of such things as you might encounter space exhaustion issues if you are not attentive enough. Running `docker volume prune` every once in a while can help reclaim that space, but be careful with this command as it will destroy all volumes not tied to containers.

Relocatable volumes

All of these options that we discussed earlier are fine when working on a single host, but what they lack is real data portability between different physical hosts. For example, the current methods of keeping data persistent can realistically scale up to but not beyond (without some extreme hacking) a single physical server with single Docker Engine and shared attached storage. This might be fine for a powerful server but starts to lack any sort of use in a true clustering configuration since you might be dealing with an unknown number of servers, mixed virtual and physical hosts, different geographic areas, and so on.

Also when a container is restarted, you most likely will not be able to easily predict where it is going to get launched to have the volume backend there for it when it starts. For this use case, there are things called relocatable volumes. These go by various different names, such as "shared multi-host storage", "orchestrated data volume", and many others, but the idea is pretty much the same across the board: have a data volume that will follow the container wherever it goes.

To illustrate the example, here, we have three hosts with two stateful services all connected using the same relocatable volume storage driver:

- **Stateful Container 1** with **Volume D** on **Host 1**
- **Stateful Container 2** with **Volume G** on **Host 3**

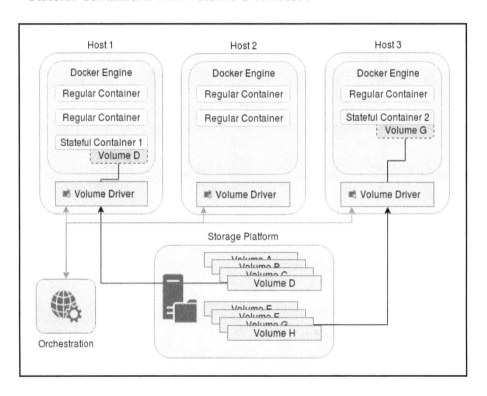

For the purpose of this example, assume that **Host 3** has died. In the normal volume driver case, all your data from **Stateful Container 2** would be lost, but because you would be using relocatable storage:

- The orchestration platform will notify your storage driver that the container has died.
- The orchestration platform will indicate that it wants to restart the killed services on a host with available resources.
- The volume driver will mount the same volume to the new host that will run the service.
- The orchestration platform will start the service, passing the volume details into the new container.

In our hypothetical example, the new system state should look a little bit like this:

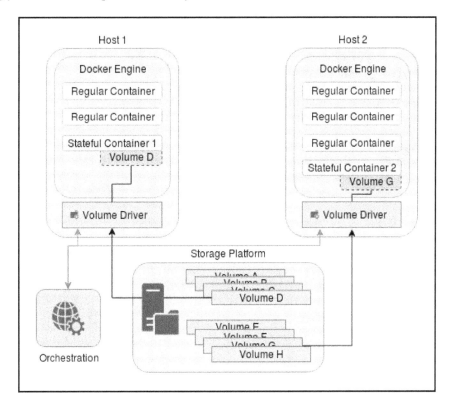

As you can see from an external point of view, nothing has changed and the data was seamlessly transitioned to the new container and kept its state, which is exactly what we wanted. For this specific purpose, there are a number of Docker volume drivers that one can choose, and each one has its own configuration method for various storage backends, but the only one included with Docker pre-built images for Azure and AWS out of the box is CloudStor, and it is only for Docker Swarm, making it super-specific and completely non-portable.

 For various reasons, including the age of technology and lackluster support by Docker and plugin developers, having to do this type of volume handling is most likely going to be the part that you sink a lot of time into when building your infrastructure. I do not want to discourage you, but at the time of writing this, the state of things is really dire regardless of what easy tutorials may like you to believe.

You can find a majority of the drivers at `https://docs.docker.com/engine/extend/legacy_plugins/#volume-plugins`. After configuration, use them in the following manner if you are doing it manually without orchestration in order to manage mounting:

```
$ # New-style volume switch (--mount)
$ docker run --mount source=<volume_name>,target=/dest/path,volume-driver=<name> \
            <image>...

$ # Old-style volume switch
$ docker run -v <volume_name>:/dest/path \
            --volume-driver <name> \
            <image>...
```

For reference, currently, I believe that the most popular plugins for handling relocatable volumes are Flocker, REX-Ray (`https://github.com/codedellemc/rexray`), and GlusterFS though there are many to choose from, with many of them having similar functionality. As mentioned earlier, the state of this ecosystem is rather abysmal for such an important feature and it seems that almost every big player running their clustering either forks and builds their own storage solution, or they make their own and keep it closed-sourced. Some deployments have even opted to using labels for their nodes to avoid this topic completely and force specific containers to go to specific hosts so that they can use locally mounted volumes.

Flocker's parent company, ClusterHQ, shut down its operations in December 2016 for financial reasons, and while the lack of support would give a bit of a push to not be mentioned here, it is still the most popular one by an order of magnitude for this type of volume management at the time of writing this book. All the code is open sourced on GitHub at `https://github.com/ClusterHQ` so you can build, install, and run it even without official support. If you want to use this plugin in an enterprise environment and would like to have support for it, some of the original developers are available for hire through a new company called ScatterHQ at `https://www.scatterhq.com/` and they have their own source code repositories at `https://github.com/ScatterHQ`.

 GlusterFS is unmaintained in its original source like Flocker, but just like Flocker, you can build, install, and run the full code from the source repository located at `https://github.com/calavera/docker-volume-glusterfs`. If you would like code versions that have received updates, you can find a few in the fork network at `https://github.com/calavera/docker-volume-glusterfs/network`.

On top of all this ecosystem fragmentation, this particular way of integrating with Docker is starting to be deprecated in favor of the `docker plugin` system which manages and installs these plugins as Docker images from Docker Hub but due to lack of availability of these new-style plugins, you might have to use a legacy plugin depending on your specific use cases.

 Sadly at the time of writing this book, `docker plugin` system is, like many of these features, so new that there are barely any available plugins for it. For example, the only plugin from the ones earlier mentioned in legacy plugins that is built using this new system is REX-Ray but the most popular storage backend (EBS) plugin does not seem to install cleanly. By the time you get to read this book, things will probably have changed here but be aware that there is a significant likelihood that in your own implementation you will be using the tried-and-tested legacy plugins.

So with all of these caveats mentioned, let's actually try to get one of the only plugins (`sshfs`) that can be found working using the new `docker plugin install` system:

 To duplicate this work, you will need access to a secondary machine (though you can run it loopback too) with SSH enabled and reachable from wherever you have Docker Engine running from, since that is the backing storage system that it uses. You will also need the target folder `ssh_movable_volume` made on the device and possibly the addition of `-o odmap=user` to the `sshfs` volume parameters depending on your setup.

```
$ # Install the plugin
$ docker plugin install vieux/sshfs

Plugin "vieux/sshfs" is requesting the following privileges:
 - network: [host]
 - mount: [/var/lib/docker/plugins/]
 - mount: []
 - device: [/dev/fuse]
 - capabilities: [CAP_SYS_ADMIN]
Do you grant the above permissions? [y/N] y
latest: Pulling from vieux/sshfs
2381f72027fc: Download complete
Digest:
sha256:72c8cfd1a6eb02e6db4928e27705f9b141a2a0d7f4257f069ce8bd813784b558
Status: Downloaded newer image for vieux/sshfs:latest
Installed plugin vieux/sshfs

$ # Sanity check
$ docker plugin ls
ID                 NAME                 DESCRIPTION             ENABLED
0d160591d86f       vieux/sshfs:latest   sshFS plugin for Docker true

$ # Add our password to a file
$ echo -n '<password>' > password_file

$ # Create a volume backed by sshfs on a remote server with SSH daemon
running
$ docker volume create -d vieux/sshfs \
                  -o sshcmd=user@192.168.56.101/ssh_movable_volume \
                  -o password=$(cat password_file) \
                  ssh_movable_volume
ssh_movable_volume

$ # Sanity check
$ docker volume ls
DRIVER             VOLUME NAME
```

```
vieux/sshfs:latest    ssh_movable_volume

$ # Time to test it with a container
$ docker run -it \
            --rm \
            --mount source=ssh_movable_volume,target=/my_volume,volume-
driver=vieux/sshfs:latest \
            ubuntu:latest \
            /bin/bash

root@75f4d1d2ab8d:/# # Create a dummy file
root@75f4d1d2ab8d:/# echo 'test_content' > /my_volume/test_file

root@75f4d1d2ab8d:/# exit
exit

$ # See that the file is hosted on the remote server
$ ssh user@192.168.56.101
user@192.168.56.101's password:
<snip>
user@ubuntu:~$ cat ssh_movable_volume/test_file
test_content

$ # Get back to our Docker Engine host
user@ubuntu:~$ exit
logout
Connection to 192.168.56.101 closed.

$ # Clean up the volume
$ docker volume rm ssh_movable_volume
ssh_movable_volume
```

Due to the way the volume is used, this volume is mostly portable and could allow us the relocatable features we need, though most other plugins use a process that runs outside of Docker and in parallel on each host in order to manage the volume mounting, un-mounting, and moving, so instructions for those will be vastly different.

Relocatable volume sync loss

One last thing that must be mentioned in this section as well is the fact that most of plugins that handle the moving of volumes can only handle being attached to a single node at any one time due to the volume being writable by multiple sources is going to generally cause serious issues so most drivers disallow it.

This however is in conflict with the main feature of most orchestration engines which, on changes to Docker services, will leave the original service running until the new one is started and passes health checks, causing the need to mount the same volume on both the old and new service task in effect, creating a chicken-egg paradox.

In most cases, this can be worked around by making sure that Docker completely kills the old service before starting the new one, but even then, you can expect that occasionally the old volume will not be unmounted quickly enough from the old node, so the new service will fail to start.

UID/GID and security considerations with volumes

This section is not in a small informational box like I would have put it elsewhere, because it is a big enough issue and problematic enough to deserve its own section. To understand what happens with container **user ID (UID)** and **group ID (GID)**, we need to understand how the host's system permission works. When you have a file with group and user permissions, they are internally all actually mapped to numbers and not kept as usernames or group names that you see when listing things with regular `ls` switches:

```
$ # Create a folder and a file that we will mount in the container
$ mkdir /tmp/foo
$ cd /tmp/foo
$ touch foofile

$ # Let's see what we have. Take note of owner and group of the file and
directory
$ ls -la
total 0
drwxrwxr-x  2 user user   60 Sep  8 20:20 .
drwxrwxrwt 56 root root 1200 Sep  8 20:20 ..
-rw-rw-r--  1 user user    0 Sep  8 20:20 foofile

$ # See what our current UID and GID are
$ id
uid=1001(user) gid=1001(user) <snip>

$ # How about we see the actual values that the underlying system uses
$ ls -na
total 0
drwxrwxr-x  2 1001 1001   60 Sep  8 20:20 .
drwxrwxrwt 56    0    0 1200 Sep  8 20:20 ..
-rw-rw-r--  1 1001 1001    0 Sep  8 20:20 foofile
```

When you do `ls`, the system reads in `/etc/passwd` and `/etc/group` to display the actual username and group name for permissions, and it is the only way in which the UID/GID is mapped to permissions but the underlying values are UIDs and GIDs.

As you might have guessed, this user-to-UID and group-to-GID mapping might not (and often does not) translate well to a containerized system as the container(s) will not have the same `/etc/passwd` and `/etc/group` files but the permissions of files on external volumes are stored with the data. For example, if the container has a group with a GID of `1001`, it will match the group permission bits `-rw` on our `foofile` and if it has a user has a UID of `1001`, it will match our `-rw` user permissions on the file. Conversely, if your UIDs and GIDs do not match up, even if you have a group or user with the same name in the container and on the host, you will not have the right UIDs and GID for proper permission processing. Time to check out what kind of a mess we can do with this:

```
$ ls -la
total 0
drwxrwxr-x   2 user user    60 Sep  8 21:16 .
drwxrwxrwt  57 root root  1220 Sep  8 21:16 ..
-rw-rw-r--   1 user user     0 Sep  8 21:16 foofile

$ ls -na
total 0
drwxrwxr-x   2 1001 1001    60 Sep  8 21:16 .
drwxrwxrwt  57    0    0  1220 Sep  8 21:16 ..
-rw-rw-r--   1 1001 1001     0 Sep  8 21:16 foofile

$ # Start a container with this volume mounted
$ # Note: We have to use the -v form since at the time of writing this
$ #       you can't mount a bind mount with absolute path :(
$ docker run --rm \
            -it \
            -v $(pwd)/foofile:/tmp/foofile \
            ubuntu:latest /bin/bash

root@d7776ec7b655:/# # What does the container sees as owner/group?
root@d7776ec7b655:/# ls -la /tmp
total 8
drwxrwxrwt 1 root root 4096 Sep  9 02:17 .
drwxr-xr-x 1 root root 4096 Sep  9 02:17 ..
-rw-rw-r-- 1 1001 1001    0 Sep  9 02:16 foofile

root@d7776ec7b655:/# # Our container doesn't know about our users
root@d7776ec7b655:/# # so it only shows UID/GID

root@d7776ec7b655:/# # Let's change the owner/group to root (UID 0) and set
setuid flag
```

```
root@d7776ec7b655:/# chown 0:0 /tmp/foofile
root@d7776ec7b655:/# chmod +x 4777 /tmp/foofile

root@d7776ec7b655:/# # See what the permissions look like now in container
root@d7776ec7b655:/# ls -la /tmp
total 8
drwxrwxrwt 1 root root 4096 Sep  9 02:17 .
drwxr-xr-x 1 root root 4096 Sep  9 02:17 ..
-rwsrwxrwx 1 root root    0 Sep  9 02:16 foofile

root@d7776ec7b655:/# # Exit the container
root@d7776ec7b655:/# exit
exit

$ # What does our unmounted volume looks like?
$ ls -la
total 0
drwxrwxr-x  2 user user   60 Sep  8 21:16 .
drwxrwxrwt 57 root root 1220 Sep  8 21:17 ..
-rwsrwxrwx  1 root root    0 Sep  8 21:16 foofile
$ # Our host now has a setuid file! Bad news!
```

> Warning! The ability to set the `setuid` flag on files is a really big security hole that executes the file with the file owner's permissions. If we decided to compile a program and set this flag on it, we could have done a massive amount of damage on the host. Refer to `https://en.wikipedia.org/wiki/Setuid` for more information on this flag.

As you can see, this can be a serious issue if we decided to be more malicious with our `setuid` flag. This issue extends to any mounted volumes we use, so make sure that you exercise proper caution when dealing with them.

> Docker has been working on getting user namespaces working in order to avoid some of these security issues, which work by re-mapping the UIDs and GIDs to something else within the container through `/etc/subuid` and `/etc/subgid` files so that there is no `root` UID clashing between the host and the container, but they're not without their problems (and there's plenty of them at the time of writing this book). For more information on using user namespaces, you can find more information at `https://docs.docker.com/engine/security/userns-remap/`.

Compounding this UID/GID problem is another issue that happens with such separate environments: even if you install all the same packages in the same order between two containers, due to users and groups usually being created by name and not a specific UID/GID, you are not guaranteed to have these consistent between the container runs, which is a serious problems if you want to remount the same volume between a container that was upgraded or rebuilt. For this reason, you must ensure that UIDs and GIDs are stable on volumes by doing something similar to the following, as we have done in some earlier examples, before you install the package(s) with the users and groups that will be dealing with the volume data:

```
RUN groupadd -r -g 910 mongodb && \
    useradd -r -u 910 -g 910 mongodb && \
    mkdir -p /data/db && \
    chown -R mongodb:mongodb /data/db && \
    chmod -R 700 /data/db && \
    apt-get install mongodb-org
```

Here, we create a group `mongodb` with GID `910` and a user `mongodb` with UID `910` and then make sure that our data directory is owned by it before we install MongoDB. By doing this, when the `mongodb-org` package is installed, the group and user for running the database is already there and with the exact UID/GID that will not change. With a stable UID/GID, we can mount and remount the volume on any built container with the same configuration as both of the numbers will match and it should work on any machine that we move the volume to.

The only final thing to possibly worry about (which is also somewhat of a problem in that last example) is that mounting a folder will overlay itself over an already created folder on the host and replace its permissions. This means that if you mount a new folder onto the container, either you have to manually change the volume's permissions or change the ownership when the container starts. Let's see what I mean by that:

```
$ mkdir /tmp/some_folder
$ ls -la /tmp | grep some_folder
drwxrwxr-x  2 sg    sg         40 Sep  8 21:56 some_folder

$ # Mount this folder to a container and list the content
$ docker run -it \
            --rm \
            -v /tmp/some_folder:/tmp/some_folder \
            ubuntu:latest \
            ls -la /tmp
total 8
drwxrwxrwt 1 root root 4096 Sep  9 02:59 .
drwxr-xr-x 1 root root 4096 Sep  9 02:59 ..
drwxrwxr-x 2 1000 1000   40 Sep  9 02:56 some_folder
```

```
$ # Somewhat expected but we will do this now by overlaying
$ # an existing folder (/var/log - root owned) in the container

$ # First a sanity chech
$ docker run -it \
            --rm \
            ubuntu:latest \
            ls -la /var | grep log
drwxr-xr-x 4 root root  4096 Jul 10 18:56 log

$ # Seems ok but now we mount our folder here
$ docker run -it \
            --rm \
            -v /tmp/some_folder:/var/log \
            ubuntu:latest \
            ls -la /var | grep log
drwxrwxr-x 2 1000  1000    40 Sep  9 02:56 log
```

As you can see, whatever permissions were already set on the folder within the container got completely trampled by our mounted directory volume. As mentioned earlier, the best way to avoid having permission errors with limited users running services in the container and mounted volumes is to change the permissions on the mounted paths on container start with a wrapper script or start the container with a mounted volume and change it manually, with the former being the much preferable option. The simplest wrapper script goes something like this:

```
#!/bin/bash -e

# Change owner of volume to the one we expect
chown mongodb:mongodb /path/to/volume

# Optionally you can use this recursive version too
# but in most cases it is a bit heavy-handed
# chown -R mongodb:mongodb /path/to/volume

su - <original limited user> -c '<original cmd invocation>'
```

Placing this in /usr/bin/wrapper.sh of the container and adding the following snippet somewhere to the Dockerfile where it runs as root should be good enough to fix the issue:

```
<snip>
CMD [ "/usr/bin/wrapper.sh" ]
```

When the container starts, the volume will be mounted already and the script will change the user and group of the volume to the proper one before passing the command to the original runner for the container, fixing our issue.

The biggest takeaway from this section should be that you should be mindful of user permissions when you deal with volumes as they may cause usability and security issues if you are not careful. As you develop your services and infrastructure, these types of pitfalls can cause everything from minor headaches to catastrophic failures but now that you know more about them, we have hopefully prevented the worst.

Summary

In this chapter, you have learned a massive amount of new stuff revolving around Docker's data handling including Docker image internals and running your own Docker Registry. We have also covered transient, node-local, and relocatable data storage and the associated volume management that you will need to effectively deploy your services in the cloud. Later we have spent some time covering the volume orchestration ecosystem to help you navigate the changing landscape of Docker volume drivers as things have been changing quickly in this space. As we got to the end, coverage of various pitfalls (like UID/GID issues) was included so that you can avoid them in your own deployments.

As we continue into the next chapter, we will cover cluster hardening and how to pass data between a large volume of services in an orderly fashion.

6
Advanced Deployment Topics

We have spent a decent amount of time talking about container communication and security, but in this chapter, we will take a look at taking deployments even further by covering the following:

- Advanced debugging techniques.
- Implementing queue messaging.
- Running security checks.
- Container security in depth.

We will also look at a few other tools and techiniques that will help you manage your deployments better.

Advanced debugging

The ability to debug containers in the wild is a very important topic and we previously covered some of the more basic techniques that can be of use here. But there are cases where `docker ps` and `docker exec` just aren't enough, so in this section, we will examine a few more tools you can add to your toolbox that can help resolve those tricky issues.

Attaching to a container's process space

There may be times when a container is running with a minimalist distribution such as Alpine Linux (`https://www.alpinelinux.org/`) and the container in question has an issue with a process that you would like to debug but also lacks the most basic tooling you need for debugging included. By default, Docker isolates all containers in their individual process namespace so our current debugging workflow, which we used before by attaching to that container directly and trying to figure out what was wrong with very limited tooling is not going to help us much here.

Luckily for us though, Docker is fully capable of joining the process namespaces of two containers with the `docker run --pid "container:<name_or_id>"` flag, so that we can attach a debug tooling container directly onto the affected one:

```
$ # Start an NGINX container
$ docker run -d --rm nginx
650a1baedb0c274cf91c086a9e697b630b2b60d3c3f94231c43984bed1073349

$ # What can we see from a new/separate container?
$ docker run --rm \
            ubuntu \
            ps -ef

UID         PID  PPID  C STIME TTY          TIME CMD
root          1     0  0 16:37 ?        00:00:00 ps -ef

$ # Now let us try the same thing but attach to the NGINX's PID space
$ docker run --rm \
            --pid "container:650a1bae" \
            ubuntu \
            ps -ef

UID         PID  PPID  C STIME TTY      TIME CMD
root          1     0  0 16:37 ?        00:00:00 nginx: master process nginx -g
daemon off;
systemd+      7     1  0 16:37 ?        00:00:00 nginx: worker process
root          8     0  0 16:37 ?        00:00:00 ps -ef
```

As you can see, we can just attach a debugging container into the same PID namespace and debug any oddly behaving process this way and can keep the original container pristine from the installation of debug tooling! Using this technique, the original container can be kept small since the tooling can be shipped separately and the container remains running throughout the debugging process so your task will not be rescheduled. That said, whenever you are debugging different containers using this method, be careful not to kill the processes or the threads within it as they have a likely chance of cascading and killing the whole container, halting your investigation.

Interestingly enough, this `pid` flag can also be invoked with `--pid host` to share the host's process namespace if you have a tool that does not run on your distribution and there is a Docker container for it (or, alternatively, if you want to use a container for the management of the host's processes):

```
$ # Sanity check
$ docker run --rm \
            ubuntu \
            ps -ef

UID        PID  PPID  C STIME TTY          TIME CMD
root         1     0  0 16:44 ?        00:00:00 ps -ef

$ # Now we try to attach to host's process namespace
$ docker run --rm \
            --pid host \
            ubuntu \
            ps -ef

UID        PID  PPID  C STIME TTY          TIME CMD
root         1     0  0 15:44 ?        00:00:02 /sbin/init splash
root         2     0  0 15:44 ?        00:00:00 [kthreadd]
root         4     2  0 15:44 ?        00:00:00 [kworker/0:0H]
<snip>
root      5504  5485  3 16:44 ?        00:00:00 ps -ef
```

It should be apparent as to how much capability this flag's functionality can provide for both running and debugging applications, so do not hesitate to use it.

 Warning! Sharing the host's process namespace with the container is a big security hole as a malicious container can easily commandeer or DoS the host by manipulating processes, especially if the container's user is running as a root. Due to this, exercise extreme caution when utilizing `--pid host` and ensure that you use this flag only on containers you trust completely.

Debugging the Docker daemon

If none of these techniques have helped you so far, you can try to run the Docker container and check what the daemon API is doing with `docker system events`, which tracks almost all actions that are triggered on its API endpoint. You can use this for both auditing and debugging, but generally, the latter is its primary purpose as you can see in the following example.

On the first terminal, run the following command and leave it running so that we can see what information we can collect:

```
$ docker system events
```

On another Terminal, we will run a new container:

```
$ docker run -it \
            --rm \
            ubuntu /bin/bash

$ root@563ad88c26c3:/# exit
exit
```

After you have done this start and stop of the container, the `events` command in the first terminal should have output something similar to this:

```
$ docker system events
2017-09-27T10:54:58.943347229-07:00 container create
563ad88c26c3ae7c9f34dfe05c77376397b0f79ece3e233c0ce5e7ae1f01004f
(image=ubuntu, name=thirsty_mccarthy)
2017-09-27T10:54:58.943965010-07:00 container attach
563ad88c26c3ae7c9f34dfe05c77376397b0f79ece3e233c0ce5e7ae1f01004f
(image=ubuntu, name=thirsty_mccarthy)
2017-09-27T10:54:58.998179393-07:00 network connect
1e1fd43bd0845a13695ea02d77af2493a449dd9ee50f2f1372f589dc4968410e
(container=563ad88c26c3ae7c9f34dfe05c77376397b0f79ece3e233c0ce5e7ae1f01004f
, name=bridge, type=bridge)
2017-09-27T10:54:59.236311822-07:00 container start
563ad88c26c3ae7c9f34dfe05c77376397b0f79ece3e233c0ce5e7ae1f01004f
(image=ubuntu, name=thirsty_mccarthy)
2017-09-27T10:54:59.237416694-07:00 container resize
563ad88c26c3ae7c9f34dfe05c77376397b0f79ece3e233c0ce5e7ae1f01004f
(height=57, image=ubuntu, name=thirsty_mccarthy, width=176)
2017-09-27T10:55:05.992143308-07:00 container die
563ad88c26c3ae7c9f34dfe05c77376397b0f79ece3e233c0ce5e7ae1f01004f
(exitCode=0, image=ubuntu, name=thirsty_mccarthy)
2017-09-27T10:55:06.172682910-07:00 network disconnect
1e1fd43bd0845a13695ea02d77af2493a449dd9ee50f2f1372f589dc4968410e
```

```
(container=563ad88c26c3ae7c9f34dfe05c77376397b0f79ece3e233c0ce5e7ae1f01004f
, name=bridge, type=bridge)
2017-09-27T10:55:06.295496139-07:00 container destroy
563ad88c26c3ae7c9f34dfe05c77376397b0f79ece3e233c0ce5e7ae1f01004f
(image=ubuntu, name=thirsty_mccarthy)
```

Its use is fairly niche but this type of tracing, along with the other tips and tricks we have discussed so far, should provide you with the tools to tackle almost any type of problem on a Docker-based cluster. Everything already mentioned aside, in my personal experience, there have also been a couple of times where gdb was required as well as a couple of times when a problem turned out to be an upstream bug. Because of that, be prepared to get your hands dirty when scaling up as the chance of novel problems increases too.

Advanced networking

Networking is one of the most important things for Docker clusters and it needs to be kept operational and running smoothly on clusters for the whole system to operate in any capacity. With that in mind, it stands to reason that it behooves us to cover a few of the topics that we have not talked about yet but that are important in most real-world deployments, big and small. There is a big chance you will encounter at least one of these use cases in your own deployments so I would recommend a full read-through, but your mileage may vary.

Static host configuration

In some specific configurations, you may have a host on your network that needs to be mapped or re-mapped to a specific IP address for the container that is trying to reach it. This allows a flexible configuration of named servers and can be a real life-saver for static hosts on the network without a good network DNS server.

To add such a host mapping to a container, you can run the container with docker run --add-host and using this flag, an entry in /etc/hosts is added that matches your input so that you can properly route your requests to it:

```
$ # Show what the default /etc/hosts has
$ docker run --rm \
            -it \
            ubuntu \
            /bin/cat /etc/hosts

127.0.0.1    localhost
```

```
::1     localhost ip6-localhost ip6-loopback
fe00::0     ip6-localnet
ff00::0     ip6-mcastprefix
ff02::1     ip6-allnodes
ff02::2     ip6-allrouters
172.17.0.2      3c46adb8a875

$ # We now will add our fake server1 host mapping
$ docker run --rm \
          -it \
          --add-host "server1:123.45.67.89" \
          ubuntu \
          /bin/cat /etc/hosts

127.0.0.1     localhost
::1     localhost ip6-localhost ip6-loopback
fe00::0     ip6-localnet
ff00::0     ip6-mcastprefix
ff02::1     ip6-allnodes
ff02::2     ip6-allrouters
123.45.67.89      server1
172.17.0.2      dd4d7c6ef7b8

$ # What does the container see when we have an additional host?
$ docker run --rm \
          -it \
          --add-host "server1:123.45.67.89" \
          ubuntu /bin/bash

root@0ade7f3e8a80:/# getent hosts server1
123.45.67.89      server1

root@0ade7f3e8a80:/# exit
exit
```

As mentioned, this can be very useful when you have a non-containerized service for which you do not want to hardcode the IP into the container that also is not resolvable from the Internet DNS servers.

DNS configuration

Speaking of DNS, we should probably talk a bit about Docker DNS handling. By default, Docker Engine uses the DNS settings from the host, but in some advanced deployment settings where the network that the cluster is being deployed in is within an already built-out network, there may be times when the engine or the container needs to be configured with a custom DNS setting or the DNS search prefix (also know as the domain name). In such cases, you are able to override the default DNS settings of the Docker Engine easily by adding the dns and/or dns-search parameters to /etc/docker/daemon.json and restarting the daemon. Both parameters allow multiple values and are pretty self-explanatory:

```
{
...

        "dns": ["1.2.3.4", "5.6.7.8", ...],
        "dns-search": ["domain.com", ...],
...
}
```

In all networking setups that I have ever worked on, I have not seen a situation where overriding DNS server IPs or DNS search prefixes is a better option to deploying your own DHCP server within the network and setting the appropriate options for the DNS server(s) (option 6) and domain name (option 15), which the machine will pick up when initializing the network interface. If you would like to find out more about these DHCP flags, I would highly recommend that you visit https://en.wikipedia.org/wiki/Dynamic_Host_Configuration_Protocol#DHCP_options and read up on them before using the parameters we mentioned previously.

Caution! In some cases where the engine host's DNS servers are pointed to localhost ranges, as they are in most systemd-resolve and dnsmasq setups, the container cannot access the host's localhost address and is thus replaced with Google's DNS servers (8.8.8.8 and 8.8.4.4) by default for all containers running on that instance. If you would like to retain the host's DNS setting within the container, you must ensure that the DNS resolver in the configuration is not one on the localhost IP range and is accessible by container networks. You can find more information about this at https://docs.docker.com/engine/userguide/networking/default_network/configure-dns/.

If you are not interested in engine-wide configuration and are only trying to override a single container's DNS settings, you can do the equivalent action by adding `--dns` and `--dns-search` options to the `docker run` command, which ends up replacing the default `/etc/resolv.conf` settings in the relevant container:

```
$ # Since my default DNS is pointed to localhost, the default should be
Google's DNS servers
$ docker run --rm \
          -it \
          ubuntu \
          /bin/cat /etc/resolv.conf

# Dynamic resolv.conf(5) file for glibc resolver(3) generated by
resolvconf(8)
#     DO NOT EDIT THIS FILE BY HAND -- YOUR CHANGES WILL BE OVERWRITTEN
# 127.0.0.53 is the systemd-resolved stub resolver.
# run "systemd-resolve --status" to see details about the actual
nameservers.
nameserver 8.8.8.8
nameserver 8.8.4.4

$ # Now we will specify a custom DNS and DNS search prefix and see what the
same file looks like
$ docker run --rm \
          -it \
          --dns 4.4.4.2 \
          --dns-search "domain.com" \
          ubuntu \
          /bin/cat /etc/resolv.conf

search domain.com
nameserver 4.4.4.2
```

As you can see, the settings in the container have been changed to match our parameters. In our case, any DNS resolution will flow to the `4.4.4.2` server and any unqualified hostname will first be attempted to get resolved as `<host>.domain.com`.

Overlay networks

We only briefly touched on this in Chapter 4, *Scaling the Containers*, but in order to get our containers to work with the Swarm service discovery, we had to create this type of network though we didn't really spend much time explaining what it is. In the context of Docker Swarm, containers on one machine cannot reach containers on a different machine as their networks are routed directly to the next hop as they traverse the network and a bridge network prevents each container from reaching its neighbor on the same node. To hook all of the containers together in this multi-host setup seamlessly, you can create an overlay network that spans any Swarm nodes that are part of the cluster. Sadly, this type of network is only available in Docker Swarm clusters, so in general, it has limited portability across the orchestration tooling but you can create one with `docker network create -d overlay network_name`. Since we have already covered an example of a deployment using this type of a network in Chapter 4, *Scaling the Containers*, you can look it up there to see it in action.

 Caution! Overlay networks do not communicate data securely by default with other nodes, so using the `--opt encrypted` flag when creating one is highly encouraged where network transport cannot be trusted fully. Using this option will incur some processing cost and will require you to allow port 50 communication within your cluster, but in most cases, it should be worth it turning it on.

Docker built-in network mappings

In previous chapters, we were mostly working with containers with the default network settings, which were utilizing the `bridge` network in most cases since that is the default, but this is not the only type of networking that can be used for a container. The following is a list of the available network connections, and almost all of them can be set through the `docker run --network` parameter:

- `bridge`: As mentioned in earlier chapters, this type of network creates an independent virtual interface on the host for communicating with the container, and the container can communicate with the host and the Internet. Generally, inter-container communication is prevented in this type of a network.
- `none`: Disables all networking communication for the container. This is useful with containers that only contain tooling and have no need for network communication.
- `host`: Uses the host's networking stack and does not create any virtual interfaces.

- `<network_name_or_id>`: Connects to a named network. This flag is useful when you create a network and want to put multiple containers in the same networking grouping. For example, this would be useful for hooking up multiple chatty containers such as Elasticsearch into their own isolated network.
- `<container_name_or_id>`: This allows you to connect to a networking stack of the specified container. Just like the `--pid` flag, this is very useful for debugging running containers without directly attaching to them, though the network may need to be created with the `--attachable` flag depending on the network driver used.

> Warning! Using the `host` networking switch gives the container full access to local system services and as such is a liability when used in any context other than testing. Use extreme caution when this flag is used, but luckily, there are only very few cases (if any) where there will be a legitimate use for this mode.

Docker communication ports

Unless you are running Docker Swarm, you will probably never need to worry about what ports Docker uses to communicate, but this is something that is relatively good to know as a point of reference should you ever encounter such configurations in the field or you want to have such deployments within your clusters. The list is pretty short, but each port is very important for the operation of most Swarm clusters:

```
2377 TCP - Used for Swarm node communication
4789 UDP - Container ingress network
7946 TCP/UDP - Container network discovery
50 IP - Used for secure communication of overlay networks if you use "--opt
encrypted" when creating the overlay network
```

High availability pipelines

Previously, we spent the majority of our time working with socket-based communication between nodes on a cluster, which is generally something that makes sense to most people and has tooling built around it in almost every programming language. So, it is the first tool that people transitioning their classic infrastructure to containers usually go for, but for large-and-beyond scales where you are dealing with pure data processing, it simply does not work well due to the back-pressure caused by exceeding the capacity of a particular stage on the rest of the processing pipeline.

If you imagine each cluster service as a consecutive set of transformation steps, the socket-based system would go through a loop of steps similar to these:

- Opening a listening socket.
- Looping forever doing the following:
    - Waiting for data on a socket from the previous stage.
    - Processing that data.
    - Sending the processed data to the next stage's socket.

But what happens in that last step if the next stage is already at the maximum capacity? What most socket-based systems will do is either throw an exception and completely fail the processing pipeline for this particular piece of data or prevent the execution from continuing and keep retrying to send the data to the next stage until it succeeds. Since we don't want to fail the processing pipeline as the result was not an error and we do not want to keep our worker waiting around for the next stage to unblock, we need something that can hold inputs to stages in an ordered structure so that the previous stage can continue working on its own new set of inputs.

Container messaging

For the scenario that we just talked about, where back-pressure on individual processing stages causes cascade backflow stoppages, message queues (often alternatively referred to as pub/sub messaging systems) are here to provide us with the exact solution we need. Message queues generally store data as messages in a **First-In**, **First-Out** (**FIFO**) queue structure and work by allowing the sender to add the desired inputs to a particular stage's queue ("enqueue") and the worker (listener) to trigger on new messages within that queue. When the worker is processing a message, the queue hides it from the rest of the workers and when the worker is complete and successful, the message is removed from the queue permanently. By operating on results in an asynchronous manner, we can allow the senders to keep working on their own tasks and completely modularize the data processing pipeline.

To see queues in action, let's say we have two running containers and within a very short period of time, messages **A**, **B**, **C**, and **D** arrive one after another as inputs from some imaginary processing step (red indicating the top of the queue):

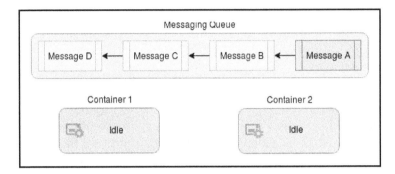

Internally, the queue tracks their ordering, and initially, neither of the container queue listeners have noticed the messages, but very quickly, they get a notification that there is new work to be done, so they get the messages in the order in which they were received. The messaging queue (depending on the exact implementation) marks those messages as unavailable for other listeners and sets a timeout for the worker to complete. In this example **Message A** and **Message B** have been marked for processing by the available workers:

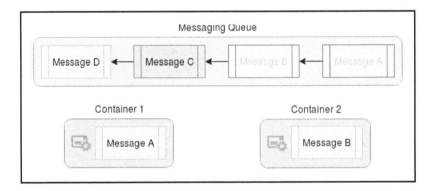

During this process, let's assume that **Container** 1 had a catastrophic failure and it just died. **Message A** timeout on the queue expires without it being finished so the queue puts it back on top and makes it available again for listeners while our other container keeps on working:

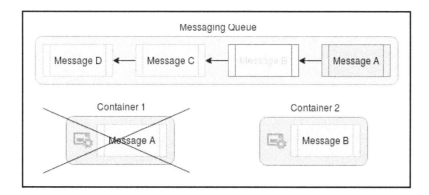

With **Message B** successfully completed, **Container 2** notifies the queue that the task is done and the queue removes it completely from its lists. With that out of the way, the container now takes the topmost message, which turns out to be the unfinished **Message A** and the process continues just like before:

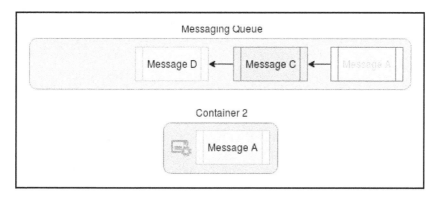

While this cluster stage has been dealing with failures and overloading, the previous stage that put all of these messages in the queue kept working on its dedicated workload. Our current stage also has not lost any data even though half of our processing capability got forcefully removed at a random point in time.

The new pseudocode loop for a worker would be a bit more like this now:

- Register as a listener on a queue.
- Loop forever doing the following:
    - Wait for a message from the queue.
    - Process the data from the queue.
    - Send the processed data to the next queue.

With this new system, if there is any kind of processing slowdown in the pipeline, the queues for those overloaded stages will start to grow in size, but if the earlier stages slow down, the queues will shrink until they are empty. As long as the maximum queue size can handle the volume of messages and the overloaded stages can handle the average demands, you can ascertain that all the data that is in the pipeline will be eventually processed and your triggers for scaling up stages are pretty much as simple as noticing larger queues that are not caused by bugs. This not only helps mitigate differences in pipeline stage scaling, but it also helps preserve data if pieces of your cluster go down since the queues will grow during failure time and then empty as you bring your infrastructure back to fully working - and all of this will happen without data loss.

If this bundle of benefits was not enough of a positive, consider that you can now have a guarantee that the data was processed since the queue keeps the data around so if a worker dies, the queue will (as we've seen earlier) put the message back in the queue to possibly get processed by another worker, unlike socket-based processing which would just silently die in that case. The increase in processing density, increase in failure tolerance, and better handling of burst data makes queues extremely attractive to container developers. If all your communication is also done with queues, service discovery might not even be needed for these workers except to tell them where the queue manager is since the queue is doing that discovery work for you.

Unsurprisingly, most queues come at a development cost, which is why they are not as widely in use as one might expect. In most cases, you will not only need to add custom queue client libraries to your worker code, but in many types of deployments, you will also need a process or a daemon somewhere that will be the main queue arbitrator that handles the messages. In fact, I would probably go as far as to say that choosing the messaging system alone is a research task onto itself, but if you're looking for quick answers, generally Apache Kafka (`https://kafka.apache.org/`), RabbitMQ (`https://www.rabbitmq.com/`), and Redis-backed custom implementations (`https://redis.io/`) seem to be more popular in clustering contexts for in-house messaging queues going from the biggest deployments to the smallest, respectively.

As with all things we have been covering so far, most cloud providers offer some type of service for this (AWS SQS, Google Cloud Pub/Sub, Azure Queue Storage, and so on) so that you don't have to build it yourself. If you are OK with spending a little bit more money, you can utilize these and not worry about hosting the daemon process yourself. Historically, messaging queues have been hard to maintain and manage properly in house, so I would venture to say that many, if not most, cloud systems use these services instead of deploying their own.

Implementing our own messaging queue

With the theory out of the way, let's see how we can build our own little queue publisher and listener. For our example here, we will use one of the simpler messaging systems based on Redis called `bull` (`https://www.npmjs.com/package/bull`). First we will write the code that will run this whole system, and to make things easy for us, we will use the same image for both the consumer and the producer.

In a new directory, create the following:

 As a reminder, this code is also in the GitHub repository and you can view it or clone it from `https://github.com/sgnn7/deploying_with_docker/tree/master/chapter_6/redis_queue` if you do not want to type the full text.

package.json

This file is pretty much just a copy of our older example with the addition of the `bull` package and a name change:

```
{
  "name": "queue-worker",
  "version": "0.0.1",
  "scripts": {
    "start": "node index.js"
  },
  "dependencies": {
    "bull": "^3.2.0"
  }
}
```

index.js

`index.js` is a single-file app that either sends a timestamp every 1.5 seconds to the queue or reads from the queue depending on the invocation argument. The queue location is defined by the `QUEUE_HOST` environment variable:

```
'use strict'

const Queue = require('bull');

const veryImportantThingsQueue = new Queue('very_important_things',
                                          { redis: { port: 6379,
                                                     host:
process.env.QUEUE_HOST }});
```

```
// Prints any message data received
class Receiver {
    constructor () {
        console.info('Registering listener...');
        veryImportantThingsQueue.process(job => {
            console.info('Got a message from the queue with data:',
job.data);
            return Promise.resolve({});
        });
    }
}

// Sends the date every 1.5 seconds
class Sender {
    constructor () {
        function sendMessage() {
            const messageValue = new Date();
            console.info('Sending a message...', messageValue);
            veryImportantThingsQueue.add({ 'key': messageValue });
        }

        setInterval(sendMessage, 1500);
    }
}

// Sanity check
if (process.argv.length < 2) {
    throw new Error(`Usage: ${process.argv.slice(2).join(' ')} <sender |
receiver>`);
}


// Start either receiver or sender depending of CLI arg
console.info('Starting...');
if (process.argv[2] === 'sender') {
    new Sender();
} else if (process.argv[2] === 'receiver') {
    new Receiver();
} else {
    throw new Error(`Usage: ${process.argv.slice(0, 2).join(' ')} <sender |
receiver>`);
}
```

Dockerfile

Nothing special here: the file is pretty much a trimmed-down version of our older Node.js app:

```
FROM node:8

# Make sure we are fully up to date
RUN apt-get update -q && \
    apt-get dist-upgrade -y && \
    apt-get clean && \
    apt-get autoclean

# Container port that should get exposed
EXPOSE 8000

ENV SRV_PATH /usr/local/share/queue_handler

# Make our directory
RUN mkdir -p $SRV_PATH && \
    chown node:node $SRV_PATH

WORKDIR $SRV_PATH

USER node

COPY . $SRV_PATH/

RUN npm install

CMD ["npm", "start"]
```

We will build the image now:

```
$ docker build -t queue-worker .
Sending build context to Docker daemon   7.168kB
<snip>
 ---> 08e33a32ba60
Removing intermediate container e17c836c5a33
Successfully built 08e33a32ba60
Successfully tagged queue-worker:latest
```

With the image building out of the way, we can now write out our stack definition file: swarm_application.yml. We are pretty much creating the queue server, the queue listener, and the queue sender on a single network and making sure that they can find each other here:

```
version: "3"
services:
  queue-sender:
    image: queue-worker
    command: ["npm", "start", "sender"]
    networks:
      - queue_network
    deploy:
      replicas: 1
    depends_on:
      - redis-server
    environment:
      - QUEUE_HOST=redis-server

  queue-receiver:
    image: queue-worker
    command: ["npm", "start", "receiver"]
    networks:
      - queue_network
    deploy:
      replicas: 1
    depends_on:
      - redis-server
    environment:
      - QUEUE_HOST=redis-server

  redis-server:
    image: redis
    networks:
      - queue_network
    deploy:
      replicas: 1
    networks:
      - queue_network
    ports:
      - 6379:6379

networks:
  queue_network:
```

Having both image built and the stack definition, we can launch our queue cluster to see whether it works:

```
$ # We need a Swarm first
$ docker swarm init
Swarm initialized: current node (c0tq34hm6u3ypam9cjr1vkefe) is now a
manager.
<snip>

$ # Now we deploy our stack and name it "queue_stack"
$ docker stack deploy \
            -c swarm_application.yml \
            queue_stack
Creating service queue_stack_queue-sender
Creating service queue_stack_queue-receiver
Creating service queue_stack_redis-server

$ # At this point, we should be seeing some traffic...
$ docker service logs queue_stack_queue-receiver
<snip>
queue_stack_queue-receiver.1.ozk2uxqnbfqz@machine    | Starting...
queue_stack_queue-receiver.1.ozk2uxqnbfqz@machine    | Registering
listener...
queue_stack_queue-receiver.1.ozk2uxqnbfqz@machine    | Got a message from
the queue with data: { key: '2017-10-02T08:24:21.391Z' }
queue_stack_queue-receiver.1.ozk2uxqnbfqz@machine    | Got a message from
the queue with data: { key: '2017-10-02T08:24:22.898Z' }
<snip>

$ # Yay! It's working!

$ # Let's clean things up to finish up
$ docker stack rm queue_stack
Removing service queue_stack_queue-receiver
Removing service queue_stack_queue-sender
Removing service queue_stack_redis-server
Removing network queue_stack_redis-server
Removing network queue_stack_queue_network
Removing network queue_stack_service_network

$ docker swarm leave --force
Node left the swarm.
```

At this point, we could add any number of senders and listeners (within reason) and our system will work just fine in a very asynchronous style, increasing throughput at both ends. As a reminder, though, if you decide to go this route, another queue type is highly advised (Kafka, SQS, and so on) but the underlying principles are pretty much the same.

Advanced security

We have covered some security issues in previous chapters, but for some issues that seem to be frequently ignored, we need to cover them with a little bit more depth than the small info box in the middle of the text and see why they are such large issues when used improperly. While it might seem like a lot of work to implement all the things we pointed out in various warnings and info boxes, the smaller the attack surface you provide to your potential intruders, the better you will be in the long run. That said, unless you are working on deploying this system for a government agency, I expect that there will be some compromises but I urge you to strongly weigh the pros and cons for each otherwise you risk getting that dreaded midnight call about an intrusion.

Ironically, hardened systems usually take so much time to develop and deploy that they are often obsolete or provide marginal business value by the time they are in production environments, and due to their carefully assembled pieces, they are rarely (if ever) updated with a newer functionality, have patches applied to them quickly, or code improvements done on the source so it is a truly a double-edged sword. There is *never* a perfect solution, only a range of things you are comfortable with to some degree of dealing with. Historically, I have mostly seen horrible execution on either extremes of the fence so my advice here is that you look for a blend of the two if possible.

Mounting the Docker socket into the container

This is by far the most egregious security hole that developers completely disregard when deploying containerized solutions. For various things related to container management, often advice on the Internet is generally leaning toward bind-mounting the Docker socket (`/var/run/docker.sock`) into the container, but the thing rarely mentioned is effectively giving the host's root-level access to such a container when you do this. Since the Docker's socket is actually just an API endpoint and the Docker daemon runs as the root, the container can simply escape its containment by launching other containers with the host's system folders being mounted on them and then executing arbitrary commands on them.

For more information on using the Docker socket as a RESTful endpoint, you can take a look at the source code or explore a bit through the documentation for Docker Engine API at `https://docs.docker.com/engine/api/v1.31/`. The only thing you will generally need to do to use it through a tool such as `curl` is to add `--unix-socket <socket_path>` and, optionally `-H "Content-Type: application/json"` for `POST` requests.

 Docker has been making strides at turning its service into a userspace one from a root-level one, but so far, this feature has not materialized in any practical manner. While personally I have reservations about this happening anytime soon, keep an eye out for this feature as at some point it may actually get released and become a usable feature which would be a huge step forward for container security.

With the theory of how to misuse the Docker socket, now we will break out of our container though we will stop short of actually doing anything damaging to the system:

```
$ Start a "benign" container with the Docker socket mounted and run Bash
$ docker run --rm \
             -it \
             -v /var/run/docker.sock:/var/run/docker.sock \
             ubuntu /bin/bash

root@686212135a17:/# # Sanity check - make sure that the socket is there
root@686212135a17:/# ls -la /var/run/docker.sock
srw-rw---- 1 root 136 0 Sep 20 05:03 /var/run/docker.sock

root@686212135a17:/# # Install curl but almost any other HTTP client will
work
root@686212135a17:/# # Even a base Python can do this but curl is fine for
brevity
root@686212135a17:/# apt-get update && apt-get install -y curl
<snip>
done

root@686212135a17:/# # Create a container through the socket and bind-mount
root to it
root@686212135a17:/# # with a "malicious" touch command to run
root@686212135a17:/# curl -s \
                      --unix-socket /var/run/docker.sock \
                      -H "Content-Type: application/json" \
                      -d '{"Image": "ubuntu", "Cmd": ["touch",
"/mnt/security_breach"], "Mounts": [{"Type": "bind", "Source": "/",
"Target":"/mnt", "RW": true}]}' \
                      -X POST \
```

```
                              http:/v1.29/containers/create
{"Id":"894c4838931767462173678aacc51c3bb98f4dffe15eaf167782513305c72558","W
arnings":null}

root@686212135a17:/# # Start our escaped container
root@686212135a17:/# curl --unix-socket /var/run/docker.sock \
                          -X POST \
                          http:/v1.29/containers/894c4838/start

root@686212135a17:/# # Exit out of our "benign" container back to host
root@686212135a17:/# exit
exit

$ # Let's see what happened on our host
$ ls -la / | grep breach
-rw-r--r--   1 root root        0 Sep 20 23:14 security_breach

$ # Oops!
```

It should be apparent now how the benign container was able to root the host with just a few CLI commands. While some of it is predicated on the container process running as the root, the same could possibly be done if the Docker group ID clashes with a non-privileged group within the container, but with nitpicks aside, suffice it to say that mounting the Docker socket without fully understanding the implications can lead to a very painful breach. With that in mind, there are (albeit rare) legitimate uses of this technique so use your best judgment here.

Host security scans

As part of a drive to increase the security of deployments, a tool was released by Docker that can help easily identify the most common security issues with a host running a Docker Engine called **Docker Bench for Security**. This tool will scan and verify a large number of possible weaknesses in your configuration and will present them in a very easy-to-read listing. You can download and run this image just like you would one of the other regular containers available on Docker Hub:

Warning! This security scan requires many permissions (`--net host`, `--pid host`, Docker socket mounting, and so on) that we have covered as generally really bad ideas to run on a host since they present a pretty large attack vector for malicious actors but on the other hand, the scan needs those permissions to check the settings you have. As such, I would highly recommend running this type of security scan on a clone of the host machine that you are trying to test in a network-isolated environment in order to prevent compromises of your infrastructure if the scanning image is maliciously modified.

```
$ docker run --rm \
            -it \
            --net host \
            --pid host \
            --cap-add audit_control \
            -e DOCKER_CONTENT_TRUST=$DOCKER_CONTENT_TRUST \
            -v /var/lib:/var/lib \
            -v /var/run/docker.sock:/var/run/docker.sock \
            -v /usr/lib/systemd:/usr/lib/systemd \
            -v /etc:/etc \
            docker/docker-bench-security
# -------------------------------------------------------------------------
-----
# Docker Bench for Security v1.3.3
#
# Docker, Inc. (c) 2015-
#
# Checks for dozens of common best-practices around deploying Docker
containers in production.
# Inspired by the CIS Docker Community Edition Benchmark v1.1.0.
# -------------------------------------------------------------------------
-----


Initializing Mon Oct  2 00:03:29 CDT 2017

[INFO] 1 - Host Configuration
[WARN] 1.1  - Ensure a separate partition for containers has been created
[NOTE] 1.2  - Ensure the container host has been Hardened
date: invalid date '17-10-1 -1 month'
sh: out of range
sh: out of range
[PASS] 1.3  - Ensure Docker is up to date
[INFO]       * Using 17.09.0 which is current
[INFO]       * Check with your operating system vendor for support and
security maintenance for Docker
[INFO] 1.4  - Ensure only trusted users are allowed to control Docker
daemon
```

```
[INFO]       * docker:x:999
[WARN] 1.5   - Ensure auditing is configured for the Docker daemon
[WARN] 1.6   - Ensure auditing is configured for Docker files and
directories - /var/lib/docker
[WARN] 1.7   - Ensure auditing is configured for Docker files and
directories - /etc/docker
[INFO] 1.8   - Ensure auditing is configured for Docker files and
directories - docker.service
<snip>
[PASS] 2.10 - Ensure base device size is not changed until needed
[WARN] 2.11 - Ensure that authorization for Docker client commands is
enabled
[WARN] 2.12 - Ensure centralized and remote logging is configured
[WARN] 2.13 - Ensure operations on legacy registry (v1) are Disabled
[WARN] 2.14 - Ensure live restore is Enabled
[WARN] 2.15 - Ensure Userland Proxy is Disabled
<snip>
[PASS] 7.9  - Ensure CA certificates are rotated as appropriate (Swarm mode
not enabled)
[PASS] 7.10 - Ensure management plane traffic has been separated from data
plane traffic (Swarm mode not enabled)
```

The list is pretty long, so most of the output lines were removed, but you should have a pretty good idea about what this tool does and how to use it. Note that this is not the only product in this space (e.g. Clair from CoreOS at `https://github.com/coreos/clair`) so try to use as many of them as you can in order to see where your weaknesses in the infrastructure lie.

Read-only containers

In the development of our previous examples spanning most of the chapters, we did not really pay much attention to whether containers changed the state of the filesystem while running. This is not such a problem for test and development systems, but in production, it is very important to lock things down even further in order to prevent malicious runtime exploitation from both internal and external sources. For this purpose, there is a `docker run --read-only` flag, which (unsurprisingly) mounts the container's root filesystem as read-only. By doing this, we ensure that all data that is not mounted with volumes is as pristine as when we built the image, ensuring consistency and protecting your cluster. The only thing that you might need to be careful of if you run the containers in this manner is that locations for temporary storage of files in places such as `/run`, `/tmp`, and `/var/tmp` are extremely likely to be required by the container during execution, so these mounts should be additionally mounted as `tmpfs` volumes:

```
$ # Start a regular container
$ docker run -it \
            --rm \
            ubuntu /bin/bash

root@79042a966943:/# # Write something to /bin
root@79042a966943:/# echo "just_a_test" > /bin/test

root@79042a966943:/# # Check if it's there
root@79042a966943:/# ls -la /bin | grep test
-rw-r--r-- 1 root root      12 Sep 27 17:43 test

root@79042a966943:/# exit
exit

$ # Now try a read-only container
$ docker run -it \
            --rm \
            --tmpfs /run \
            --tmpfs /tmp \
            --tmpfs /var/tmp \
            --read-only \
            ubuntu /bin/bash

root@5b4574a46c09:/# # Try to write to /bin
root@5b4574a46c09:/# echo "just_a_test" > /bin/test
bash: /bin/test: Read-only file system

root@5b4574a46c09:/# # Works as expected! What about /tmp?
root@5b4574a46c09:/# echo "just_a_test" > /tmp/test
root@5b4574a46c09:/# ls /tmp
test

root@5b4574a46c09:/# exit
exit
```

If you do not expect your container to change anything on the filesystem and since containers should generally not need to write to paths such as /usr, using this flag in production is highly recommended, so apply it liberally to all your static services if possible.

Base system (package) updates

We talked a little about this previously, but it seems that in most online documentation and blogs, package updates have been sorely neglected in coverage within the context of Docker containers. While there are supporters of both camps, it is important to remember that there is no guarantee that the tagged images available from places such as Docker Hub have been built with the latest updates, and even in cases where they are, the tagged image might have been built a while ago and, as such, won't contain the latest security patches.

While it is true that within Docker containers, the host's kernel is used to run the context of the container, a security hole in any of the supporting libraries within the container can (and usually does) result in a breach that can often cascade onto the host and into your whole network. Due to this fact, my personal recommendation for containers that will be deployed to production is that you should always make sure that the container is built with the latest libraries if possible. There are definite risks, albeit small, in manually upgrading packages on some base images that are caused by library incompatibilities that occur when you do the upgrade, but as a general rule, it is a risk worth taking.

In most cases, in order to do this kind of upgrade, just like we covered earlier in most of our Docker examples, you pretty much need to invoke the system upgrade lines specific to the base OS distribution of the image in `Dockerfile`. For our default deployment OS (Ubuntu LTS), this operation is done with `apt-get update` and `apt-get dist-upgrade`:

```
...
RUN apt-get update && apt-get -y dist-upgrade
...
```

 Caution! Do not forget that by default, `docker build` will cache all individual layers that have unchanged `Dockerfile` directives, so this command will work as expected the first time, but its layer will be pulled from the cache any subsequent time it is used if none of the lines preceding it have changed due to the fact that this line will stay the same regardless of packages changing upstream. If you want to ensure that you get the latest updates, you will have to break the cache either by changing a line above `apt-get` in your `Dockerfile` or by adding `--no-cache` to your `docker build` command. Also, note that using `--no-cache`, all layers will be regenerated, possibly causing a prolonged build cycle and/or registry disk use.

Privileged mode versus --cap-add and --cap-drop

Some advanced things that you might want to do within a container, such as **Docker-in-Docker (DinD)**, NTP, mounting loopback devices, and many others, will require higher privileges than the ones given to the root user of the container by default. As such, additional privileges need to be allowed for the container to run without issues, so for that use case, Docker has a very simple but extremely broad privileged mode that adds the complete host's capabilities to the container. To use this mode, just append `--privileged` to the `docker run` command:

 Docker-in-Docker (commonly known as **DinD**) is a special configuration of a container that allows you to run the Docker Engine within the container that is already running on a Docker Engine but without sharing the Docker socket, which allows (if precautions are taken) a more secure and robust way to build containers within your infrastructure that is already containerized. The prevalence of this configuration is somewhat rare but is very powerful when used as part of a **Continuous Integration (CI)** and **Continuous Delivery (CD)** setup.

```
$ # Run an NTP daemon without the extra privileges and see what happens
$ docker run -it \
          --rm \
          cguenther/ntpd

ntpd: can't set priority: Permission denied
reset adjtime failed: Operation not permitted
creating new /var/db/ntpd.drift
adjtimex failed: Operation not permitted
adjtimex adjusted frequency by 0.000000ppm
ntp engine ready
reply from 38.229.71.1: offset -2.312472 delay 0.023870, next query 8s
settimeofday: Operation not permitted
reply from 198.206.133.14: offset -2.312562 delay 0.032579, next query 8s
reply from 96.244.96.19: offset -2.302669 delay 0.035253, next query 9s
reply from 66.228.42.59: offset -2.302408 delay 0.035170, next query 7s
^C

$ And now with our new privileged mode
$ docker run -it \
          --rm \
          --privileged \
          cguenther/ntpd

creating new /var/db/ntpd.drift
adjtimex adjusted frequency by 0.000000ppm
```

```
ntp engine ready
^C
```

As you can see, adding this flag removes all errors from the output as we can now change the system time.

With the functionality of this mode explained, we can now talk about why ideally, if possible, you should never use the privileged mode. By default, the privileged mode allows practically full access to most of the host's systems and is not granular enough to make sense in most circumstances, so after you figure out that your container needs additional privileges, you should selectively add them with `--cap-add` instead. These flags are standard Linux capability identifiers that you can find in places such as `http://man7.org/linux/man-pages/man7/capabilities.7.html` and allow fine-tuning to the level of access you desire. If we now convert our previous NTP daemon example into this new style, it should look a bit more like this:

```
$ # Sanity check
$ docker run -it \
            --rm \
            cguenther/ntpd

ntpd: can't set priority: Permission denied
<snip>
settimeofday: Operation not permitted
<snip>
^C

$ # Now with the added SYS_TIME capability
$ docker run -it \
            --rm \
            --cap-add SYS_TIME \
            cguenther/ntpd

ntpd: can't set priority: Permission denied
creating new /var/db/ntpd.drift
adjtimex adjusted frequency by 0.000000ppm
ntp engine ready
reply from 204.9.54.119: offset 15.805277 delay 0.023080, next query 5s
set local clock to Mon Oct  2 06:05:47 UTC 2017 (offset 15.805277s)
reply from 38.229.71.1: offset 0.005709 delay 31.617842, next query 9s
^C
```

If you noticed, we still have an error visible due to another missing capability, but the `settimeofday` error is gone, which is the most important problem that we needed to fix for this container to run.

Interestingly enough, we can also drop capabilities from our container that are not being used with `--cap-drop` if we want to increase security. For this flag, there is also a special keyword, `ALL`, that can be used to drop all available privileges. If we use this to fully lock down our NTP container but have everything working, let us see what that will look like:

```
docker run -it \
        --rm \
        --cap-drop ALL \
        --cap-add SYS_TIME \
        --cap-add SYS_CHROOT \
        --cap-add SETUID \
        --cap-add SETGID \
        --cap-add SYS_NICE \
        cguenther/ntpd

creating new /var/db/ntpd.drift
adjtimex adjusted frequency by 0.000000ppm
ntp engine ready
reply from 216.229.0.49: offset 14.738336 delay 1.993620, next query 8s
set local clock to Mon Oct  2 06:16:09 UTC 2017 (offset 14.738336s)
reply from 216.6.2.70: offset 0.523095 delay 30.422572, next query 6s
^C
```

Here, we have removed all capabilities first and then added back the few that are really needed to run the container, and as you can see, things are working just fine. In your own deployments, I would strongly suggest that if you have spare development capacity or are security-oriented, take some time to lock your running containers in this manner as they will be much more secure and you will be much more sure that the container is running with the principle of least privilege.

The **Principle of Least Privilege** is a concept in computer security where you allow only the minimal privileges needed to run a component to the user or a service. This principle is very much a staple of high-security implementations but is often not found elsewhere due to the assumed overhead of managing the access even though it is a great way to increase the security and stability of your systems. If you would like to find out more about this concept, you should definitely make your way to `https://en.wikipedia.org/wiki/Principle_of_least_privilege` and check it out.

Summary

In this chapter, we have learned many advanced tools and techniques needed to deploy robust clusters, such as the following:

- Additional debugging options to manage container issues.
- Deep dives into Docker's advanced networking topics.
- Implementing our own queue messaging.
- Various security hardening tips and tricks.

All of these topics combined with previous material should cover the gamut of deployment needs for most clusters. But in the next chapter, we will see what issues we need to worry about when the number of hosts, services, and tasks reaches levels that aren't generally expected and we start seeing the clusters fall apart and what we can do to mitigate such problems.

7
The Limits of Scaling and the Workarounds

When you scale up your systems, every tool or framework you are using will reach a point where it will break or just not function as expected. For some things that point will be high and for some it will be low, and the intent of this chapter is to cover strategies and workarounds for the most likely scalability issues you will encounter when working with microservice clusters. In this chapter we will cover the following topics:

- Increasing service density and stability.
- Avoiding and mitigating common issues with large-scale deployments.
- Multi-service containers.
- Best practices for zero-downtime deployments.

Limiting service resources

So far, we have not really spent any time talking about service isolation with regard to the resources available to the services, but it is a very important topic to cover. Without limiting resources, a malicious or misbehaving service could be liable to bring the whole cluster down, depending on the severity, so great care needs to be taken to specify exactly what allowance individual service tasks should use.

The generally accepted strategy for handling cluster resources is the following:

- Any resource that may cause errors or failures to other services if used beyond intended values is highly recommended to be limited on the service level. This is usually the RAM allocation, but may include CPU or others.
- Any resources, specifically the hardware ones, for which you have an external limit should also be limited for Docker containers too (e.g. you are only allowed to use a specific portion of a 1-Gbps NAS connection).
- Anything that needs to run on a specific device, machine, or host should be locked to those resources in the same fashion. This kind of setup is very common when only a certain number of machines have the right hardware for a service, such as in GPU computing clusters.
- Any resource that you would like specifically rationed within the cluster generally should have a limit applied. This includes things such as lowering the CPU time percentage for low-priority services.
- In most cases, the rest of the resources should be fine using normal allocations of the available resources of the host.

By applying these rules, we will ensure that our cluster is more stable and secure, with the exact division of resources that we want among the services. Also, if the exact resources required for a service are specified, the orchestration tool usually can make better decisions about where to schedule newly created tasks so that the service density per Engine is maximized.

RAM limits

Strangely enough, even though CPU might be considered the most important computing resource, RAM allocation for clustered services is even more important due to the fact that RAM overuse can (and will) cause **Out of Memory** (**OOM**) process and task failures for anything running on the same host. With the prevalence of memory leaks in software, this usually is not a matter of "if" but "when", so setting limits for RAM allocation is generally very desirable, and in some orchestration configurations it is even mandatory. Suffering from this issue is usually indicated by seeing `SIGKILL`, `"Process killed"`, or `exit code -9` on your service.

Keep in mind, though, that these signals could very well be caused by other things but the most common cause is OOM failures.

By limiting the available RAM, instead of a random process on the host being killed by OOM manager, only the offending task's processes will be targeted for killing, so the identification of faulty code is much easier and faster because you can see the large number of failures from that service and your other services will stay operational, increasing the stability of the cluster.

OOM management is a huge topic and is much more broad than it would be wise to include in this section, but it is a very important thing to know if you spend a lot of time in the Linux kernel. If you are interested in this topic, I highly recommend that you visit `https://www.kernel.org/doc/gorman/html/understand/understand016.html` and read up on it.

WARNING! On some of the most popular kernels, memory and/or swap cgroups are disabled due to their overhead. To enable memory and swap limiting on these kernels, your hosts kernel must be started with `cgroup_enable=memory` and `swapaccount=1` flags. If you are using GRUB for your bootloader, you can enable them by editing `/etc/default/grub` (or, on the latest systems, `/etc/default/grub.d/<name>`), setting `GRUB_CMDLINE_LINUX="cgroup_enable=memory swapaccount=1"`, running `sudo update-grub`, and then restarting your machine.

To use the RAM-limiting `cgroup` configuration, run the container with a combination of the following flags:

- `-m` / `--memory`: A hard limit on the maximum amount of memory that a container can use. Allocations of new memory over this limit will fail, and the kernel will terminate a process in your container that will usually be the main one running the service.
- `--memory-swap`: The total amount of memory including swap that the container can use. This must be used with the previous option and be larger than it. By default, a container can use up to twice the amount of allowed memory maximum for a container. Setting this to `-1` allows the container to use as much swap as the host has.

- `--memory-swappiness`: How eager the system will be to move pages from physical memory to on-disk swap space. The value is between `0` and `100`, where `0` means that pages will try to stay in resident RAM as much as possible, and vice versa. On most machines this value is `80` and will be used as the default, but since swap space access is very slow compared to RAM, my recommendation is to set this number as close to `0` as you can afford.

- `--memory-reservation`: A soft limit for the RAM usage of a service, which is generally used only for the detection of resource contentions with the generally expected RAM usage so that the orchestration engine can schedule tasks for maximum usage density. This flag does not have any guarantees that it will keep the service's RAM usage below this level.

There are a few more flags that can be used for memory limiting, but even the preceding list is a bit more verbose than you will probably ever need to worry about. For most deployments, big and small, you will probably only need to use `-m` and set a low value of `--memory-swappiness`, the latter usually being done on the host itself through the `sysctl.d` boot setting so that all services will utilize it.

> You can check what your `swappiness` setting is by running `sysctl vm.swappiness`. If you would like to change this, and in most cluster deployments you will, you can set this value by running the following command:
> ```
> $ echo "vm.swappiness = 10" | sudo tee -a
> /etc/sysctl.d/60-swappiness.conf
> ```

To see this in action, we will first run one of the most resource-intensive frameworks (JBoss) with a limit of 30 MB of RAM and see what happens:

```
$ docker run -it \
            --rm \
            -m 30m \
            jboss/wildfly

Unable to find image 'jboss/wildfly:latest' locally
latest: Pulling from jboss/wildfly
<snip>
Status: Downloaded newer image for jboss/wildfly:latest
========================================================================

   JBoss Bootstrap Environment

   JBOSS_HOME: /opt/jboss/wildfly

   JAVA: /usr/lib/jvm/java/bin/java
```

```
   JAVA_OPTS:  -server -Xms64m -Xmx512m -XX:MetaspaceSize=96M -
XX:MaxMetaspaceSize=256m -Djava.net.preferIPv4Stack=true -
Djboss.modules.system.pkgs=org.jboss.byteman -Djava.awt.headless=true


=======================================================================


*** JBossAS process (57) received KILL signal ***
```

As expected, the container used up too much RAM and was promptly killed by the kernel. Now, what if we try the same thing but give it 400 MB of RAM?

```
$ docker run -it \
          --rm \
          -m 400m \
          jboss/wildfly
=======================================================================


   JBoss Bootstrap Environment

   JBOSS_HOME: /opt/jboss/wildfly

   JAVA: /usr/lib/jvm/java/bin/java

   JAVA_OPTS:  -server -Xms64m -Xmx512m -XX:MetaspaceSize=96M -
XX:MaxMetaspaceSize=256m -Djava.net.preferIPv4Stack=true -
Djboss.modules.system.pkgs=org.jboss.byteman -Djava.awt.headless=true


=======================================================================


14:05:23,476 INFO  [org.jboss.modules] (main) JBoss Modules version
1.5.2.Final
<snip>
14:05:25,568 INFO  [org.jboss.ws.common.management] (MSC service thread
1-6) JBWS022052: Starting JBossWS 5.1.5.Final (Apache CXF 3.1.6)
14:05:25,667 INFO  [org.jboss.as] (Controller Boot Thread) WFLYSRV0060:
Http management interface listening on http://127.0.0.1:9990/management
14:05:25,667 INFO  [org.jboss.as] (Controller Boot Thread) WFLYSRV0051:
Admin console listening on http://127.0.0.1:9990
14:05:25,668 INFO  [org.jboss.as] (Controller Boot Thread) WFLYSRV0025:
WildFly Full 10.1.0.Final (WildFly Core 2.2.0.Final) started in 2532ms -
Started 331 of 577 services (393 services are lazy, passive or on-demand)
```

Our container can now start without any issues!

If you have worked a lot with applications in bare metal environments, you might be asking yourselves why exactly the JBoss JVM didn't know ahead of time that it wouldn't be able to run within such a constrained environment and fail even sooner. The answer here lies in a really unfortunate quirk (though I think it might be considered a feature depending on your point of view) of `cgroups` that presents the host's resources unaltered to the container even though the container itself is constrained. You can see this pretty easily if you run a memory-limited container and print out the available RAM limits:

```
$ # Let's see what a low allocation shows
$ docker run -it --rm -m 30m ubuntu /usr/bin/free -h
              total        used        free      shared  buff/cache
available
Mem:           7.6G        1.4G        4.4G         54M        1.8G
5.9G
Swap:            0B          0B          0B

$ # What about a high one?
$ docker run -it --rm -m 900m ubuntu /usr/bin/free -h
              total        used        free      shared  buff/cache
available
Mem:           7.6G        1.4G        4.4G         54M        1.8G
5.9G
Swap:            0B          0B          0B
```

As you can imagine, this causes all kinds of cascade issues with applications launched in a `cgroup` limited container such as this, the primary one being that the application does not know that there is a limit at all so it will just go and try to do its job assuming that it has full access to the available RAM. Once the application reaches the predefined limits, the app process will usually be killed and the container will die. This is a huge problem with apps and runtimes that can react to high memory pressures as they might be able to use less RAM in the container but because they cannot identify that they are running constrained, they tend to gobble up memory at a much higher rate than they should.

Sadly, things are even worse on this front for containers. You must not only give the service a big enough RAM limit to start it, but also enough that it can handle any dynamically allocated memory during the full duration of the service. If you do not, the same situation will occur but at a much less predictable time. For example, if you ran an NGINX container with only a 4 MB of RAM limit, it will start just fine but after a few connections to it, the memory allocation will cross the threshold and the container will die. The service may then restart the task and unless you have a logging mechanism or your orchestration provides good tooling for it, you will just end up with a service that has a `running` state but, in actuality, it is unable to process any requests.

If that wasn't enough, you also really should not arbitrarily assign high limits either. This is due to the fact that one of the purposes of containers is to maximize service density for a given hardware configuration. By setting limits that are statistically nearly impossible to be reached by the running service, you are effectively wasting those resources because they can't be used by other services. In the long run, this increases both the cost of your infrastructure and the resources needed to maintain it, so there is a high incentive to keep the service limited by the minimum amount that can run it safely instead of using really high limits.

Orchestration tooling generally prevents overcommiting resources, although there has been some progress to support this feature in both Docker Swarm and Kubernetes, where you can specify a soft limit (memory request) versus the true limit (memory limit). However, even with those parameters, tweaking the RAM setting is a really challenging task because you may get either under-utilization or constant rescheduling, so all the topics covered here are still very relevant. For more information on orchestration-specific handling of overcommiting, I suggest you read the latest documentation for your specific orchestration tool.

So, when looking at all the things we must keep in mind, tweaking the limits is closer to an art form than anything else because it is almost like a variation of the famous bin-packing problem (`https://en.wikipedia.org/wiki/Bin_packing_problem`), but also adds the statistical component of the service on top of it, because you might need to figure out the optimum service availability compared to wasted resources due to loose limits.

Let's say we have a service with the following distribution:

- Three physical hosts with 2 GB RAM each (yes, this is really low, but it is to demonstrate the issues on smaller scales)
- **Service 1** (database) that has a memory limit of 1.5 GB, two tasks, and has a 1 percent chance of running over the hard limit
- **Service 2** (application) that has a memory limit of 0.5 GB, three tasks, and has a 5 percent chance of running over the hard limit
- **Service 3** (data processing service) that has a memory limit of 0.5 GB, three tasks, and has a 5 percent chance of running over the hard limit

A scheduler may allocate the services in this manner:

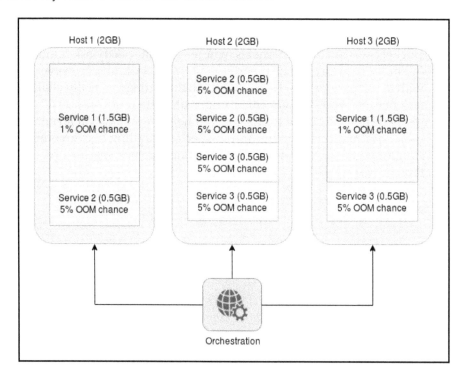

WARNING! You should always have spare capacity on your clusters for rolling service updates, so having the configuration similar to the one shown in the diagram would not work well in the real world. Generally, this extra capacity is also a fuzzy value, just like RAM limits. Generally, my formula for it is the following, but feel free to tweak it as needed:
```
overcapacity = avg(service_sizes) * avg(service_counts) *
avg(max_rolling_service_restarts)
```
We will discuss this a bit more further in the text.

What if we take our last example and now say that we should just run with 1 percent OOM failure rates across the board, increasing our **Service 2** and **Service 3** memory limit from 0.5 GB to 0.75 GB, without taking into account that maybe having higher failure rates on the data processing service and application tasks might be acceptable (or even not noticeable if you are using messaging queues) to the end users?

The new service spread would now look like this:

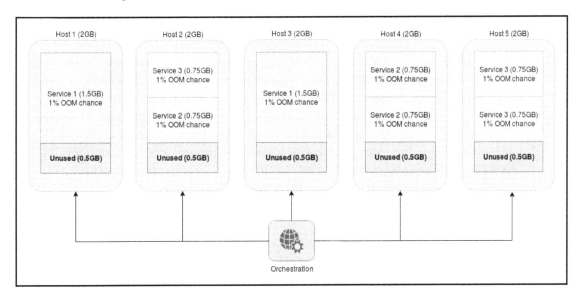

Our new configuration has a massive amount of pretty obvious issues:

- 25 percent reduction in service density. This number should be as high as possible to get all the benefits of using microservices.
- 25 percent reduction in hardware utilization. Effectively, 1/4 of the available hardware resources are being wasted in this setup.

- Node count has increased by 66 percent. Most cloud providers charge by the number of machines you have running assuming they are the same type. By making this change you have effectively raised your cloud costs by 66 percent and may need that much extra ops support to keep your cluster working.

Even though this example has been intentionally rigged to cause the biggest impact when tweaked, it should be obvious that slight changes to these limits can have massive repercussions on your whole infrastructure. While in real-world scenarios this impact will be reduced because there will be larger host machines than in the example which will make them better able to stack smaller (relative to total capacity) services in the available space, *do not* underestimate the cascading effects of increasing service resource allocations.

CPU limits

Just like in our previous section about memory limits for services, `docker run` also supports a variety of CPU settings and parameters to tweak the computational needs of your services:

- `-c/--cpu-shares`: On a high-load host, all tasks are weighted equally by default. Setting this on a task or service (from the default of `1024`) will increase or decrease the percentage of CPU utilization that the task can be scheduled for.
- `--cpu-quota`: This flag sets the number of microseconds that a task or service can use the CPU within a default block of time of 100 milliseconds (100,000 microseconds). For example, to only allow a maximum of 50% of a single CPU's core usage to a task, you would set this flag to `50000`. For multiple cores, you would need to increase this value accordingly.
- `--cpu-period`: This changes the previous quota flag default interval in microseconds over which the `cpu-quota` is being evaluated (100 milliseconds/100,000 microseconds) and either reduces it or increases it to inversely affect the CPU resource allocation to a service.
- `--cpus`: A float value that combines parts of both `cpu-quota` and `cpu-period` to limit the number of CPU core allocations to the task. For example, if you only want a task to use up to a quarter of a single CPU resource, you would set this to `0.25` and it would have the same effect as `--cpu-quota 25000 --cpu-period 100000`.

- `--cpuset-cpus`: This array flag allows the service to only run on specified CPUs indexed from 0. If you wanted a service to use only CPUs 0 and 3, you could use `--cpuset-cpus "0,3"`. This flag also supports entering values as a range (that is `1-3`).

While it might seem like a lot of options to consider, in most cases you will only need to tweak the `--cpu-shares` and `--cpus` flags, but it is possible that you will need much more granular control over the resources that they provide.

How about we see what the `--cpu-shares` value can do for us? For this, we need to simulate resource contention and in the next example, we will try to do this by incrementing an integer variable as many times as we can within a period of 60 seconds in as many containers as there are CPUs on the machine. The code is a bit gnarly, but most of it is to get the CPU to reach resource contention levels on all cores.

Add the following to a file called `cpu_shares.sh` (also available on `https://github.com/sgnn7/deploying_with_docker`):

```bash
#!/bin/bash -e

CPU_COUNT=$(nproc --all)
START_AT=$(date +%s)
STOP_AT=$(( $START_AT + 60 ))

echo "Detected $CPU_COUNT CPUs"
echo "Time range: $START_AT -> $STOP_AT"

declare -a CONTAINERS

echo "Allocating all cores but one with default shares"
for ((i = 0; i < $CPU_COUNT - 1; i++)); do
  echo "Starting container $i"
  CONTAINERS[i]=$(docker run \
                  -d \
                  ubuntu \
                  /bin/bash -c "c=0; while [ $STOP_AT -gt \$(date +%s) ];
do c=\$((c + 1)); done; echo \$c")
done

echo "Starting container with high shares"
  fast_task=$(docker run \
              -d \
              --cpu-shares 8192 \
              ubuntu \
              /bin/bash -c "c=0; while [ $STOP_AT -gt \$(date +%s) ]; do
c=\$((c + 1)); done; echo \$c")
```

```
    CONTAINERS[$((CPU_COUNT - 1))]=$fast_task

  echo "Waiting full minute for containers to finish..."
  sleep 62

  for ((i = 0; i < $CPU_COUNT; i++)); do
    container_id=${CONTAINERS[i]}
    echo "Container $i counted to $(docker logs $container_id)"
    docker rm $container_id >/dev/null
  done
```

Now we will run this code and see the effects of our flag:

```
$ # Make the file executable
$ chmod +x ./cpu_shares.sh

$ # Run our little program
$ ./cpu_shares.sh
Detected 8 CPUs
Time range: 1507405189 -> 1507405249
Allocating all cores but one with default shares
Starting container 0
Starting container 1
Starting container 2
Starting container 3
Starting container 4
Starting container 5
Starting container 6
Starting container with high shares
Waiting full minute for containers to finish...
Container 0 counted to 25380
Container 1 counted to 25173
Container 2 counted to 24961
Container 3 counted to 24882
Container 4 counted to 24649
Container 5 counted to 24306
Container 6 counted to 24280
Container 7 counted to 31938
```

While the container with the high --cpu-share value didn't get the full increase in count that might have been expected, if we ran the benchmark over a longer period of time with a tighter CPU-bound loop, the difference would be much more drastic. But even in our small example you can see that the last container had a distinct advantage over all the other running containers on the machine.

To see how the `--cpus` flag compares, let's take a look at what it can do on an uncontended system:

```
$ # First without any limiting
$ time docker run -it \
                  --rm \
                  ubuntu \
                  /bin/bash -c 'for ((i=0; i<100; i++)); do sha256sum
/bin/bash >/dev/null; done'
real    0m1.902s
user    0m0.030s
sys     0m0.006s

$ # Now with only a quarter of the CPU available
$ time docker run -it \
                  --rm \
                  --cpus=0.25 \
                  ubuntu \
                  /bin/bash -c 'for ((i=0; i<100; i++)); do sha256sum
/bin/bash >/dev/null; done'
real    0m6.456s
user    0m0.018s
sys     0m0.017s
```

As you can see, the `--cpus` flag is really good for ensuring that a task will not use any more CPU than the specified value even if there is no contention for resources on the machine.

> Keep in mind that there are a few more options for limiting resource usage for containers that are a bit outside of the scope of the general ones that we have covered already, but they are mainly for device-specific limitations (such as device IOPS). If you are interested in seeing all of the available ways to limit resources to a task or a service, you should be able to find them all at `https://docs.docker.com/engine/reference/run/#runtime-constraints-on-resources`.

Pitfall avoidance

In most small and medium deployments, you will never see the same problems that you will start seeing when you scale up beyond them, so this section is to show you the most common issues that you will encounter and how to work around them in the cleanest way possible. While this list should cover most of the glaring issues you will encounter, some of your own will need custom fixes. You shouldn't be scared to make those changes because almost all host OS installations are just not geared towards the configuration that a high-load multi-container would need.

 WARNING! Many of the values and tweaks in this section have been based on personal experiences with deploying Docker clusters in the cloud. Depending on your combination of cloud provider, OS distribution, and infrastructure-specific configurations, the values may not need changing from the defaults, and some may even be detrimental to your system if used verbatim without spending some time learning what they mean and how to modify them. If you continue reading this section, please use the examples only as examples on how to change the values and not as something to copy/paste directly into configuration management tooling.

ulimits

`ulimit` settings are little-known settings to most Linux desktop users, but they are a really painful and often-encountered issue when working with servers. In a nutshell, `ulimit` settings control many aspects around a process' resource usage just like our Docker resource tweaks we covered earlier and they are applied to every process and shell that has been started. These limits are almost always set on distributions to prevent a stray process from taking down your machine, but the numbers have usually been chosen with regular desktop usage in mind, so trying to run server-type code on unchanged systems is bound to hit at least the open file limit, and possibly some other limits.

We can use `ulimit -a` to see what our current (also called **soft**) settings are:

```
$ ulimit -a
core file size          (blocks, -c) 0
data seg size           (kbytes, -d) unlimited
scheduling priority             (-e) 0
file size               (blocks, -f) unlimited
pending signals                 (-i) 29683
max locked memory       (kbytes, -l) 64
max memory size         (kbytes, -m) unlimited
open files                      (-n) 1024
pipe size            (512 bytes, -p) 8
POSIX message queues     (bytes, -q) 819200
real-time priority              (-r) 0
stack size              (kbytes, -s) 8192
cpu time               (seconds, -t) unlimited
max user processes              (-u) 29683
virtual memory          (kbytes, -v) unlimited
file locks                      (-x) unlimited
```

As you can see, there are only a few things set here, but there is one that stands out: our "open files" limit (`1024`) is fine for general applications, but if we run many services that handle a large number of open files (such as a decent amount of Docker containers), this value must be changed or you will hit errors and your services will effectively die.

You can change this value for your current shell with `ulimit -S <flag> <value>`:

```
$ ulimit -n
1024

$ # Set max open files to 2048
$ ulimit -S -n 2048

$ # Let's see the full list again
$ ulimit -a
<snip>
open files                      (-n) 2048
<snip>
```

But what if we try to set this to something really high?

```
$ ulimit -S -n 10240
bash: ulimit: open files: cannot modify limit: Invalid argument
```

Here, we have now encountered the hard limit imposed by the system. This limit is something that will need to be changed at the system level if we want to modify it beyond those values. We can check what these hard limits are with `ulimit -H -a`:

```
$ ulimit -H -a | grep '^open files'
open files                      (-n) 4096
```

So, if we want to increase our open files number beyond `4096`, we really need to change the system-level settings. Also, even if the soft limit of `4086` is fine with us, the setting is only for our own shell and its child processes, so it won't affect any other service or process on the system.

If you really wanted to, you actually can change the `ulimit` settings of an already-running process with `prlimit` from the `util-linux` package, but this method of adjusting the values is discouraged because the settings do not persist during process restarts and are thus pretty useless for that purpose. With that said, if you want to find out whether your `ulimit` settings have been applied to a service that is already running, this CLI tool is invaluable, so don't be afraid to use it in those cases.

To change this setting, you need to do a combination of options that is dependent on your distribution:

- Create a security limits configuration file. You can do this rather simply by adding a few lines to something like `/etc/security/limits.d/90-ulimit-open-files-increase.conf`. The following example sets the open file soft limit on `root` and then on all other accounts (`*` does not apply to the `root` account) to `65536`. You should find out what the appropriate value is for your system ahead of time:

  - ```
    root soft nofile 65536
    root hard nofile 65536
    * soft nofile 65536
    * hard nofile 65536
    ```

- Add the `pam_limits` module to **Pluggable Authentication Module (PAM)**. This will, in turn, affect all user sessions with the previous ulimit change setting because some distributions do not have it included otherwise your changes might not persist. Add the following to `/etc/pam.d/common-session`:

  - ```
    session required pam_limits.so
    ```

- Alternatively, on some distributions, you can directly add the setting to the affected service definition in `systemd` in an override file:

  - **LimitNOFILE=65536**

Overriding `systemd` services is a somewhat lengthy and distracting topic for this section, but it is a very common strategy for tweaking third-party services running on cluster deployments with that init system, so it is a very valuable skill to have. If you would like to know more about this topic, you can find a condensed version of the process at `https://askubuntu.com/a/659268`, and if you want the detailed version the upstream documentation can be found at `https://www.freedesktop.org/software/systemd/man/systemd.service.html`.

CAUTION! In the first example, we used the * wildcard, which affects all accounts on the machine. Generally, you want to isolate this setting to only the affected service accounts, if possible, for security reasons. We also used `root` because root values are specifically set by name in some distributions, which overrides the * wildcard setting due to the higher specificity. If you want to learn more about limits, you can find more information on these settings at `https://linux.die.net/man/5/limits.conf`.

Max file descriptors

In the same way that we have a maximum open file limit for sessions and processes, the kernel itself has a limit for the maximum open file descriptors across the whole system. If this limit is reached, no other files will be able to be opened, and thus this needs tweaking on machines that may have a large number of files open at any one time.

This value is part of the kernel parameters and as such can be seen with `sysctl`:

```
$ sysctl fs.file-max
fs.file-max = 757778
```

While on this machine the value seems reasonable, I have seen a few older distributions with a surprisingly low value that will get easily hit with errors if you are running a number of containers on the system.

Most kernel configuration settings we discuss here and later in this chapter can be temporarily changed with `sysctl -w <key>="<value>"`. However, since those values are reset back to defaults on each reboot, they usually are of no long-term use for us and are not going to be covered here, but keep in mind that you can use such techniques if you need to debug a live system or apply a temporary time-sensitive fix.

To change this to a value that will persist across reboots, we will need to add the following to the `/etc/sysctl.d` folder (that is, `/etc/sysctl.d/10-file-descriptors-increase.conf`):

```
fs.file-max = 1000000
```

After this change, reboot, and you should now be able to open up to 1 million file handles on the machine!

Socket buffers

To increase performance, it is usually highly advantageous to increase the size of the socket buffers because they are no longer doing the work of a single machine but the work of as many Docker containers as you have running on top of regular machine connectivity. For this, there are a few settings that you should probably set to make sure that the socket buffers are not struggling to keep up with all the traffic passing through them. At the time of writing this book, most of these default buffer settings are generally pretty tiny when the machine starts (200 KB in a few machines that I've checked) and they are supposed to be dynamically scaled, but you can force them to be much larger from the start.

On an Ubuntu LTS 16.04 installation, the following are the default ones for the buffer settings (though yours may vary):

```
net.core.optmem_max = 20480
net.core.rmem_default = 212992
net.core.rmem_max = 212992
net.core.wmem_default = 212992
net.core.wmem_max = 212992
net.ipv4.tcp_rmem = 4096 87380 6291456
net.ipv4.tcp_wmem = 4096 16384 4194304
```

We will dial these values up to some sensible defaults by adding the following to
`/etc/sysctl.d/10-socket-buffers.conf`, but be sure to use values that make sense in
your environment:

```
net.core.optmem_max = 40960
net.core.rmem_default = 16777216
net.core.rmem_max = 16777216
net.core.wmem_default = 16777216
net.core.wmem_max = 16777216
net.ipv4.tcp_rmem = 4096 87380 16777216
net.ipv4.tcp_wmem = 4096 87380 16777216
```

By increasing these values, our buffers start large and should be able to handle quite a bit of
traffic with much better throughput, which is what we want in a clustering environment.

Ephemeral ports

If you aren't familiar with ephemeral ports, they are the port numbers that all outbound
connections get assigned if the originating port is not explicitly specified on the connection,
which is the vast majority of them. For example, if you do any kind of outbound HTTP
request with almost every client library, you will most likely have one of these ephemeral
ports assigned as the return communication port for your connection.

To see some sample ephemeral port usage on your machine, you can use `netstat`:

```
$ netstat -an | grep ESTABLISHED
tcp        0      0 192.168.56.101:46496    <redacted>:443
ESTABLISHED
tcp        0      0 192.168.56.101:45512    <redacted>:443
ESTABLISHED
tcp        0      0 192.168.56.101:42014    <redacted>:443
ESTABLISHED
<snip>
tcp        0      0 192.168.56.101:45984    <redacted>:443
ESTABLISHED
tcp        0      0 192.168.56.101:56528    <redacted>:443
ESTABLISHED
```

As you develop systems with multiple services with numerous outbound connections
(which is practically mandatory when working with Docker services), you may notice that
there are limits on the number of ports you are allowed to use and are likely to find that
these ports may overlap with the ranges that some of your internal Docker services are
using, causing intermittent and often annoying connectivity issues. In order to fix these
issues, changes need to be made to the ephemeral port range.

Since these are also kernel settings, we can see what our current ranges are with `sysctl`, just like we did in a couple of earlier examples:

```
$ sysctl net.ipv4.ip_local_port_range
net.ipv4.ip_local_port_range = 32768     60999
```

You can see that our range is in the upper half of the port allocations, but any service that may start listening within that range could be in trouble. It is also possible that we may need more than 28,000 ports.

 You may be curious how you get or set the `ipv6` settings for this parameter, but luckily (at least for now) this same setting key is used for both `ipv4` and `ipv6` ephemeral port ranges. At some point, this setting name may change, but I think we are at least a couple of years away from that.

To change this value, we can either use `sysctl -w` for a temporary change or `sysctl.d` for a permanent change:

```
$ # First the temporary change to get us up to 40000
$ # ports. For our services, we separately have to
$ # ensure none listen on any ports above 24999.
$ sudo sysctl -w net.ipv4.ip_local_port_range="25000 65000"
net.ipv4.ip_local_port_range = 25000 65000

$ # Sanity check
$ sysctl net.ipv4.ip_local_port_range
net.ipv4.ip_local_port_range = 25000     65000

$ # Now for the permanent change (requires restart)
$ echo "net.ipv4.ip_local_port_range = 25000 65000" | sudo tee
/etc/sysctl.d/10-ephemeral-ports.conf
```

With this change, we have effectively increased the number of outbound connections we can support by over 30%, but we could have just as easily used the same setting to ensure that ephemeral ports do not collide with other running services.

Netfilter tweaks

Sadly, the settings we have seen so far are not the only things that need tweaking with increased network connections to your server. As you increase the load on your server, you may also begin to see `nf_conntrack: table full` errors in your `dmesg` and/or kernel logs. For those unfamiliar with `netfilter`, it is a kernel module that tracks all **Network Address Translation** (**NAT**) sessions in a hashed table that adds any new connections to it and clears them after they are closed and a predefined timeout is reached, so as you increase the connection volume from and to a single machine, you will most likely find that the majority of these related settings are defaulted rather conservatively and are in need of tweaking (though your distribution may vary--make sure to verify yours!):

```
$ sysctl -a | grep nf_conntrack
net.netfilter.nf_conntrack_buckets = 65536
<snip>
net.netfilter.nf_conntrack_generic_timeout = 600
<snip>
net.netfilter.nf_conntrack_max = 262144
<snip>
net.netfilter.nf_conntrack_tcp_timeout_close = 10
net.netfilter.nf_conntrack_tcp_timeout_close_wait = 60
net.netfilter.nf_conntrack_tcp_timeout_established = 432000
net.netfilter.nf_conntrack_tcp_timeout_fin_wait = 120
net.netfilter.nf_conntrack_tcp_timeout_last_ack = 30
net.netfilter.nf_conntrack_tcp_timeout_max_retrans = 300
net.netfilter.nf_conntrack_tcp_timeout_syn_recv = 60
net.netfilter.nf_conntrack_tcp_timeout_syn_sent = 120
net.netfilter.nf_conntrack_tcp_timeout_time_wait = 120
net.netfilter.nf_conntrack_tcp_timeout_unacknowledged = 300
<snip>
```

Quite a few of these can be changed, but the usual suspects for errors that need tweaking are as follows:

- `net.netfilter.nf_conntrack_buckets`: Controls the size of the hash table for the connections. Increasing this is advisable, although it can be substituted with a more aggressive timeout. Note that this cannot be set with regular `sysctl.d` settings, but instead needs to be set with a kernel module parameter.
- `net.netfilter.nf_conntrack_max`: The number of entries to hold. By default, this is four times the value of the previous entry.

- `net.netfilter.nf_conntrack_tcp_timeout_established`: This keeps the mapping for an open connection for up to five days (!). This is generally almost mandatory to reduce in order to not overflow your connection tracking table, but don't forget that it needs to be above the TCP `keepalive` timeout or you will get unexpected connection breaks.

To apply the last two settings, you need to add the following to `/etc/sysctl.d/10-conntrack.conf` and adjust the values for your own infrastructure configuration:

```
net.netfilter.nf_conntrack_tcp_timeout_established = 43200
net.netfilter.nf_conntrack_max = 524288
```

 netfilter is a massively complex topic to cover in a small section, so reading up on its impacts and configuration settings is highly recommended before changing these numbers. To get an idea of each of the settings, you can visit `https://www.kernel.org/doc/Documentation/networking/nf_conntrack-sysctl.txt` and read up about it.

For a bucket count, you need to directly change the `nf_conntrack hashsize` kernel module parameter:

```
echo '131072' | sudo tee /sys/module/nf_conntrack/parameters/hashsize
```

Finally, to ensure that the right order is followed when loading the netfilter module so these values persist correctly, you will probably also need to add the following to the end of `/etc/modules`:

```
nf_conntrack_ipv4
nf_conntrack_ipv6
```

If everything was done correctly, your next restart should have all of the netfilter settings we talked about set.

Multi-service containers

Multi-service containers are a particularly tricky topic to broach, as the whole notion and recommended use of Docker is that you are only running single-process services within the container. Because of that, there is quite a bit of implicit pressure not to cover this topic because it can easily be misused and abused by developers who do not understand the reasons why this practice is strongly discouraged.

However, with that said and out of the way, there will be times where you will need to run multiple processes in a tight logical grouping where a multi-container solution would not make sense or it would be overly kludgey, which is why this topic is still important to cover. Having said all that, I cannot stress enough that you should only use this type of service collocation as a last resort.

Before we even write a single line of code, we must discuss an architectural issue with multiple processes running within the same container, which is called the `PID 1` problem. The crux of this issue is that Docker containers run in an isolated environment in which they do not get help from the host's `init` process in reaping orphaned child processes. Consider an example process `Parent Process`, that is a basic executable that starts another process called `Child Process`, but as some point after that, if the associated `Parent Process` exits or is killed you will be left with the zombie `Child Process` loitering around in your container since `Parent Process` is gone and there is no other orphan reaping process running within the container sandbox. If the container exits, then the zombie processes will get cleaned up because they are all wrapped in a namespace, but for long-running tasks this can present a serious problem for running multiple processes inside a single image.

 Terminology here might be confusing, but what was meant in simple terms is that every process is supposed be removed (also known as `reaped`) from the process table after it exits, either by the parent process or some other designated process (usually `init`) in the hierarchy that will take ownership of of it in order to finalize it. A process that does not have a running parent process in this context is called an orphan process.

Some tools have the ability to reap these zombie processes (such as Bash and a few other shells), but even they aren't good enough init processes for our containers because they do not pass signals such as `SIGKILL`, `SIGINT`, and others to child processes, so stopping the container or pressing things such as *Ctrl + C* in the Terminal are of no use and will not terminate the container. If you really want to run multiple processes inside the container, your launching process must do orphan reaping and signal passing to children. Since we don't want to use the full init system like `systemd` from the container, there are a couple of alternatives here, but in the recent versions of Docker we now have the `--init` flag, which can run our containers with a real init runner process.

Let's see this in action and try to exit a program where the starting process is `bash`:

```
$ # Let's try to run 'sleep' and exit with <Ctrl>-C
$ docker run -it \
            ubuntu \
            bash -c 'sleep 5000'
^C^C^C^C^C^C^C^C^C^C
```

```
<Ctrl-C not working>

$ # On second terminal
$ docker ps
CONTAINER ID IMAGE   COMMAND                   CREATED           STATUS
c7b69001271d ubuntu "bash -c 'sleep 5000'" About a minute ago Up About a
minute

$ # Can we stop it?
$ docker stop c7b69001271d
<nothing happening>
^C

$ # Last resort - kill the container!
$ docker kill c7b69001271d
c7b69001271d
```

This time, we'll run our container with the `--init` flag:

```
$ docker run -it \
            --init \
            ubuntu \
            bash -c 'sleep 5000'
^C

$ # <Ctrl>-C worked just fine!
```

As you can see, `--init` was able to take our signal and pass it to all the listening children processes, and it works well as an orphan process reaper, though the latter is really hard to show in a basic container. With this flag and its functionality, you should now be able to run multiple processes with either a shell such as Bash or upgrade to a full process management tool such as `supervisord` (`http://supervisord.org/`) without any issues.

Zero-downtime deployments

With every cluster deployment, you will at some point need to think about code redeployment while minimizing the impact on your users. With small deployments, it is feasible that you might have a maintenance period in which you turn off everything, rebuild the new images, and restart the services, but this style of deployment is really not the way that medium and large clusters should be managed because you want to minimize any and all direct work needed to maintain the cluster. In fact, even for small clusters, handling code and configuration upgrades in a seamless manner can be invaluable for increased productivity.

Rolling service restarts

If the new service code does not change the fundamental way that it interacts with other services (inputs and outputs), often the only thing that is needed is a rebuild (or replacement) of the container image that is then placed into the Docker registry, and then the service is restarted in an orderly and staggered way. By staggering the restarts, there is always at least one task that can handle the service request available, and from an external point of view, this changeover should be completely seamless. Most orchestration tooling will do this automatically for you if you change or update any settings for a service, but since they are very implementation-specific we will focus on Docker Swarm for our examples:

```
$ # Create a new swarm
$ docker swarm init
Swarm initialized: current node (j4p08hdfou1tyrdqj3eclnfb6) is now a
manager.
<snip>

$ # Create a service based on mainline NGINX and update-delay
$ # of 15 seconds
$ docker service create \
                --detach=true \
                --replicas 4 \
                --name nginx_update \
                --update-delay 15s \
                nginx:mainline
s9f44kn9a4g6sf3ve449fychv

$ # Let's see what we have
$ docker service ps nginx_update
ID              NAME              IMAGE            DESIRED STATE    CURRENT STATE
rbvv37cg85ms    nginx_update.1    nginx:mainline   Running          Running 56
seconds ago
y41761d41olf    nginx_update.2    nginx:mainline   Running          Running 56
seconds ago
gza13g9ar7jx    nginx_update.3    nginx:mainline   Running          Running 56
seconds ago
z7dhy6zu4jt5    nginx_update.4    nginx:mainline   Running          Running 56
seconds ago

$ # Update our service to use the stable NGINX branch
$ docker service update \
                --detach=true \
                --image nginx:stable \
                nginx_update
nginx_update
```

```
$ # After a minute, we can now see the new service status
$ docker service ps nginx_update
ID                 NAME               IMAGE             DESIRED STATE   CURRENT
STATE
qa7evkjvdml5   nginx_update.1       nginx:stable    Running      Running
about a minute ago
rbvv37cg85ms  \_ nginx_update.1   nginx:mainline  Shutdown     Shutdown
about a minute ago
qbg0hsd4nxyz   nginx_update.2       nginx:stable    Running      Running
about a minute ago
y41761d41olf  \_ nginx_update.2   nginx:mainline  Shutdown     Shutdown
about a minute ago
nj5gcf541fgj   nginx_update.3       nginx:stable    Running      Running 30
seconds ago
gza13g9ar7jx  \_ nginx_update.3   nginx:mainline  Shutdown     Shutdown 31
seconds ago
433461xm4roq   nginx_update.4       nginx:stable    Running      Running 47
seconds ago
z7dhy6zu4jt5  \_ nginx_update.4   nginx:mainline  Shutdown     Shutdown 48
seconds ago

$ # All our services now are using the new image
$ # and were started staggered!

$ # Clean up
$ docker service rm nginx_update
nginx_update

$ docker swarm leave --force
Node left the swarm.
```

As you can see, it should be simple enough to do the same thing with your own code changes without any downtime!

> If you want to be able to restart multiple tasks instead of one at a time, Docker Swarm has an --update-parallelism <count> flag as well that can be set on a service. When using this flag, --update-delay is still observed but instead of a single task being restarted, they are done in batches of <count> size.

Blue-green deployments

Rolling restarts are nice, but sometimes the changes that you need to apply are on the hosts themselves and will need to be done to every Docker Engine node in the cluster, for example, if you need to upgrade to a newer orchestration version or to upgrade the OS release version. In these cases, the generally accepted way of doing this without a large team for support is usually by something called **blue-green deployments**. It starts by deploying a secondary cluster in parallel to the currently running one, possibly tied to the same data store backend, and then at the most opportune time switching the entry routing to point to the new cluster. Once all the processing on the original cluster has died down it is deleted, and the new cluster becomes the main processing group. If done properly, the impact on the users should be imperceptible and the whole underlying infrastructure has been changed in the process.

The process starts with the creation of the secondary cluster. At that point there is no effective change other than testing that the new cluster behaves as expected:

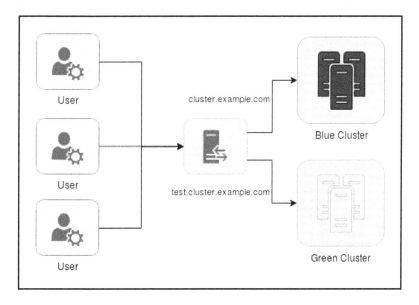

After the secondary cluster is operational, the router swaps the endpoints and the processing continues on the new cluster:

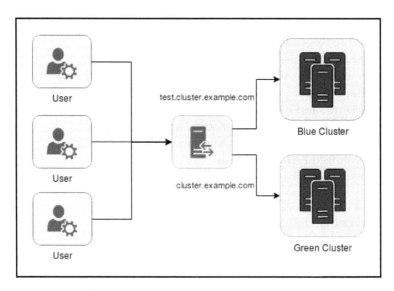

With the swap made, after all the processing is done, the original cluster is decommissioned (or left as an emergency backup):

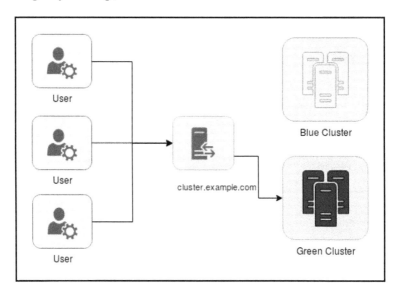

But the application of this deployment pattern on full clusters is not the only use for it--in some cases, it is possible to do this at the service level within the same cluster, using the same pattern to swap in a newer component, but there is a better system for that, which we will cover next.

Blue-turquoise-green deployments

With deployments of code, things get a bit trickier because changing APIs on either the input or output sides or the database schema can wreak havoc on a cluster with interspersed versions of code. To get around this problem, there is a modified blue-green deployment pattern called **blue-turquoise-green deployment** where the code is attempted to be kept compatible with all running versions until the new code is deployed, after which the service is again updated by removing the compat code.

The process here is pretty simple:

1. The service that uses API version x is replaced with a new version of the service that supports both API version x and API version $(x+1)$ in a rolling fashion. This provides zero downtime from the user's perspective, but creates a new service that has the newer API support.
2. After everything is updated, the service that has the old API version x is removed from the codebase.
3. Another rolling restart is done on the service to remove traces of the deprecated API so only API version $(x+1)$ support is left.

This approach is extremely valuable when the services you are using need to be persistently available, and in many cases you could easily replace the API version with the messaging queue format, if your cluster is based on queues. The transitions are smooth, but there is overhead in needing to twice modify the service compared to a single time with a hard-swap, but it is a decent trade-off. This approach is also extremely valuable when the services in use deal with a database that might need a migration, so you should probably use this approach when others are not good enough.

Summary

In this chapter, we covered various tools and techniques that you will need as you increase your infrastructure scale beyond the simple prototypes. By now we should have learned how to limit service access to host's resources, handle the most common pitfalls with ease, run multiple services in a single container, and handle zero-downtime deployments and configuration changes.

In the next chapter, we will spend time working on deploying our own mini version of **Platform-as-a-Service** (**PAAS**) using many of the things we have learned so far.

8
Building Our Own Platform

In previous chapters, we spent a lot of time working on individual pieces of infrastructure building up little isolated pieces here and there, but in this chapter, we will try to put as many concepts together and build a minimally-viable **Platform-as-a-Service** (**PaaS**). In the following sections, we will cover these topics:

- **Configuration Management** (**CM**) tooling
- **Amazon Web Service** (**AWS**) deployment
- Continuous integration/Continuous delivery (CI/CD)

As we build up the core of our services, we will see what it takes to take a small service and deploy it into the real cloud.

One thing to note here is that this chapter is provided as only a quick primer and a basic example on real deployments in the cloud since creating a full PaaS infrastructure with all the bells and whistles is something that is usually so complex that it takes large teams months or years sometime to work out all the problems. Compounding the issue, the solutions are usually very specifically tailored to the choices of services and orchestration tooling running on top of this and as such, consider things you see in this chapter as a sample of the current ecosystem that you could use in your own deployment but other tools may be better suited to your specific needs.

Configuration management

With every system that depends on a large number of similarly configured machines (regardless of whether they are physical or virtual ones), there always arises a need for simple and easy rebuild tooling to help automate the majority of the tasks that have in the past been done by hand. In the case of PaaS clusters, ideally, all pieces of the infrastructure are capable of being rebuilt with minimal user intervention into the exact state that is wanted. In the case of bare-metal PaaS server nodes, this is critically important as any operation that you have to do manually gets multiplied by the number of nodes you have, so streamlining this process should be of utmost importance for any kind of production-ready clustering infrastructure.

Now you may ask yourself, "Why do we care about covering CM tooling?" and the truth of the matter is that if you do not have proper CM around your container infrastructure, you are guaranteeing yourself after-hour emergency calls due to various issues such as: the nodes never joining the cluster, mismatched configurations, unapplied changes, version incompatibilities, and many other problems that will make you pull your hair out. So to prevent this set of situations from happening to you, we will really dive deep into this ecosystem of supporting software.

With that explained and out of the way, we can see some of the options we have available to choose from for the CM tooling:

- Ansible (`https://www.ansible.com`)
- Puppet (`https://puppet.com`)
- Chef (`https://www.chef.io/chef/`)
- SaltStack (`https://saltstack.com`)
- A few others that are mostly far weaker in terms of functionality and stability.

Due to the fact that both Puppet and Chef require an agent-based deployment and SaltStack is trailing in Ansible popularity by a huge margin, for our work here, we will cover Ansible as the CM tooling of choice but as your needs will probably vary. Use your own requirements to select the most appropriate tool for the job.

As a relevant side note from my interactions with the DevOps online communities, it seems that at the time of writing this material, Ansible is becoming the de facto standard for CM tooling but it is not without its flaws. While I would love to recommend its use everywhere for a myriad of great features, expect complex edge cases of bigger modules to be marginally reliable and keep in mind that most bugs you will find are likely to have been already fixed by an unmerged pull request on GitHub that you might have to apply locally as needed.

WARNING! Choice of configuration management tooling should not be taken lightly and you should weigh the pros and cons of each before committing to a single one as this tooling is the hardest to switch out once you have a few machines managed with it! While many IT and DevOps professionals treat this choice almost as a way of life (similar to polarization between `vim` and `emacs` users), make sure that you evaluate your options carefully and logically due to the high costs of switching to a different one down the road. I have personally never heard of a company switch CM tooling after running with one for a while though I am sure there are a few out there.

Ansible

If you have not worked with Ansible before, it is has the following benefits:

- It is relatively easy to use (YAML/Ninja2 based)
- It only needs an SSH connection to the target
- It contains a huge amount of pluggable modules to extend its functionality (`https://docs.ansible.com/ansible/latest/modules_by_category.html`), many of which are in the base install so you usually do not have to worry about dependencies

If this list doesn't sound good enough, the whole Ansible architecture is extensible, so if there are no available modules that satisfy your requirements, they are somewhat easy to write and integrate, and thus Ansible is able to accommodate almost any infrastructure you may have or want to build. Under the covers, Ansible uses Python and SSH to run commands directly on the target host but in a much higher-level **domain-specific language** (**DSL**) that makes it very easy and quick for someone to write a server configuration versus scripting SSH commands directly through something like Bash.

The current Ubuntu LTS version (16.04) comes with Ansible 2.0.0.2, which should be adequate for most purposes, but using versions that are closer to upstream ones is often advised for both bug fixes and for new module additions. If you choose the latter route, make sure to have the version pinned to ensure consistently working deployments.

Installation

To install Ansible on most Debian-based distributions, generally the process is extremely simple:

```
$ # Make sure we have an accurate view of repositories
$ sudo apt-get update

<snip>
Fetched 3,971 kB in 22s (176 kB/s)
Reading package lists... Done

$ # Install the package
$ sudo apt-get install ansible

Reading package lists... Done
Building dependency tree
Reading state information... Done
The following NEW packages will be installed:
  ansible
0 upgraded, 1 newly installed, 0 to remove and 30 not upgraded.
<snip>
Setting up ansible (2.0.0.2-2ubuntu1) ...

$ # Sanity check
$ ansible --version

ansible 2.0.0.2
  config file = /home/user/checkout/eos-administration/ansible/ansible.cfg
  configured module search path = /usr/share/ansible
```

Basics

The standard layout for a project is usually split into roles that define functionality slices with the rest of the configurations basically just supporting those roles. The basic file structure of Ansible projects looks something like this (though more complex setups are often needed):

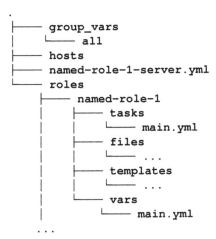

```
├──── group_vars
│     └──── all
├──── hosts
├──── named-role-1-server.yml
└──── roles
      ├──── named-role-1
      │     ├──── tasks
      │     │     └──── main.yml
      │     ├──── files
      │     │     └──── ...
      │     ├──── templates
      │     │     └──── ...
      │     └──── vars
      │           └──── main.yml
      ...
```

Let us break down the basic structure of this filesystem tree and see how each piece is used in the bigger picture:

- `group_vars/all`: This file is used to define variables that are used for all of your playbooks. These can be used in playbooks and templates with variable expansions (`"{{ variable_name }}"`).
- `hosts/`: This file or a directory lists hosts and groups that you want to manage and any specific connectivity details like protocol, username, SSH key, and so on. In documentation, this file is often called the inventory file.
- `roles/`: This holds a list of role definitions that can be applied in a hierarchical and layered way to a target machine. Usually, it is further subdivided into `tasks/`, `files/`, `vars/`, and other layout-sensitive structures within each role:
    - `<role_name>/tasks/main.yml`: A YAML file that lists the main steps to execute as part of the role.
    - `<role_name>/files/...`: Here you would add static files that would be copied to target a machine that do not require any pre-processing.

- `<role_name>/templates/...`: In this directory, you would add template files for role-related tasks. These usually contain templates that will be copied to the target machine with variable substitutions.
- `<role_name>/vars/main.yml`: Just like the parent directory implies, this YAML file holds role-specific variable definitions.

- `playbooks/`: In this directory, you would add all top-level ancillary playbooks that do not fit well in role definitions.

Usage

Now that we have been introduced to what Ansible looks like and how it operates, it is time to do something practical with it. What we will do at this point is make an Ansible deployment configuration to apply some of the system tweaks we covered in the previous chapter and have Docker ready for us on the machine after running the playbook.

This example is relatively simple but it should show pretty well the ease of use and power of a decent configuration management tooling. Ansible is also a massive topic that a small section like this just can not cover in as much detail as I would like to but the documentation is relatively good and you can find it at `https://docs.ansible.com/ansible/latest/index.html`.

This example (and others) can be found at `https://github.com/sgnn7/deploying_with_docker/tree/master/chapter_8/ansible_deployment` if you want to skip the manual typing; however, it might be good practice to do it once to get the hang of the Ansible YAML file structure.

First, we will need to create our file structure for holding files. We will call our main role `swarm_node` and since our whole machine is just going to be a swarm node, we will name our top-level deployment playbook the same:

```
$ # First we create our deployment source folder and move there
$ mkdir ~/ansible_deployment
$ cd ~/ansible_deployment/

$ # Next we create the directories we will need
$ mkdir -p roles/swarm_node/files roles/swarm_node/tasks

$ # Make a few placeholder files
$ touch roles/swarm_node/tasks/main.yml \
        swarm_node.yml \
```

```
        hosts

$ # Let's see what we have so far
$ tree
.
├──── hosts
├──── roles
│       └───── swarm_node
│              ├───── files
│              └───── tasks
│                     └───── main.yml
└───── swarm_node.yml
4 directories, 3 files
```

Now let's add the following content to the top-level `swarm_node.yml`. This will be the main entry point for Ansible and it basically just defines target hosts and roles that we want to be run on them:

```
---
- name: Swarm node setup
  hosts: all

  become: True

  roles:
    - swarm_node
```

 YAML files are whitespace structured so make sure that you do not omit any spacing when editing this file. In general, all nesting levels are two spaces farther than the parent, key/values are defined with colons, and lists are itemized with a – (minus) prefix. For more information, about the YAML structure go to `https://en.wikipedia.org/wiki/YAML#Syntax`.

What we are doing here should be mostly obvious:

- `hosts: all`: Run this on all the defined servers in the inventory file. Generally, this would be just a DNS name but since we will only have a single machine target, `all` should be fine.
- `become: True`: Since we use SSH to run things on the target and the SSH user is usually not root, we need to tell Ansible that it needs to elevate permissions with `sudo` for the commands that we will run. If the user requires a password to use `sudo`, you can specify it when invoking the playbook with the `ansible-playbook -K` flag, but we will be using AWS instances later in the chapter which do not require one.

- roles: swarm_mode: This is a list of roles we want to apply to the targets which is for now just a single one called swarm_node. This name *must* match a folder name in roles/.

Next in line for defining will be our system tweaking configuration files that we covered in the previous chapter for things like increases in file descriptor maximum, ulimits, and a couple of others. Add the following files and their respective content to the roles/swarm_node/files/ folder:

- conntrack.conf:

```
net.netfilter.nf_conntrack_tcp_timeout_established = 43200
net.netfilter.nf_conntrack_max = 524288
```

- file-descriptor-increase.conf:

```
fs.file-max = 1000000
```

- socket-buffers.conf:

```
net.core.optmem_max = 40960
net.core.rmem_default = 16777216
net.core.rmem_max = 16777216
net.core.wmem_default = 16777216
net.core.wmem_max = 16777216
net.ipv4.tcp_rmem = 4096 87380 16777216
net.ipv4.tcp_wmem = 4096 87380 16777216
```

- ulimit-open-files-increase.conf:

```
root soft nofile 65536
root hard nofile 65536
* soft nofile 65536
* hard nofile 65536
```

With those added, our tree should look a bit more like this now:

```
.
├──── hosts
├──── roles
│     └──── swarm_node
│           ├──── files
│           │     ├──── conntrack.conf
│           │     ├──── file-descriptor-increase.conf
│           │     ├──── socket-buffers.conf
│           │     └──── ulimit-open-files-increase.conf
│           └──── tasks
│                 └──── main.yml
└──── swarm_node.yml
```

With most of the files in place, we can now finally move onto the main configuration file--`roles/swarm_mode/tasks/main.yml`. In it, we will lay out our configuration steps one by one using Ansible's modules and DSL to:

- `apt-get dist-upgrade` the image for security.
- Apply various improvements to machine configuration files in order to perform better as a Docker host.
- Install Docker.

To simplify understanding the following Ansible configuration code, it would be good to also keep this structure in mind since it underpins each discrete step we will use and is pretty easy to understand after you see it a couple of times:

```
- name: A descriptive step name that shows in output
  module_name:
    module_arg1: arg_value
    module_arg2: arg2_value
    module_array_arg3:
      - arg3_item1
      ...
    ...
```

You can find all module documentation we use in the playbook below at the main Ansible website (`https://docs.ansible.com/ansible/latest/list_of_all_modules.html`). We will avoid getting too deep in module documentation here due to the sheer volume of information that will generally be a distraction to the purpose of this section.

You can also find module-specific documentation that we used here too:
- `https://docs.ansible.com/ansible/latest/apt_module.html`
- `https://docs.ansible.com/ansible/latest/copy_module.html`
- `https://docs.ansible.com/ansible/latest/lineinfile_module.html`
- `https://docs.ansible.com/ansible/latest/command_module.html`
- `https://docs.ansible.com/ansible/latest/apt_key_module.html`
- `https://docs.ansible.com/ansible/latest/apt_repository_module.html`

Let us see what that main installation playbook (`roles/swarm_mode/tasks/main.yml`) should look like:

```
---
- name: Dist-upgrading the image
  apt:
    upgrade: dist
    force: yes
    update_cache: yes
    cache_valid_time: 3600

- name: Fixing ulimit through limits.d
  copy:
    src: "{{ item }}.conf"
    dest: /etc/security/limits.d/90-{{ item }}.conf
  with_items:
    - ulimit-open-files-increase

- name: Fixing ulimits through pam_limits
  lineinfile:
    dest: /etc/pam.d/common-session
    state: present
    line: "session required pam_limits.so"

- name: Ensuring server-like kernel settings are set
  copy:
    src: "{{ item }}.conf"
    dest: /etc/sysctl.d/10-{{ item }}.conf
```

```
  with_items:
    - socket-buffers
    - file-descriptor-increase
    - conntrack

# Bug: https://github.com/systemd/systemd/issues/1113
- name: Working around netfilter loading order
  lineinfile:
    dest: /etc/modules
    state: present
    line: "{{ item }}"
  with_items:
    - nf_conntrack_ipv4
    - nf_conntrack_ipv6

- name: Increasing max connection buckets
  command: echo '131072' > /sys/module/nf_conntrack/parameters/hashsize

# Install Docker
- name: Fetching Docker's GPG key
  apt_key:
    keyserver: hkp://pool.sks-keyservers.net
    id: 58118E89F3A912897C070ADBF76221572C52609D

- name: Adding Docker apt repository
  apt_repository:
    repo: 'deb https://apt.dockerproject.org/repo {{ ansible_distribution |
lower }}-{{ ansible_distribution_release | lower }} main'
    state: present

- name: Installing Docker
  apt:
    name: docker-engine
    state: installed
    update_cache: yes
    cache_valid_time: 3600
```

 WARNING! This configuration has *no* hardening for the image to be comfortably placed on the internet live so use care and add whatever securing steps and tooling you require into this playbook before doing your real deployment. At the absolute least I would suggest installing the `fail2ban` package but you may have alternative strategies (e.g. seccomp, grsecurity, AppArmor, etc).

In this file, we sequentially ordered the steps one by one to configure the machine from base to a system fully capable of running Docker containers by using some of the core Ansible modules and the configuration files we created earlier. One thing that might not be very obvious is our use of the `{{ ansible_distribution | lower }}` type variables but in those, we are using Ansible facts (`https://docs.ansible.com/ansible/latest/playbooks_variables.html`) gathered about the system we are running on and passing them though a Ninja2 `lower()` filter to ensure that the variables are lowercase. By doing this for the repository endpoint, we can use the same configuration without problems on almost any deb-based server target without much trouble as the variables will be substituted to the appropriate values.

At this point, the only thing we would need to do in order to apply this configuration to a machine is to add our server IP/DNS to `hosts` file and run the playbook with `ansible-playbook <options> swarm_node.yml`. But since we want to run this on an Amazon infrastructure, we will stop here and see how we can take these configuration steps and from them create an **Amazon Machine Image** (**AMI**) on which we can start any number of **Elastic Compute Cloud** (**EC2**) instances that are identical and have already been fully configured.

Amazon Web Services setup

To continue onto our Amazon Machine Image (AMI) building section, we cannot go any further without having a working AWS account and an associated API key so we will do that first before continuing further. To avoid ambiguity, be aware that almost all AWS services cost money to use and your use of the API may incur charges for you even for things that you might not readily expect (that is, bandwidth usage, AMI snapshot storage, and on) so use it accordingly.

 AWS is a massively complex piece of machinery, exponentially more than Ansible, and covering everything that you might need to know about it is impossible to do within the scope of this book. But we will try here to provide you with enough relevant instructions for you to have a place to start from. If you decide you want to learn more about AWS, their documentation is generally pretty great and you can find it at `https://aws.amazon.com/documentation/`.

Creating an account

While the process is pretty straightforward, it has changed a couple of times in very significant ways, so detailing the full process here with no way to update it would would end up being a disservice to you so to create the account, I will guide you to the link that has the most up-to-date information on how to do it, which is `https://aws.amazon.com/premiumsupport/knowledge-center/create-and-activate-aws-account/`. In general, the start of the process is at `https://aws.amazon.com/` and you can begin it by clicking on the yellow **Sign Up** or **Create an AWS Account** button on the top right of the screen and following the instructions:

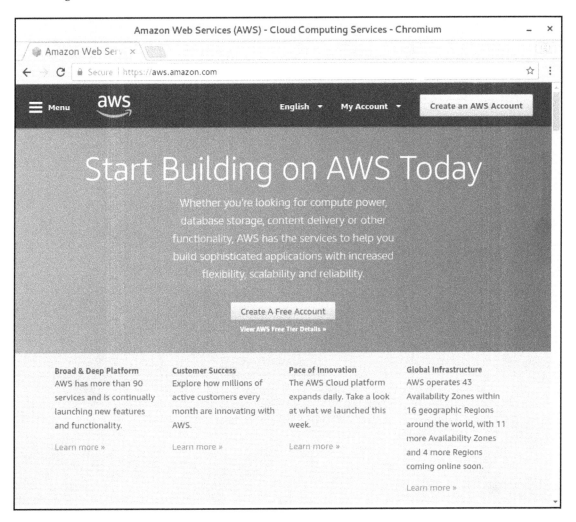

Getting API keys

With the AWS account created, we now need to get our API keys so that we can access and use our resources through the various tools we want to use:

1. Sign in to your console by going to `https://<account_id or alias>.signin.aws.amazon.com/console`. Note that you may need to sign in as the root account initially to do this (small blue link below the **Sign In** button, as shown in the following screenshot) if you did not create a user when you registered the account:

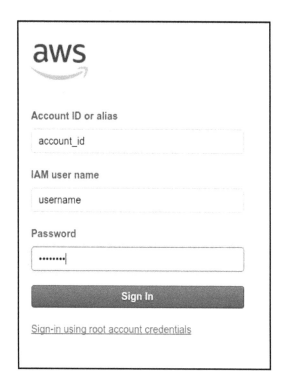

2. Navigate to the IAM page at `https://console.aws.amazon.com/iam/` and click on the **Users** link on the left-hand side of the screen.

3. Click on **Add user** to start the user creation process.

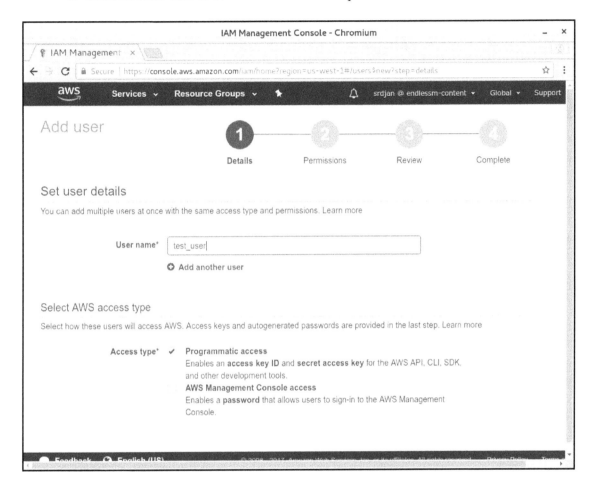

CAUTION! Make sure that the **Programmatic access** checkbox is ticked, or else your AWS API keys will not work for our examples.

4. For the permissions, we will give this user full administrator access. For production services, you will want to limit this to only the needed level of access:

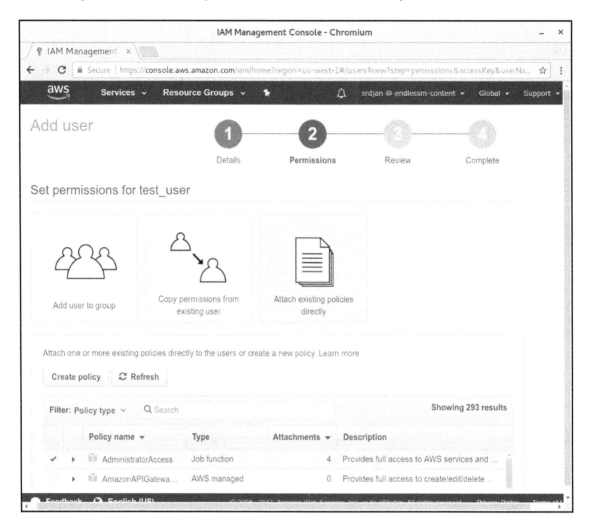

5. Follow the rest of the wizard and make a record of the key ID and key secret, as these will be your API credentials for AWS:

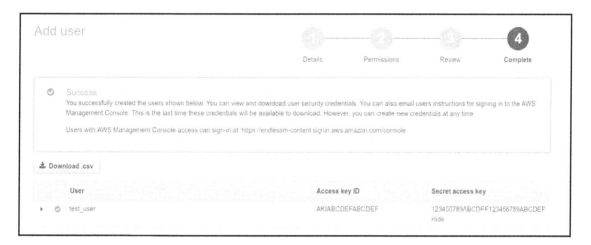

Using the API keys

To use the API keys in the easiest way, you can export variables in your shell that will get picked up by the tooling; however, you will need to do this on every Terminal where you are working with AWS APIs:

```
$ export AWS_ACCESS_KEY_ID="AKIABCDEFABCDEF"
$ export AWS_SECRET_ACCESS_KEY="123456789ABCDEF123456789ABCDEF"
$ export AWS_REGION="us-west-1"
```

Alternatively, if you have the `awscli` tool installed (`sudo apt-get install awscli`), you can just run `aws configure`:

```
$ aws configure
AWS Access Key ID [None]: AKIABCDEFABCEF
AWS Secret Access Key [None]: 123456789ABCDEF123456789ABCDEF
Default region name [None]: us-west-1
Default output format [None]: json
```

There are many other ways to set your credentials as well through things like profiles but it really all depends on your expected usage case. For more information on these options, you can refer to the official documentation at `https://docs.aws.amazon.com/cli/latest/userguide/cli-chap-getting-started.html`.

So with the key available and configured for CLI use, we can now proceed onto building custom AMI images with Packer.

HashiCorp Packer

As we previously implied, our CM scripts are really not that optimal if we have to run them every time on a new machine that we add to the cluster or the cloud infrastructure in general. While we can do that, we really shouldn't, since in a perfect world the cluster nodes should be a flexible group that can spawn and kill instances depending on the usage with minimal user intervention so requiring a manual setup of each new machine is simply untenable even at the smallest cluster scales. With AMI image creation we can pre-bake a templated base system image with Ansible a single time, when the image is being made. By doing that, we can launch any new machine with this same image and our interaction with a running system would be kept at a minimum since everything would ideally be already configured.

To make these machine images, HashiCorp Packer (`https://www.packer.io/`) allows us to do exactly that by applying a provisioning run of our CM tool of choice (Ansible) and outputting a ready-to-use image for any of the big cloud providers. By doing this, you could have the desired state of the cluster nodes (or any other server configuration) permanently enshrined in an image, and for any node addition needs for the cluster all you would need to do is spawn more VM instances based on the same Packer image.

Installation

Due to the fact that Packer is written in Go programming language, to install Packer, you only need to download the binary from their website found at `https://www.packer.io/downloads.html`. You can usually do something like the following for a quick installation:

```
$ # Get the archive
$ wget -q --show-progress
https://releases.hashicorp.com/packer/1.1.1/packer_<release>.zip
packer_<release>.zip 100%[==============================================>]
15.80M 316KB/s in 40s

$ # Extract our binary
$ unzip packer_<release>.zip
Archive: packer_<release>.zip
  inflating: packer

$ # Place the binary somewhere in your path
$ sudo mv packer /usr/local/bin/
```

```
$ packer --version
1.1.1
```

 CAUTION! Packer binaries only provide TLS authentication for their runner without any form of signature checking, so the assurance that the program was published by HashiCorp itself is orders of magnitude lower than a GPG-signed `apt` repository that Docker uses; so, exercise extra care when getting it this way or build it from source (`https://github.com/hashicorp/packer`).

Usage

Using Packer is actually relatively easy as all you need in most cases is the Ansible setup code and a relatively small `packer.json` file. Add this content to `packer.json` in our Ansible deployment configuration from the earlier section:

```
{
  "builders": [
    {
      "ami_description": "Cluster Node Image",
      "ami_name": "cluster-node",
      "associate_public_ip_address": true,
      "force_delete_snapshot": true,
      "force_deregister": true,
      "instance_type": "m3.medium",
      "region": "us-west-1",
      "source_ami": "ami-1c1d217c",
      "ssh_username": "ubuntu",
      "type": "amazon-ebs"
    }
  ],
  "provisioners": [
    {
      "inline": "sudo apt-get update && sudo apt-get install -y ansible",
      "type": "shell"
    },
    {
      "playbook_dir": ".",
      "playbook_file": "swarm_node.yml",
      "type": "ansible-local"
    }
  ]
}
```

If it is not obvious, what we have here in this configuration file is the `provisioners` and `builders` sections, which in general correspond to Packer inputs and outputs, respectively. In our preceding example, we first install Ansible through the `shell` provisioner since the next step requires it, and then run the `main.yml` playbook from our current directory with the `ansible-local` provisioner on a base AMI. After applying all the changes, we save the result as a new **Elastic Block Store** (**EBS**) optimized AMI image.

AWS **Elastic Block Store** (**EBS**) is a service that provides block device storage to EC2 instances (these instances are basically just VMs). To the machine, these look like regular hard disks and can be formatted to whatever filesystem you want and are used to persist data in a permanent manner in the Amazon Cloud. They have configurable size and levels of performance; however, as you might expect, the price goes up as those two settings increase. The only other thing to keep in mind is that while you can move the drive around EC2 instances just like you would move a physical disk, you cannot move an EBS volume across availability zones. A simple workaround is to copy the data over.

"AMI image" phrase expands into "Amazon Machine Image image", which is a really quirky way to phrase things, but just like the sister phrase "PIN number", it flows much better when used that way and will be intentionally referred to in that way in this section. If you're curious about this particularity of the English language, you should peruse the Wiki page for RAS syndrome at `https://en.wikipedia.org/wiki/RAS_syndrome`.

For the builders section, it will be helpful to explain some of the parameters in more detail as they may not be obvious from reading the JSON file:

```
- type: What type of image are we building (EBS-optimized one in our case).
- region: What region will this AMI build in.
- source_ami: What is our base AMI? See section below for more info on
this.
- instance_type: Type of instance to use when building the AMI - bigger
machine == faster builds.
- ami_name: Name of the AMI that will appear in the UI.
- ami_description: Description for the AMI.
- ssh_username: What username to use to connect to base AMI. For Ubuntu,
this is usually "ubuntu".
- associate_public_ip_address: Do we want this builder to have an external
IP. Usually this needs to be true.
- force_delete_snapshot: Do we want to delete the old block device snapshot
if same AMI is rebuilt?
- force_deregister: Do we want to replace the old AMI when rebuilding?
```

You can find more information on this particular builder type and its available options at `https://www.packer.io/docs/builders/amazon-ebs.html`.

Choosing the right AMI base image

Unlike selecting the base Docker image to extend that we covered in earlier chapters, choosing the correct AMI to use Packer on is sadly not a simple task. Some distributions are regularly updated, so the IDs change. The IDs are also unique per AWS region and you may want hardware or paravirtualization (HVM vs PV). On top of all this, you also have to chose the right one for your storage needs (`instance-store`, `ebs`, and `ebs-ssd` at the time of writing this book), creating an absolutely un-intuitive matrix of options.

If you have not worked with Amazon **Elastic Compute Cloud** (**EC2**) and EBS, the storage options are a bit confusing to newcomers but they mean the following:

- `instance-store`: This type of storage is local to the EC2 VM that is running, has space varied depending on the VM type (usually very little though), and gets completely discarded anytime the VM is terminated (a stopped or rebooted VM retains its state though). Instance store is great for nodes that do not need to keep any state but should not be used for machines that you want to have data retained on; however, you can mount a separate EBS drive to an instance--store VM independently if you want to have persistent storage and also utilize the stateless storage.
- `ebs`: This storage type creates and associates an EBS volume backed by older magnetic spinning hard drives (relatively slow vs solid-state drives) anytime an EC2 instance is started with this specific image, so the data is always kept around. This option is good if you want to have your data persisted or the `instance-store` volumes are not big enough. As of today though, this option is being actively deprecated, so it is likely that it will disappear in the future.
- `ebs-ssd`: This option is pretty much the same as the preceding one, but using **Solid State Devices** (SSD) that are much faster but much more expensive per gigabyte of allocation as the backing store.

Another thing that we need to choose is the virtualization type:

- Paravirtualization / `pv`: This type of virtualization is older and uses software to chain load your image, so it was capable to run on a much more diverse hardware. While it was faster long time ago, today it is generally slower than the hardware virtualization.
- Hardware virtualization / `hvm`: This type of virtualization uses CPU-level instructions to run your image in a completely isolated environment akin to running the image directly on bare-metal hardware. While it depends on specific Intel VT CPU technology implementations, it is generally much better performant than `pv` virtualization, so in most cases, you should probably use it over other options, especially if you are not sure which one to choose.

With our new knowledge of the available options, we can now figure out what image we will use as the base. For our designated OS version (Ubuntu LTS), you can use the helper page at `https://cloud-images.ubuntu.com/locator/ec2/` to find the right one:

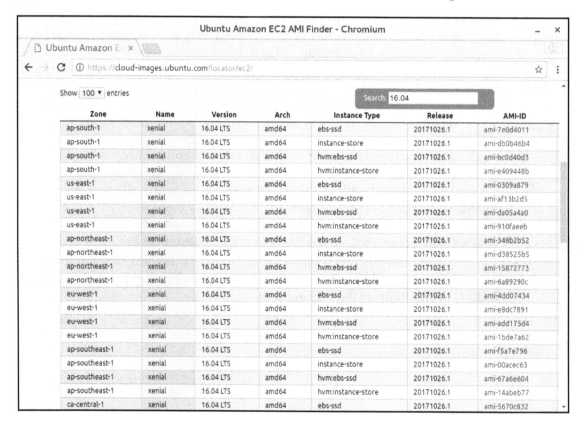

For our test builds, we will be using `us-west-1` region, Ubuntu 16.04 LTS version (`xenial`), 64-bit architecture (`amd64`), `hvm` virtualization, and `ebs-ssd` storage so we can use the filters at the bottom of the page to narrow things down:

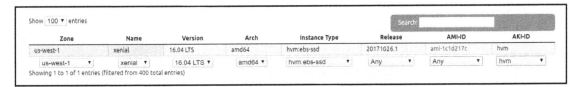

As you can see, the list collapses to one choice and in our `packer.json` we will use `ami-1c1d217c`.

 Since this list is updated with AMIs that have newer security patches, it is very likely that by the time you are reading this section the AMI ID will be something else on your end. Because of that, do not be alarmed if you see discrepancies between values we have found here and what you have available to you while reading of this chapter.

Building the AMI

 WARNING! Running this Packer build will for sure incur some (albeit barely a couple of US dollars at the time of writing this book) charges on your AWS account due to usage of non-free instance type, snapshot use, and AMI use, some possibly recurring. Refer to the pricing documentation of AWS for those services to estimate the amount that you will be charged. As an additional note, it is also good practice to clean up everything either from the console or CLI after you finish working with AWS objects that will not be kept around since it will ensure that you do not get additional charges after working with this code.

With the `packer.json` in place, we can now do a build of our image. We will first install the pre-requisites (`python-boto` and `awscli`), then check the access, and finally build our AMI:

```
$ # Install python-boto as it is a prerequisite for Amazon builders
$ # Also get awscli to check if credentials have been set correctly
$ sudo apt-get update && sudo apt-get install -y python-boto awscli
<snip>

$ # Check that AWS API credentials are properly set.
$ # If you see errors, consult the previous section on how to do this
$ aws ec2 describe-volumes
```

```
{
    "Volumes": [
    ]
}

$ # Go to the proper directory if we are not in it
$ cd ~/ansible_deployment

$ # Build our AMI and use standardized output format
$ packer build -machine-readable packer.json

<snip>
1509439711,,ui,say,==> amazon-ebs: Provisioning with shell script:
/tmp/packer-shell105349087
<snip>
1509439739,,ui,message, amazon-ebs: Setting up ansible (2.0.0.2-2ubuntu1)
...
1509439741,,ui,message, amazon-ebs: Setting up python-selinux (2.4-3build2)
...
1509439744,,ui,say,==> amazon-ebs: Provisioning with Ansible...
1509439744,,ui,message, amazon-ebs: Uploading Playbook directory to Ansible
staging directory...
<snip>
1509439836,,ui,message, amazon-ebs: TASK [swarm_node : Installing Docker]
******************************************
1509439855,,ui,message, amazon-ebs: [0;33mchanged: [127.0.0.1][0m
1509439855,,ui,message, amazon-ebs:
1509439855,,ui,message, amazon-ebs: PLAY RECAP
***********************************************************************
1509439855,,ui,message, amazon-ebs: [0;33m127.0.0.1[0m :
[0;32mok[0m[0;32m=[0m[0;32m10[0m [0;33mchanged[0m[0;33m=[0m[0;33m9[0m
unreachable=0 failed=0
1509439855,,ui,message, amazon-ebs:
1509439855,,ui,say,==> amazon-ebs: Stopping the source instance...
<snip>
1509439970,,ui,say,Build 'amazon-ebs' finished.
1509439970,,ui,say,--> amazon-ebs: AMIs were created:\nus-west-1: ami-
a694a8c6\n
```

Success! With this new image ID that you can see at the end of the output (`ami-a694a8c6`), we can now launch instances in EC2 with this AMI and they will have all the tweaks we have applied as well as have Docker pre-installed!

Deployments to AWS

With just the bare images and no virtual machines to run them on, our previous Packer work has not gotten us yet fully into an automated working state. To really get there, we will now need to tie everything together with more Ansible glue to complete the deployment. The encapsulation hierarchy of the different stages should conceptually look something like this:

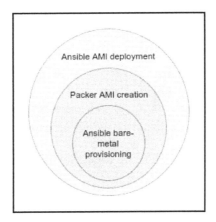

As you can see from the diagram, we will take a layered approach to deployments:

- In the innermost level, we have the Ansible scripts to take a bare machine, VM, or an AMI to the configuration state we want it to be in.
- Packer encapsulates that process and produces static AMI images that are further usable on Amazon EC2 cloud offerings.
- Ansible then finally encapsulates everything mentioned previously by deploying machines with those static, Packer-created images.

The road to automated infrastructure deployment

Now that we know what we want, how can we do it? Luckily for us, as hinted in the previous list, Ansible can do that part for us; we just need to write a couple of configuration files. But AWS is very complex here so it will not be as simple as just starting an instance since we want an isolated VPC environment. However, since we will only manage one server, we don't really care much for inter-VPC networking, so that will make things a bit easier.

We first need to consider all the steps that will be required. Some of these will be very foreign to most of you as AWS is pretty complex and most developers do not usually work on networking, but they are the minimum necessary steps to have an isolated VPC without clobbering the default settings of your account:

- Set up the VPC for a specific virtual network.
- Create and tie a subnet to it. Without this, our machines will not be able to use the network on it.
- Set up a virtual Internet gateway and attach it to the VPC for unresolvable addresses with a routing table. If we do not do this, the machines will not be able to use the Internet.
- Set up a security group (firewall) whitelist of ports that we want to be able to access our server (SSH and HTTP ports). By default all ports are blocked so this makes sure that the launched instances are reachable.
- Finally, provision the VM instance using the configured VPC for networking.

To tear down everything, we will need to do the same thing, but just in reverse.

First, we need some variables that will be shared across both deploy and teardown playbooks. Create a `group_vars/all` file in the same directory as the big Ansible example that we have been working on in this chapter:

```
# Region that will accompany all AWS-related module usages
aws_region: us-west-1

# ID of our Packer-built AMI
cluster_node_ami: ami-a694a8c6

# Key name that will be used to manage the instances. Do not
# worry about what this is right now - we will create it in a bit
ssh_key_name: swarm_key

# Define the internal IP network for the VPC
swarm_vpc_cidr: "172.31.0.0/16"
```

Now we can write our `deploy.yml` in the same directory that `packer.json` is in, using some of those variables:

 The difficulties of this deployment is starting to scale up significantly from our previous examples and there is no good way to cover all the information that is spread between dozens of AWS, networking, and Ansible topics to describe it in a concise way, but here are some links to the modules we will use that, if possible, you should read before proceeding:

- https://docs.ansible.com/ansible/latest/ec2_vpc_net_module.html
- https://docs.ansible.com/ansible/latest/set_fact_module.html
- https://docs.ansible.com/ansible/latest/ec2_vpc_subnet_module.html
- https://docs.ansible.com/ansible/latest/ec2_vpc_igw_module.html
- https://docs.ansible.com/ansible/latest/ec2_vpc_route_table_module.html
- https://docs.ansible.com/ansible/latest/ec2_group_module.html
- https://docs.ansible.com/ansible/latest/ec2_module.html

```yaml
- hosts: localhost
  connection: local
  gather_facts: False

  tasks:
    - name: Setting up VPC
      ec2_vpc_net:
        region: "{{ aws_region }}"
        name: "Swarm VPC"
        cidr_block: "{{ swarm_vpc_cidr }}"
      register: swarm_vpc

    - set_fact:
        vpc: "{{ swarm_vpc.vpc }}"

    - name: Setting up the subnet tied to the VPC
      ec2_vpc_subnet:
        region: "{{ aws_region }}"
        vpc_id: "{{ vpc.id }}"
        cidr: "{{ swarm_vpc_cidr }}"
        resource_tags:
          Name: "Swarm subnet"
      register: swarm_subnet

    - name: Setting up the gateway for the VPC
      ec2_vpc_igw:
        region: "{{ aws_region }}"
        vpc_id: "{{ vpc.id }}"
      register: swarm_gateway

    - name: Setting up routing table for the VPC network
      ec2_vpc_route_table:
        region: "{{ aws_region }}"
        vpc_id: "{{ vpc.id }}"
        lookup: tag
        tags:
          Name: "Swarm Routing Table"
```

```
      subnets:
        - "{{ swarm_subnet.subnet.id }}"
      routes:
        - dest: 0.0.0.0/0
          gateway_id: "{{ swarm_gateway.gateway_id }}"


    - name: Setting up security group / firewall
      ec2_group:
        region: "{{ aws_region }}"
        name: "Swarm SG"
        description: "Security group for the swarm"
        vpc_id: "{{ vpc.id }}"
        rules:
          - cidr_ip: 0.0.0.0/0
            proto: tcp
            from_port: 22
            to_port: 22
          - cidr_ip: 0.0.0.0/0
            proto: tcp
            from_port: 80
            to_port: 80
        rules_egress:
          - cidr_ip: 0.0.0.0/0
            proto: all
      register: swarm_sg

    - name: Provisioning cluster node
      ec2:
        region: "{{ aws_region }}"
        image: "{{ cluster_node_ami }}"
        key_name: "{{ ssh_key_name }}"
        instance_type: "t2.medium"
        group_id: "{{ swarm_sg.group_id }}"
        vpc_subnet_id: "{{ swarm_subnet.subnet.id }}"
        source_dest_check: no
        assign_public_ip: yes
        monitoring: no
        instance_tags:
          Name: cluster-node
        wait: yes
        wait_timeout: 500
```

What we are doing here closely matches our earlier plan but now we have concrete deployment code to match it up against:

1. We set up the VPC with the `ec2_vpc_net` module.

2. We create our subnet and associate it to the VPC with the `ec2_vpc_subnet` module.

3. The Internet virtual gateway for our cloud is created with `ec2_vpc_igw`.

4. Internet gateway is then made to resolve any addresses that are not within the same network.

5. `ec2_group` module is used to enable ingress and egress networking but only port `22` (SSH) and port `80` (HTTP) are allowed in.

6. Finally, our EC2 instance is created within the newly configured VPC with the `ec2` module.

As we mentioned earlier, the tear-down should be very similar but in reverse and contain a lot more `state: absent` arguments. Let's put the following in `destroy.yml` in the same folder:

```
- hosts: localhost
  connection: local
  gather_facts: False

  tasks:
    - name: Finding VMs to delete
      ec2_remote_facts:
        region: "{{ aws_region }}"
        filters:
          "tag:Name": "cluster-node"
      register: deletable_instances

    - name: Deleting instances
      ec2:
        region: "{{ aws_region }}"
        instance_ids: "{{ item.id }}"
        state: absent
        wait: yes
        wait_timeout: 600
      with_items: "{{ deletable_instances.instances }}"
      when: deletable_instances is defined

    # v2.0.0.2 doesn't have ec2_vpc_net_facts so we have to fake it to get
VPC info
    - name: Finding route table info
      ec2_vpc_route_table_facts:
        region: "{{ aws_region }}"
        filters:
          "tag:Name": "Swarm Routing Table"
      register: swarm_route_table
```

```
  - set_fact:
      vpc: "{{ swarm_route_table.route_tables[0].vpc_id }}"
    when: swarm_route_table.route_tables | length > 0

  - name: Removing security group
    ec2_group:
      region: "{{ aws_region }}"
      name: "Swarm SG"
      state: absent
      description: ""
      vpc_id: "{{ vpc }}"
    when: vpc is defined

  - name: Deleting gateway
    ec2_vpc_igw:
      region: "{{ aws_region }}"
      vpc_id: "{{ vpc }}"
      state: absent
    when: vpc is defined

  - name: Deleting subnet
    ec2_vpc_subnet:
      region: "{{ aws_region }}"
      vpc_id: "{{ vpc }}"
      cidr: "{{ swarm_vpc_cidr }}"
      state: absent
    when: vpc is defined

  - name: Deleting route table
    ec2_vpc_route_table:
      region: "{{ aws_region }}"
      vpc_id: "{{ vpc }}"
      state: absent
      lookup: tag
      tags:
        Name: "Swarm Routing Table"
    when: vpc is defined

  - name: Deleting VPC
    ec2_vpc_net:
      region: "{{ aws_region }}"
      name: "Swarm VPC"
      cidr_block: "{{ swarm_vpc_cidr }}"
      state: absent
```

If the deploy playbook was readable, then this playbook should be generally easy to understand and as we mentioned, it just runs the same steps in reverse, removing any infrastructure pieces we already created.

Running the deployment and tear-down playbooks

If you remember, earlier in our `group_vars` definition, we had a key variable (`ssh_key_name: swarm_key`) that at this point becomes relatively important as without a working key we can neither deploy nor start our VM, so let's do that now. We will use `awscli` and `jq`--a JSON parsing tool that will reduce the amount of work we do, but it is possible to do without it as well through the GUI console:

```
$ # Create the key with AWS API and save the private key to ~/.ssh
directory
$ aws ec2 create-key-pair --region us-west-1 \
                          --key-name swarm_key | jq -r '.KeyMaterial' >
~/.ssh/ec2_swarm_key

$ # Check that its not empty by checking the header
$ head -1 ~/.ssh/ec2_swarm_key
-----BEGIN RSA PRIVATE KEY-----

$ # Make sure that the permissions are correct on it
$ chmod 600 ~/.ssh/ec2_swarm_key

$ # Do a sanity check that it has the right size and permissions
$ ls -la ~/.ssh/ec2_swarm_key
-rw------- 1 sg sg 1671 Oct 31 16:52 /home/sg/.ssh/ec2_swarm_key
```

With the key in place, we can finally run our deploy script:

```
$ ansible-playbook deploy.yml
 [WARNING]: provided hosts list is empty, only localhost is available


PLAY
***********************************************************************

TASK [Setting up VPC]
********************************************************
ok: [localhost]

TASK [set_fact]
*********************************************************
ok: [localhost]

TASK [Setting up the subnet]
**************************************************
ok: [localhost]

TASK [Setting up the gateway]
```

```
**************************************************
ok: [localhost]

TASK [Setting up routing table]
**************************************************
ok: [localhost]

TASK [Setting up security group]
**************************************************
ok: [localhost]

TASK [Provisioning cluster node]
**************************************************
changed: [localhost]

PLAY RECAP
************************************************************************
localhost : ok=7 changed=1 unreachable=0 failed=0

$ # Great! It looks like it deployed the machine!

$ # Let's see what we have. First we need to figure out what the external
IP is
$ aws ec2 describe-instances --region us-west-1 \
                              --filters Name=instance-state-
name,Values=running \
                              --query
'Reservations[*].Instances[*].PublicIpAddress'
[
    [
        "52.53.240.17"
    ]
]

$ # Now let's try connecting to it
ssh -i ~/.ssh/ec2_swarm_key ubuntu@52.53.240.17

<snip>
Are you sure you want to continue connecting (yes/no)? yes
Warning: Permanently added '52.53.240.17' (ECDSA) to the list of known
hosts.
<snip>

ubuntu@ip-172-31-182-20:~$ # Yay! Do we have Docker?
ubuntu@ip-172-31-182-20:~$ sudo docker ps
CONTAINER ID IMAGE COMMAND CREATED STATUS PORTS NAMES

ubuntu@ip-172-31-182-20:~$ # Create our single-server swarm
```

```
ubuntu@ip-172-31-182-20:~$ sudo docker swarm init
Swarm initialized: current node (n2yc2tedm607rvnjs72fjgl11) is now a
manager.
<snip>

ubuntu@ip-172-31-182-20:~$ # Here we can now do anything else that's needed
ubuntu@ip-172-31-182-20:~$ # Though you would normally automate everything
```

 If you see errors similar to "`No handler was ready to authenticate. 1 handlers were checked. ['HmacAuthV4Handler'] Check your credentials`", ensure that you have your AWS credentials set properly.

Looks like everything is working! At this point, we could literally deploy our previously built 3-tier application if we wanted to. As we are done with our example and since we have our mini PaaS working, we can go back and clean up things by running the `destroy.yml` playbook:

```
ubuntu@ip-172-31-182-20:~$ # Get out of our remote machine
ubuntu@ip-172-31-182-20:~$ exit
logout
Connection to 52.53.240.17 closed.

$ # Let's run the cleanup script
ansible-playbook destroy.yml
 [WARNING]: provided hosts list is empty, only localhost is available


PLAY
************************************************************************

TASK [Finding VMs to delete]
*************************************************
ok: [localhost]

TASK [Deleting instances]
*************************************************
changed: [localhost] => <snip>

TASK [Finding route table info]
*********************************************
ok: [localhost]

TASK [set_fact]
****************************************************************
ok: [localhost]
```

```
TASK [Removing security group]
***************************************************
changed: [localhost]

TASK [Deleting gateway]
*********************************************************
changed: [localhost]

TASK [Deleting subnet]
*********************************************************
changed: [localhost]

TASK [Deleting route table]
****************************************************
changed: [localhost]

TASK [Deleting VPC]
*************************************************************
changed: [localhost]

PLAY RECAP
***********************************************************************
localhost : ok=9 changed=6 unreachable=0 failed=0
```

And with that, we have automated deployments and teardowns of our infrastructure with single commands. While the example is pretty limited in scope, it should give you some ideas on how to expand beyond that with auto-scaling groups, orchestration management AMIs, registry deployment, and data persistence that would turn this into a full-fledged PaaS.

Continuous integration/Continuous delivery

As you make more services, you will notice that manual deployments of changes from source control and builds are taking up more time due to the need to figure out which image dependencies belong where, which image actually needs rebuilding (if you run a mono-repo), if the service changed at all, and many other ancillary issues. In order to simplify and streamline our deployment process, we will need to find a way to make this whole system fully automated so that the only thing needed to deploy a new version of services is a commit of a change to a branch of your code repository.

As of today, the most popular automation server called Jenkins is generally used in such function to do this build automation and deployment of Docker images and infrastructure but others like Drone, Buildbot, Concoure, etc have been rising fast through the ranks of very capable software CI/CD tooling too but none have so far reached the same acceptance levels from the industry yet. Since Jenkins is also relatively easy to use, we can do a quick demonstration of its power, and while the example is a bit simplistic, it should make it obvious on how this can be used for much more.

Since Jenkins will need `awscli`, Ansible, and `python-boto`, we have to make a new Docker image based on the Jenkins that is available from Docker Hub. Create a new folder and add a `Dockerfile` with the following content in it:

```
FROM jenkins

USER root
RUN apt-get update && \
    apt-get install -y ansible \
                       awscli \
                       python-boto

USER jenkins
```

Now we build and run our server:

```
$ # Let's build our image
$ docker build -t jenkins_with_ansible

Sending build context to Docker daemon 2.048kB
Step 1/4 : FROM jenkins
<snip>
Successfully tagged jenkins_with_ansible:latest

$ # Run Jenkins with a local volume for the configuration
$ mkdir jenkins_files
$ docker run -p 8080:8080 \
             -v $(pwd)/jenkins_files:/var/jenkins_home \
             jenkins_with_ansible

Running from: /usr/share/jenkins/jenkins.war
<snip>
Jenkins initial setup is required. An admin user has been created and a
password generated.
Please use the following password to proceed to installation:

3af5d45c2bf04fffb88e97ec3e92127a

This may also be found at: /var/jenkins_home/secrets/initialAdminPassword
```

```
<snip>
INFO: Jenkins is fully up and running
```

While it is still running, let's go to the main page and enter the installation password that we got a warning for during the image start. Go to `http://localhost:8080` and enter the password that was in your logs:

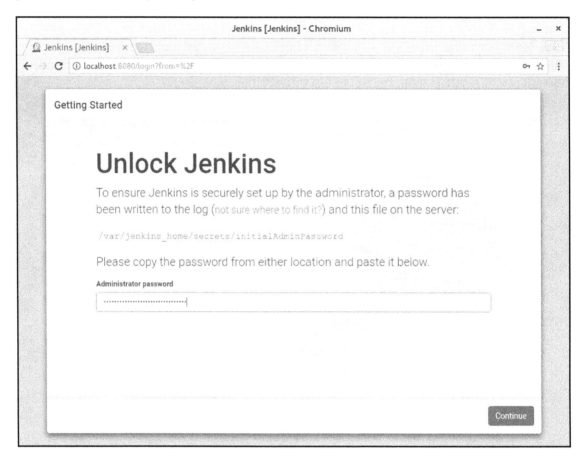

Click on **Install Suggested Plugins** on the next window and then after the relevant downloads are finished, select **Continue** as admin on the last installer page, which should lead you to the main landing page:

Click on **create new jobs**, name it `redeploy_infrastructure`, and make it a **Freestyle project**:

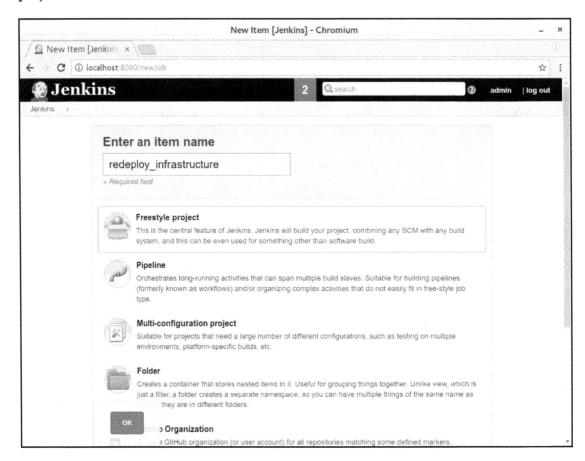

Next, we will configure the job with our Git repository endpoint so that it builds on any commits to the master branch:

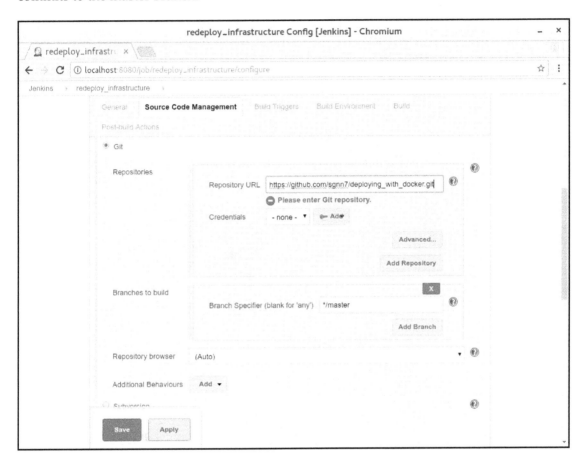

As our build step, when the repository trigger activates, we will destroy and deploy the infrastructure, effectively replacing it with a newer version. Add a new build step of **Execute Shell** type and add the following to it:

```
# Export needed AWS credentials
export AWS_DEFAULT_REGION="us-west-1"
export AWS_ACCESS_KEY_ID="AKIABCDEFABCDEF"
export AWS_SECRET_ACCESS_KEY="123456789ABCDEF123456789ABCDEF"

# Change to relevant directory
cd chapter_8/aws_deployment

# Redeploy the service by cleaning up the old deployment
```

```
# and deploying a new one
ansible-playbook destroy.yml
ansible-playbook deploy.yml
```

The job should look quite a bit similar to this:

Save the changes with Save, which should take you to the build's main page. Here, click on the Build Now button and once the build appears on the left side build list, click on its progress bar or the dropdown next to its name and select View Log:

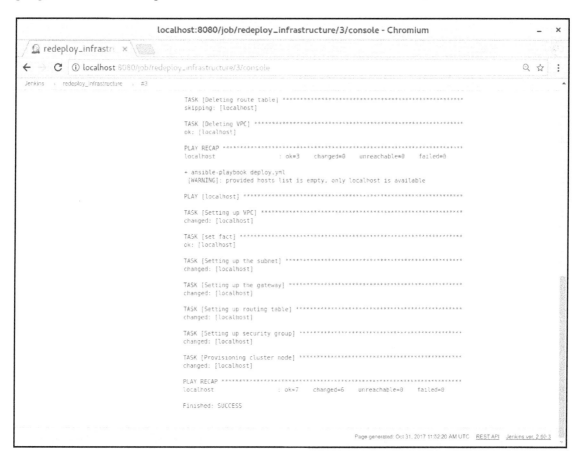

Success! As you can see, with Jenkins and a small configuration, we just made an automated deployment of our simple infrastructure. It is crude but effective though normally you would not want to redeploy everything but just the pieces that have changed and have the Jenkins live in-cluster, but that are somewhat more-involved endeavors that will be left to the reader as possible points of improvement.

Resource considerations

Since Jenkins runs on top of a Java VM, it will eat up available RAM at an alarming rate and is usually the biggest hog of usage along with being the most frequent **out-of-memory (OOM)** culprit I have had experience with. In even the lightest use cases, plan to allocate at least 1 GB of RAM to Jenkins workers or risk various failures at the most inopportune stages of your build pipelines. As a general rule, most Jenkins installation at this time will not have many problems with 2 GB of RAM allocated to them, but due to the price of RAM in VM instances, you can try to scale things back until you reach the acceptable levels of performance.

The last thing to also pay attention to is that the Jenkins image is also a bulky one relatively speaking, weighing in at about a hefty 800 MB, so keep in mind that moving this container is really not as easy nor fast as some other tooling that we have been using.

First-deploy circular dependency

When using Jenkins within your cluster as a Dockerized service to chain-build all other images, it is important for me to mention a common pitfall where you will inevitably have the issue with new deployments where Jenkins is not available initally since at the cluster initialization stage no images are usually available in the registry and the default Jenkins Docker image is not configured in any way. On top of all this, since you often need an already-running Jenkins instance to build a newer Jenkins image, you will be in the the classic Catch-22 situation. You may have a reflex to build Jenkins manually as a followup deployment step, but you must resist the urge to do so if you want to really have infrastructure that is mostly hands-off.

The general workaround to this is problem of bootstrapping Jenkins on a clean cluster has generally been something as shown in the following diagram:

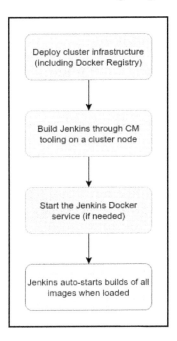

The cluster deployment is done first to ensure that we have a way t build our bootstrap image, and the **Docker Registry** is used to store the image after it is built. Following this, we build the Jenkins image on any available Docker Engine node and push it to the registry so that the service will have the right image to start with. If needed, we then launch the mentioned service using the same configuration management tool (like Ansible) or the orchestration tooling and wait for the auto-start job that will build all other remaining images which should populate the registry with all the other images needed to run the full cluster. The basic idea here is to do the initial bootstrap through CM tooling and then let the Jenkins service rebuild all the other images and (re)start the tasks.

In large-scale deployments, it is also possible to use your cluster orchestration to schedule and handle this bootstrap procedure instead of the CM tooling but due to the vast differences between each orchestration engine, these steps may vary wildly between them.

Further generic CI/CD uses

Good CI tooling like Jenkins can do much more than the things we covered here; they all require significant investment of time and effort to get working, but the benefits are pretty significant if you can get them implemented:

- **Self-building**: As mentioned in the workaround previously, you can have Jenkins build its own image when the configuration changes and have it redeploy itself.
- **Deployment of only changed Docker images**: If you use Docker caching, you can check whether the new build created a different image hash and only deploy if it did. Doing this will prevent pointless work and have your infrastructure always running the newest code.
- **Timed Docker pruning**: You can run cleanup jobs (or any other jobs similar to `cron`) on Jenkins that will free up or manage your Docker nodes to avoid manual interactions.

This list can also include: automated releases, failure notifications, build tracking, and quite a few other things that can be gained as well but suffice it to say, you really want a working CI pipeline in any non-trivial deployment.

A rule of thumb is that if you need to do something manually that can be automated with some timers and shell script, most CI tooling (like Jenkins) is there to help you out, so don't be afraid to try different and creative uses for it. With a full array of options and other tooling we have covered in this chapter, you can go to sleep soundly knowing that your clusters are going to be fine for a little while without needing constant babysitting.

Summary

In this chapter, we have covered more on how you would truly deploy a PaaS infrastructure and the following topics that were required for it were examined in depth: configuration Management tooling with Ansible, cloud image management with HashiCorp Packer, and continuous integration with Jenkins. With the knowledge gained here, you should now be able to use the various tooling we discussed and create your own mini-PaaS for your own service deployments, and with some additional work, you can turn it into a full-scale PaaS!

In the next chapter, we will take a look at how we can take our current Docker and infrastructure work and take it even bigger. We will also cover what direction this field might be moving toward, so if you would like to gain insights into the largest of deployments in the world, stick around.

9
Exploring the Largest-Scale Deployments

In earlier chapters, we covered many different aspects of deploying Docker containers, but if we are to turn our examples into a global service that would withstand the throughput of many millions of requests a second, a few things will still need to be addressed and this chapter was specifically written to go over the most important ones in some detail. Since implementations of topics covered here would involve enough material to be books on their own and infrastructure would differ wildly depending on a multitude of factors, the text here will be mostly on the theory side, but the previous understanding of services we gained in the text leading up to this chapter should be good enough to give you ideas on how you can proceed with the least amount of pain.

In its core, the topics we will cover revolve around choosing the right technologies and then following three basic ideas:

- Automate everything!
- Really, automate it all!
- Yes, automate even those one-off things you do every few weeks

It might be a joke, but hopefully by now it should be clear that one of the main points of all of this work (besides isolation) is to remove any human interaction from your system in regards to keeping your services running so that you and your team can focus on actually developing services and not wasting time on deployments.

Maintaining quorums

In our previous examples, we mostly worked with a single-node manager but if you want resilience, you must ensure that there are minimal points of failure that will take your whole infrastructure down and a single orchestration management node is absolutely not enough for production services regardless of whether you use Swarm, Kubernetes, Marathon, or something else as your orchestration tooling. From the best practices perspective, you would want to have at least three or more management nodes in your cluster that are spread across three or more of your cloud's **Availability Zones** (**AZ**) or equivalent grouping to really ensure stability at scales since data center outages have been known to happen and have caused serious issues to companies that did not mitigate these types of circumstances.

While in most orchestration platforms you can have any number of backing management nodes (or backing key-value stores in some cases), you will always have to balance resiliency vs speed due to the fact that with more nodes comes better capability to handle failures of larger parts of the system, but changes to this system (such as node additions and removals) must reach more points that will all have to agree, thus making it slower to process data. In most cases where this 3+ availability zone topology is required, we will need to go in details about quorums—the concept we lightly covered earlier, which is the backbone of all **high availability** (**HA**) systems.

Quorums in their basic sense are a grouping of the majority of management nodes, which together can decide whether updates to the cluster are going to be allowed or not. If the quorum is lost by the fact that half or more management nodes are unavailable, all changes to the cluster will be stopped to prevent your cluster infrastructure from having effectively split clusters. To properly divide your network topology for scale in this respect, you must make sure that you have a minimum of three nodes and/or availability zones as the quorum majority is lost with a single failure with less than that number. Taking this further, you will generally also want an odd number of nodes and availability zones since even numbers do not provide much additional protection for maintaining quorum, as we will see in a moment.

To start off, let's say that you have five management nodes. To maintain a quorum of this number, you must have three or more nodes available, but if you have only two availability zones, the best split you can do is 3-2, which will work fine if a connection is broken or the **AZ** with two management nodes goes down, but if the **AZ** with three nodes goes down, a quorum cannot be established since two is less than half of the total node count.

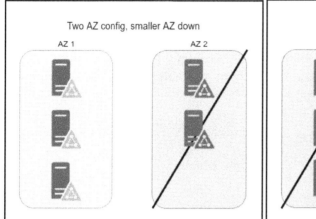
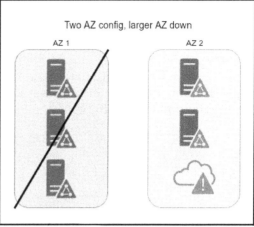

Let us now see what kind of resilience we can get with three availability zones. The optimal layout of this grouping with five management nodes would be *2-2-1* and if you take a closer look at what happens when any one of the zones goes out, you will see that the quorum is always maintained since we will either have *3 (2+1)* or *4 (2+2)* nodes still available from the rest of the cluster, ensuring that our services run without issues:

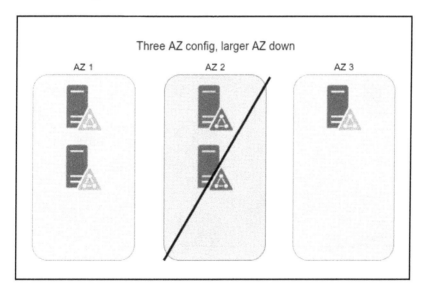

Of course, it is also good to show what kind of effect even numbers have on the effectiveness since we mentioned that they may be a bit troublesome. With four AZs, the best split that we can make would be *2-1-1-1* across them and with those numbers we can only tolerate two zones being unavailable if they both contain only one node. With this setup, we have a 50/50 chance that two zones being unavailable will include the zone with two nodes within it, putting the number of total nodes unavailable to over 3, and thus the cluster will be completely offline:

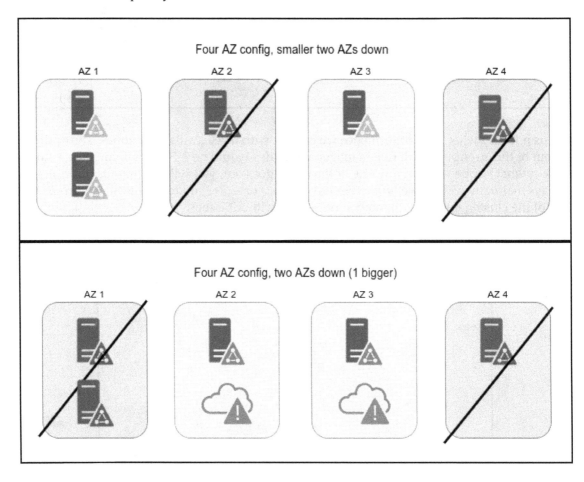

This spread of management nodes across higher counts of AZs for clusters gets much more stable if you have more availability zones and managers, but for our simple example here, we can see this effect if we have five management nodes and five availability zones (*1-1-1-1-1* layout). With such a split, due to the quorum requiring at least three nodes, we will still be fully operational if any two of the five zones are unavailable, increasing your failure tolerance by 100 percent from the 3-AZ topology; but you can assume that communication between possibly wildly disparate geographical regions will add plenty of latency to any updates.

Hopefully, with these examples, it should now be clear what kind of considerations and calculations you would use when trying to keep your cluster resilient and it is able to maintain quorum. While the tooling may differ depending on the orchestration tooling (that is `etcd` nodes versus Zookeeper nodes), the principles remain relatively the same in almost all of them, so this section should be relatively portable.

Node automation

As we have worked on making **Amazon Machine Images** (**AMIs**) with Packer, we have seen what kind of thing we can do with pre-baked instance images, but their true power is only fully harnessed when the whole infrastructure is comprised of them. If your orchestration management nodes and worker nodes have their own system images, with a couple of startup scripts also baked-in though the init system (for example, `systemd` startup services), you can make instances launched with those images auto-join your cluster during boot in their predefined roles. Taking this further to a conceptual level, if we extract all stateful configuration into the image configurations and all dynamic configurations into a separate service accessible to all nodes such as EC2 `user-data` or HashiCorp Vault, your cluster will be almost fully self-configuring besides the initial deployment and image building.

By having this powerful auto-join capability, you are eliminating most of the manual work related to scaling your cluster up or down since there is no need for interacting with the VM instance other than starting it. A rather simple illustration of this architecture is depicted in the following figure, where orchestration and worker nodes have their own respective images and self-configure on startup using a shared configuration data provider within the **VPC** itself:

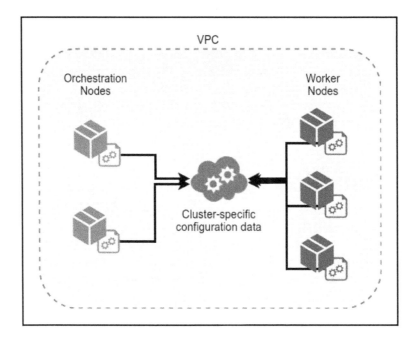

 CAUTION! To prevent serious security breaches make sure to separate and isolate any sensitive information to be accessible only by the desired systems in this configuration service layout. As we mentioned in one of the early chapters, following security best practices by using need-to-know practices will ensure that a compromise of a single point (most likely a worker node) will not be able to spread easily to the rest of your cluster. As a simple example here, this would include making sure that management secrets are not readable by worker nodes or their network.

Reactive auto-scaling

With automated self-configuration implemented, we can start looking even bigger by starting the instances automatically. If you remember auto-scaling groups from earlier chapters, even that can be automated in most cloud offerings. By using launch configurations and pre-configured images, like the ones we just talked about, adding or removing nodes with this setup would be as easy as dialing the desired nodes setting. The auto-scaling group would increase or decrease the worker instance count and because the images are self-configuring, that would be the full extent of input needed from you. With such a simple input, you can make scaling changes to your infrastructure extremely easy and done through many different ways.

Something to consider here as an even further step in automation is that with some cloud providers you can trigger these actions in your auto-scaling groups based on their metrics or even a `cron`-like schedule as well. In principle, if you have increased load on your cluster you could trigger a node count increase, and conversely, if the load on either the cluster or an individual node drops below a pre-defined value you can activate a service drain and shutdown of a fraction of your nodes to scale the system as needed. For periodic but predictable demand variations (see `https://en.wikipedia.org/wiki/Internet_Rush_Hour` for more info), the scheduled scaling changes we mentioned can make sure that you have enough resources to handle the expected demand.

Predictive auto-scaling

If you manually dial up and down the node counts and auto-scale on schedule or metric triggers, you still will have some issues bringing up services you need at exactly the time you want them to run since services take a bit of time to get online, self-configure, and start getting propagated to various load balancers in your network. With that type of architecture, it is likely that your users will be the one discovering that you do not have enough capacity and your system then reacting to compensate. If you are really striving for all-out best user experience from your services sometimes you may also need to add one more layer to your auto-scaling triggers that can predict when your service will need more resources before they are even actually needed, aptly called **predictive scaling**.

In extremely broad terms, what you would do to add this predictive layer to your infrastructure is to funnel some fraction of your metrics collected over the last x amount of time to a **machine learning** (**ML**) tool such as TensorFlow (`https://www.tensorflow.org/`) and generate a training set that would be able to make the tooling you are using able to predict with some certainty whether you will need more nodes or not. By using this method, your services can scale before they will even be needed to do so (!) and in a much smarter way than simple schedule-based approaches. Systems such as these are pretty difficult to integrate properly into your pipeline, but if you are working on global scales with crazy throughput and simple reactive auto-scaling comes up short, it is an avenue possibly worth exploring.

Training set in machine learning means just a set of training data (in our case it would be a chunk of our long-term metrics) that you can use to teach a neural network about how to correctly predict the demand that you will need.

Like many of the topics in recent chapters, there are actual books written on this material (machine learning) that would eclipse the content of this one by volume many times over and would provide only marginal utility for you here. If you would like to learn more about machine learning in detail, this Wikipedia page has a good primer on it at `https://en.wikipedia.org/wiki/Machine_learning` and you can give TensorFlow a whirl at `https://www.tensorflow.org/get_started/get_started`.

In the end, if you manage to implement some or all of these techniques together, you will barely need any interventions with your clusters to handle scaling in either direction. As an added bonus to being able to sleep soundly, you will also save resources since you will be able to closely match your processing resources with the actual usage of your services making you, your budget, and your users all happy.

Monitoring

Any service that you rely on in your service delivery should ideally have a way to notify you if something has gone wrong with it, and I do not mean user feedback here. Most service development nowadays is moving at incredible speeds and monitoring is one of those things like backups that most developers do not think about until something catastrophic happens, so it is something that we should cover a little bit. The big question that really should determine how you approach this topic is if your users can handle the downtimes that you will not see without monitoring.

Most tiny services might be OK with some outages, but for everything else, this would be at a bare minimum a couple of angry emails from users and at worst your company losing a huge percentage of your users, so monitoring at all scales is greatly encouraged.

While it is true that monitoring is maybe considered one of those boring pieces of your infrastructure to implement, having a way to gain insights into what your cloud is doing at all times is an absolutely essential part of managing the multitude of disparate systems and services. By adding monitoring to your **Key Performance Indicators** (**KPIs**) you can ensure that, as a whole, your system is performing as expected and by adding triggers to your critical monitoring targets you can be instantly alerted to any activity that can potentially impact your users. Having these type of insights into the infrastructure can both help reduce user turnover and drive better business decisions.

As we worked through our examples, you may have already come up with ideas of what you would monitor, but here are some common ones that consistently pop up as the most useful ones:

- **Node RAM utilization**: If you notice that your nodes aren't using all the RAM allocated, you can move to smaller ones and vice versa. This generally gets less useful if you use memory-constrained Docker containers, but it is still a good metric to keep as you want to make sure you never hit a system-level max memory utilization on a node or your containers will run with much slower swap instead.
- **Node CPU utilization**: You can see from this metric if your service density is too low or too high or if there are spikes in service demands.
- **Node unexpected terminations**: This one is good to track to ensure that your CI/CD pipeline is not creating bad images, that your configuration services are online, and a multitude of other issues that could take down your services.
- **Service unexpected terminations**: Finding out why a service is unexpectedly terminating is critical to ironing out bugs out of any system. Seeing an increase or a decrease in this value can be good indicators of codebase quality though they can also indicate a multitude of other problems, both internal and external to your infrastructure.
- **Messaging queue sizes**: We covered this in a bit of detail before but ballooning queue sizes indicate that your infrastructure is unable to process data as quickly as it is generated, so this metric is always good to have.

- **Connection throughputs**: Knowing exactly how much data you are dealing with can be a good indicator of service load. Comparing this to other collected stats can also tell you if the problems you are seeing are internally or externally caused.
- **Service latencies**: Just because there are no failures does not mean that the service is unusable. By tracking latencies you can see in detail what could use improving or what is not performing to your expectations.
- **Kernel panics**: Rare but extremely deadly, kernel panics can be a really disruptive force on your deployed services. Even though it is pretty tricky to monitor these, keeping track of kernel panics will alert you if there is an underlying kernel or hardware problem that you will need to start addressing.

This obviously is not an exhaustive list, but it covers some of the more useful ones. As you develop your infrastructure, you will find that adding monitoring everywhere leads to better turnarounds on issues and discovery of scalability bugs with your services. So once you have monitoring added to your infrastructure, don't be afraid to plug it into as many pieces of your system that you can. At the end of the day, by gaining visibility and transparency of your whole infrastructure through monitoring, you can make wiser decisions and build better services, which is exactly what we want.

Evaluating next-gen technologies

Something that I personally have been feeling has been left out of most documentation and learning material about containers (and most other tech topics) is proper evaluation and risk assessment of emerging technologies. While the risk of choosing a fundamentally flawed music player is trivial, choosing a fundamentally flawed cloud technology could tie you up in years of pain and development that you would otherwise not have needed. With the speed of tooling creation and development in the cloud space increasing at break-neck speed, good evaluation techniques are something that you might want to have in your toolbox of skills as they can save you effort, time, and money in the long run. Hunches are great but having a solid, repeatable, and deterministic way of evaluating technologies is a much more likely way to cause long-term success.

Please note that while the advice given here has had a pretty good track record for me and other people I have talked to over my career, you can never fully predict the course that a disparate landscape of technologies will take, especially when most tech start-ups can close their doors at a moment's notice (i.e. ClusterHQ). So keep in mind that these are all just points of interest and not a magical list that will make the most common problems with choosing technologies disappear.

Technological needs

This should be a pretty obvious one, but it needs to be written down. If you have a need for a feature that is provided by a tool that you do not want to develop in-house, you will not have much of a choice but to go with it and hope for the best. Luckily, in most cloud technologies and the tooling modules that supports them, there are usually at least two competing options fighting for the same users so things are not as dire as they may seem today even though just a single year back almost everything in this space had a version number below 1.0. As you evaluate how competing tools fit your needs, also keep in mind that not every tool is geared towards the same purpose even if they solve the same issues. If we take an example of current Kubernetes versus Marathon, even though they can both be used to solve the same service deployment problems, Kubernetes is mostly geared towards that single purpose but Marathon, for example, can also be used to do scheduling and cluster management as an additional functionality so we are in the proverbial sense really comparing apples and oranges.

In broad strokes, your service infrastructure needs will drive your tooling needs so you will not often end up dealing with your favorite programming language, having easy integration points, or working with a sane tooling codebase, but integrating a tool that will save you hundreds or thousands of man-hours is something not to be taken lightly. Sometimes it might be possible to completely skirt around a technological requirement by changing pieces of your system's architecture to avoid adding complexity to the system, but in my personal experience this was almost never easy to do so your mileage may vary.

Popularity

This is probably the most controversial dimension to consider, but also one of the most important ones to pay attention to when dealing with new technologies. While it is absolutely true that popularity does not equate to technical merit, it can be assumed that:

- More people using a particular tool will be able to provide better integration help.
- Solutions to problems will be easier to find.
- If the codebase is open source, the project will be more likely to have fixes and features added to it.

In another way of describing the problem, can you afford to risk weeks/months/years of integration work on a tool that is unproven or on track to be abandoned in the next couple of years? If you are a really big shop with massive budgets this might not be an issue but in most cases, you will not have the opportunity to play with integrating different competing technologies to see which one is the best. While there are times that there are perfectly valid cases where taking a calculated chance with a new tool is warranted and desired, in the majority of cases due to the sheer complexity and longevity of cloud systems the cost of failure is extremely high, so a pragmatic approach is generally recommended but your individual requirements may vary, so choose accordingly.

To evaluate this aspect of a project there is a variety of tooling that can be used, but the simplest and the easiest are the GitHub project forks/stars (for OSS projects), Google Trends (https://trends.google.com) projections, and general social media feedback from people that have used said technology. By looking at movements and shifts in these values, extrapolation of long-term viability can be made with a relatively good accuracy and combined together with comparisons against existing tooling can create a good picture of the general pulse of a project as well. Upwardly-mobile projects generally have been indicative of superior technological base but in some cases, this was spurred by rejection of existing tooling or a big marketing push, so don't always think the popular option is better when evaluating a tool.

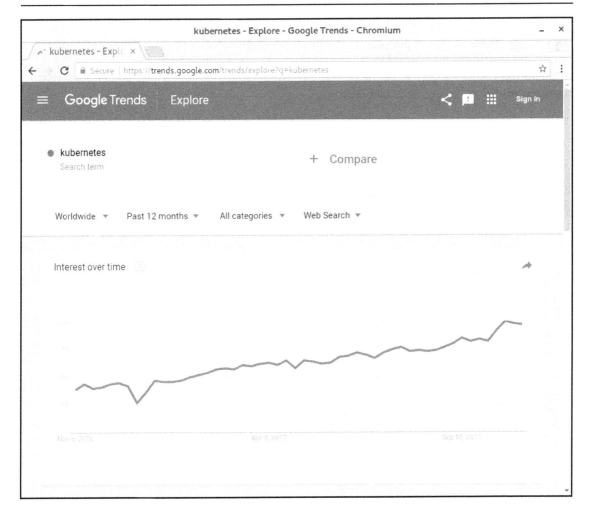

In the preceding screenshot, you can see a distinct increase over time in interest in Kubernetes that somewhat mirrors community adoption and acceptance of that orchestration tooling. If we were to implement this technology ourselves, we could be reasonably sure that for some period of time that we would be using a tool that will be easier to work with and get support for.

When comparing Kubernetes against Marathon and using the same technique, things get very messy as Marathon is also a very common long-distance running activity, so the results get muddled with unrelated Google queries. In the following screenshot, we overlaid the results versus a couple of other cloud-related keywords and you can see that there's something wrong with our data:

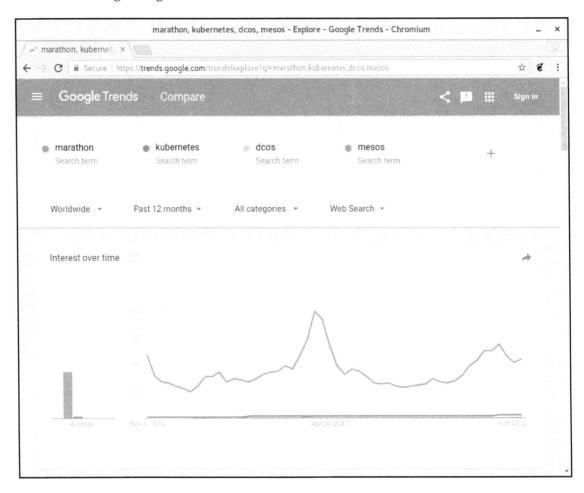

However, taking a look at the top-right side of their GitHub pages and the forks/stars we can see how they compare (**3,483** stars and **810** forks versus **28,444** stars and **10,167** forks):

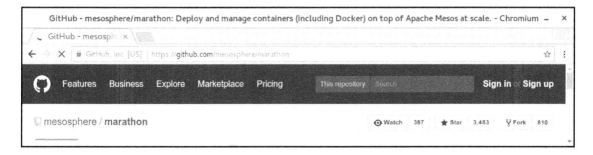

Compare the preceding GitHub page with the following page:

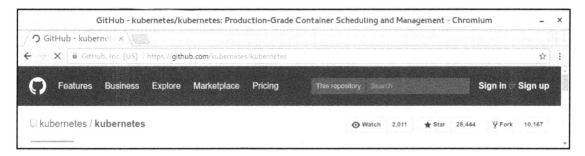

In this particular example, though, it is very hard to see long-term trends and we've mentioned that these two do not solve the same kind of problems, on top of which these two tools have vastly different setup complexity, so proper evaluation is really difficult.

Something that is really important that we should mention before moving on to the next dimension: a common and highly-recommended risk mitigation for immature tooling (this scenario is much more likely than you might think) is that your own developers can be used to fix bugs and add features to relevant upstream projects if they are capable and allowed to work on them. If a tool is such a good fit for your infrastructure and you can throw development resources behind it, it will not make much of a difference if it is popular or not as long as you can make it work for you in the way that you are satisfied with.

As a reference data point, countless times during the development of cloud implementations, the teams that I worked on have found bugs and issues in upstream projects that we fixed rather quickly and in the process also helped all the other users of that software instead of potentially waiting days or weeks for the upstream developers to make time to fix them. I would highly encourage this type of approach to contributing back being applied to your workplace if possible since it helps the whole project's community and indirectly prevents loss of project momentum due to unfixed bugs.

A team's technical competency

New tooling often has a great initial idea, but due to poor execution or architecture, it quickly turns into spaghetti code that is un-maintainable and prone to bugs. If design and implementation are kept to high standards, you can have a better assurance that you will not get unexpected breakages or at least that the bugs can be easier to find and fix. The competency of the core project developers plays a huge part in this aspect and since most of the newer tooling is open-source, taking a look at the codebase can often be very helpful in this respect.

It is near impossible to put exact guidelines for evaluating projects that span all sorts of technologies and systems, but there are some red flags that should be treated as warning signs of potential troubles in the future for the tooling that is used in critical applications:

- **Lack of tests**: Without tests, assurance that the code works is pretty much eliminated and you are hoping that the developer making changes was careful enough when implementing new features and that they did not break current functionality. I have only seen a handful of developers in my life that can be as mindful of all the edge cases as a test harness, but I would not hold my breath that the project you are looking into has one of them.
- **Clever code**: From time to time, a project will have one or more developers that are more concerned about showing their skills off than the maintainability of the project they are working on and they will almost always turn files they touch into code that only they can work on, causing future problems with adding features or fixing bugs. Almost always this type of change is one-directional and after a long enough period of time it usually ends up in the death of the project (more often than not in my experience).

- **A high count of critical bugs open for extended periods of time**: For any project, there will come a time where you will encounter a critical bug that must be fixed as soon as possible, and by seeing trends in how long fixes take, you can see whether the team is capable of quickly fixing an issue or whether it pays attention to the wider community. While more of a subjective metric, it becomes extremely important as the profile or security posture of your service increases.

You can also use any other metrics for evaluation such as: old and un-merged pull requests, arbitrarily closed bug reports, and many more as long as you get the right notion of the codebase's quality. With that knowledge in hand, you can properly evaluate what the future might hold for your candidate tooling and how your infrastructure can evolve with it.

Summary

And with that, we have reached the end of our book! In this chapter, we have covered various things that you will need to take your small service and make it global through aggressive automation, splitting things into multiple availability zones, and adding monitoring to your infrastructure. Since cloud technologies are also relatively young, we have more importantly included some tips on how to evaluate emerging tooling as objectively as you can to ensure that your projects have the greatest likelihood of success with the tooling ecosystem changes that will be common for the foreseeable future. By assuming that things will change in the future and having the tools to handle those changes, we can be ready to embrace anything that gets thrown at us.

Index